A Health Educator's Guide to Understanding Drugs of Abuse Testing

A Health Educator's Guide to Understanding Drugs of Abuse Testing

Amitava Dasgupta, PhD, DABCC

Professor of Pathology and Laboratory Medicine
University of Texas Health Sciences Center at Houston

JONES AND BARTLETT PUBLISHERS

Sudbury, Massachusetts

BOSTON   TORONTO   LONDON   SINGAPORE

World Headquarters
Jones and Bartlett Publishers
40 Tall Pine Drive
Sudbury, MA 01776
978-443-5000
info@jbpub.com
www.jbpub.com

Jones and Bartlett Publishers
Canada
6339 Ormindale Way
Mississauga, Ontario L5V 1J2
Canada

Jones and Bartlett Publishers
International
Barb House, Barb Mews
London W6 7PA
United Kingdom

Jones and Bartlett's books and products are available through most bookstores and online booksellers. To contact
Jones and Bartlett Publishers directly, call 800-832-0034, fax 978-443-8000, or visit our website www.jbpub.com.

Substantial discounts on bulk quantities of Jones and Bartlett's publications are available to corporations, professional
associations, and other qualified organizations. For details and specific discount information, contact the special sales
department at Jones and Bartlett via the above contact information or send an email to specialsales@jbpub.com.

The authors, editor, and publisher have made every effort to provide accurate information. However, they are not
responsible for errors, omissions, or for any outcomes related to the use of the contents of this book and take no
responsibility for the use of the products and procedures described. Treatments and side effects described in this
book may not be applicable to all people; likewise, some people may require a dose or experience a side effect that
is not described herein. Drugs and medical devices are discussed that may have limited availability controlled by
the Food and Drug Administration (FDA) for use only in a research study or clinical trial. Research, clinical
practice, and government regulations often change the accepted standard in this field. When consideration is
being given to use of any drug in the clinical setting, the health care provider or reader is responsible for
determining FDA status of the drug, reading the package insert, and reviewing prescribing information for the
most up-to-date recommendations on dose, precautions, and contraindications, and determining the appropriate
usage for the product. This is especially important in the case of drugs that are new or seldom used.

Production Credits
Acquisitions Editor: Shoshanna Goldberg
Associate Editor: Amy L. Flagg
Editorial Assistant: Kyle Hoover
Production Manager: Julie Champagne Bolduc
Production Assistant: Jessica Steele Newfell
Marketing Manager: Jessica Faucher

V.P., Manufacturing and Inventory Control: Therese
  Connell
Composition: Lynn L'Heureux
Cover Design: Scott Moden
Cover Image: © Olivier Le Queinec/ShutterStock, Inc.
Printing and Binding: Malloy, Inc.
Cover Printing: Malloy, Inc.

Library of Congress Cataloging-in-Publication Data
Dasgupta, Amitava, 1958–
  A health educator's guide to understanding drugs of abuse testing / Amitava Dasgupta.
    p. ; cm.
  Includes bibliographical references and index.
  ISBN 978-0-7637-6589-7 (pbk. : alk. paper)
  1. Drug testing. I. Title.
  [DNLM: 1. Substance Abuse Detection—methods. 2. Substance-Related Disorders—urine. 3. Drug Monitoring—
methods. 4. Employment—legislation & jurisprudence. 5. False Positive Reactions. QY 185 D229h 2010]
  HV5823.D37 2010
  616.86'075—dc22

6048

Printed in the United States of America
13 12 11 10 09   10 9 8 7 6 5 4 3 2 1

To my parents.

Contents

Foreword

There is a common misconception among physicians and other health care providers that screening for drugs of abuse will lead to the identification of any illicit compound in the sample collected. Because this is not true, the health care provider needs to know what drugs of abuse might be present in a person under evaluation and then seek to identify those specific compounds. An even bigger challenge for the health care provider is understanding how drugs of abuse in clinical specimens can be concealed by additives in the specimen.

While the use of drugs of abuse in society is high, there is rapid development of methods to attempt to conceal the identification of the drugs of abuse in clinical samples. Elaborate efforts in the sporting world to conceal the presence of compounds that are not permitted for athletes in competition have demonstrated the extreme scientific sophistication challenging the clinician and the laboratory test method. Underdiagnosis is a serious problem. Failing to detect a drug of abuse is an error of serious clinical, and sometimes social, importance. Similarly, when assays are performed that produce false-positive results and indicate that an individual who has not ingested a drug of abuse is positive for an illicit substance, the consequences can be equally tragic. Notably, athletes or airplane pilots falsely accused of ingesting an illicit compound can lose their careers as well as the respect of society.

Given the high frequency of positive tests for drugs of abuse and the clinical importance of knowing if such drugs are present when evaluating a patient, the clinician must have access to a thorough, reliable, and current source of information. This source must contain information about which tests to perform to identify potential drugs of abuse and the pitfalls in the interpretation of the test results.

A clinical handbook by a true authority on the topic has long been needed. This book by Amitava Dasgupta is exactly that. Dr. Dasgupta is the ultimate expert on the laboratory detection of drugs of abuse, the many means to obscure their detection, and the natural compounds that can cause false-positive tests for drugs of abuse. He has years of experience in the field and is regarded by colleagues like me as the consultant to seek in the most difficult of clinical cases.

Dr. Dasgupta is the author of a large body of literature on the detection and concealment of drugs of abuse. His writing style is clear and simple, resulting in a practical book that is most useful for health care providers. This guide needs to be in every emergency room and on the bookshelf of every laboratory director responsible for testing for drugs of abuse.

Michael Laposata, MD, PhD
Pathologist-in-Chief
Vanderbilt University Hospital
Professor of Pathology and Medicine
Vanderbilt University School of Medicine

Preface

Workplace drug testing is used to deter employees from abusing drugs as well as to prevent workplace accidents and work-related injuries. Moreover, a drug-free work environment also results in improved productivity and higher morale. Workplace drug testing has evolved from being virtually nonexistent in the 1980s to the point where there is a widespread acceptance of drug-testing programs by both government and private employers. However, workplace drug testing and pre-employment drug testing involve the complex process of proper specimen collection, analysis, and interpretation of test results.

A Health Educator's Guide to Understanding Drugs of Abuse Testing discusses all aspects of workplace drug testing from the collection to the analysis and interpretation. Chapter 1 provides a historical perspective of drug abuse and the psychoactive drugs known to ancient civilizations. A demographic aspect of drug abuse also is presented. Chapter 2 highlights pharmacology and the genetic aspects of drugs of abuse. In drugs-of-abuse testing, a drug metabolite often is targeted instead of a parent drug because the metabolite can be detected for a longer time in urine. Therefore, Chapter 2 is the basis of understanding drugs-of-abuse testing. Chapter 3 is devoted to designer drugs, including the date-rape drugs gamma-hydroxybutyric acid and rohypnol. The chapter also discusses why these drugs are difficult to detect in routine workplace drug testing. Chapters 4, 5, and 6 discuss the fundamental basis of workplace drug testing, commonly tested drugs in federally mandated drug-testing programs,

how pre-employment drug testing has evolved since President Reagan signed the executive order in 1986, and the legal issues involving workplace drug testing. Chapter 6 is appropriate for health care administrators and human resources professionals who deal with the legal aspects of workplace drug testing every day. Chapter 7, which discusses methodologies of drugs-of-abuse testing, is helpful in understanding current limitations of workplace drug testing. Chapter 8 discusses current devices available for point-of-care testing for abused drugs. Chapters 9, 10, and 11 discuss in detail how people try to beat drug tests and how health care providers can stay one step ahead of them. Chapters 12, 13, 14, and 15 deal with what could go wrong in workplace drug testing, especially when a person is wrongly accused of using a drug when the individual either took a prescription medication or ate a poppy seed–containing or related food. These chapters also are helpful for Medical Review Officers to evaluate analytical true positive drug testing cases. Point-of-care testing, although it has several limitations, is gaining acceptance in drugs-of-abuse testing because results are available within a short time period when the person being tested is present. Chapter 17 is devoted to drug testing in alternative matrices such as hair, sweat, and saliva. These matrices are used less often than urine drug testing, but in the future may gain further acceptance. Finally, Chapter 18 looks into the effects herbal remedies have on drugs-of-abuse testing.

This book covers all aspects of drug testing, and tables are provided within the chapters for quick reference to various over-the-counter and prescription medications that may produce false-positive test results. My hope is for health care providers and administrators to use this book as a comprehensive guide to all aspects of drug testing.

ACKNOWLEDGMENTS

I wish to thank Robert L. Hunter, MD, PhD, chairman of pathology and laboratory medicine at the University of Texas Medical School at Houston, for his support during this project. The vice chairman of my department, Robert E. Brown, MD, read several chapters critically and provided valuable comments. Alissa Tillery, nurse manager of occupational health at Memorial-Hermann Hospital at Texas Medical Center, the primary teaching hospital of the University of Texas Medical School, also read many chapters and made useful recommendations. Alice Wells read the entire manuscript and generously helped me in editing this book. Lastly, I want to thank my wife for her support during this project.

I would like to thank Dr. Taguchi Hiroaki for graciously drawing all the chemical structures in this book using ChemDraw (CambridgeSoft, Cambridge, MA). Proper credits are given in the references or in the text for all original sources of information provided in this book, including all governmental sources where the information is in the public domain. In addition, a few different publishers have granted permission to reprint previously published tables and figures. I greatly appreciate the generosity of these publishers for granting permission to reproduce this copyrighted material. I made all efforts to ensure that proper credits are given to all sources of information and material used in this book; I will be glad to include any omission of a reference in a subsequent edition if it is brought to my attention.

Abbreviations

1,4-BD: 1,4-butanediol

2C-B: 4-bromo-2,5-diemthoxy-β-phenylethylamine

CEDIA: Cloned-enzyme donor immunoassay

CLIA: Chemiluminescent immunoassay

CYP450: Cytochrome P-450 mixed function oxidase

ELISA: Enzyme-linked immunosorbent assay

EMIT: Enzyme-multiplied immunoassay technique

FPIA: Fluorescence polarization immunoassay

GABA: γ-aminobutyric acid

GBL: Gamma-butyrolactone

GC/MS: Gas chromatography/mass spectrometry

GHB: γ-hydroxybutyrate (a designer drug)

GLYT1: Glycine transporter 1 gene

HPLC: High-performance liquid chromatography

KIMS: Kinetic interaction of microparticles in solution (a form of immunoassay)

LSA: Lysergic acid hydroxyethylamide

LSD: Lysergic acid diethylamide

MDA: 3,4-methylenedioxyamphetamine

MDMA: 3,4-methylenedioxymethamphetamine (commonly known as ecstasy)

MEIA: Microparticle enzyme immunoassay

MRO: Medical review officer

OPRM1: Opioid receptor mu 1 gene

SAMHSA: Substance Abuse and Mental Health Services Administration (under the U.S. Department of Health and Human Services [DHHS])

THC: Δ^9-tetrahydrocannabinol

THC-COOH: 11-nor-9-carboxy Δ^9-tetrahydrocannabinol

TLC: Thin-layer chromatography

CHAPTER 1

Drugs of Abuse: Past and Present

ABSTRACT

Drug abuse has been around since the earliest recorded history. Poppy plants were cultivated as long ago as 3400 B.C. in Mesopotamia. Even the ancient Greeks and Romans used cocaine. Today, the most frequently abused drugs are marijuana, cocaine, amphetamines, 3,4-methylenedioxyamphetamine (MDMA, commonly called "ecstasy"), heroin, morphine, codeine, methadone, barbiturates, benzodiazepines, phencyclidine, and lysergic acid diethylamide (LSD). Less commonly abused drugs include magic mushrooms, peyote cactus, steroids, and volatile solvents (most frequently abused by teenagers). However, because many employers, including federal and state governments, now routinely conduct drug testing for new employees as well as workplace drug testing in order to achieve a drug-free workplace, drug abuse by the general population is on the decline. Nevertheless, drug abuse remains a serious problem worldwide, causing decreased productivity and accidents, as well as morbidity and mortality.

Any drug can be poisonous and even fatal in a high dosage, even drugs like acetaminophen and salicylate, which are relatively safe and can be purchased without a prescription. The drugs with the highest abuse potential have psychoactive properties and can cause euphoria. These drugs can have medical use (for example, narcotic analgesics such as morphine, codeine, and meperidine) but due to high abuse potential are classified as controlled substances by authorities worldwide. Some psychoactive drugs, such as heroin, have high abuse

potential and no known medical use. These drugs are often classified as Schedule I controlled substances by the U.S. Drug Enforcement Agency (DEA). Unfortunately, Schedule I drugs are imported into the United States illegally and sold in the streets. Possession, sale, and abuse of any of these substances are against the law in most countries. In some countries, such as Singapore, possession and sale of such controlled substances are punishable by death. In the United Arab Emirates a person can be imprisoned for several years just for possessing food that contains poppy seeds. Drug abuse is not only harmful to society but also is associated with accidents, morbidity, and mortality.

HISTORY OF DRUG ABUSE

Many plants contain substances capable of changing mood and producing euphoria. In 3400 B.C., Egyptians cultivated poppy plants in Mesopotamia; later the poppy plants were introduced in India and China. The first authentic reference to the milky juice of poppy plants (opium) dates to the beginning of the third century B.C. Arabian physicians used opium extensively to treat disease, and around 1000 A.D., the physician Avicenna used opium to treat eye diseases.[1] In 1799 Chinese authorities, aware of widespread opium addiction, banned opium altogether; in 1839 the smuggling of illegal opium led to what became known as the Opium War between Britain and China.

In the United States, opium was legally grown as well as imported during the nineteenth century. Opiates were widely available in myriad tonics and patent medicines, and smoking in opium dens was unhindered, resulting in an epidemic of opiate addiction by the late 1800s. During the Civil War the generous use of morphine in treating wounded soldiers also produced many addicts.

Heroin was first synthesized in 1874 in London. Heroin was considered a highly effective medicine for treating cough, chest pain, and tuberculosis.

Another well-known plant with psychoactive properties is *Cannabis sativa* (hemp). Hashish, the most potent product produced from the hemp plant, was used in China and India 5000 years ago. The earliest known reference to the plant is found in the pharmacy book of the Chinese emperor Shen Nung written in 2737 B.C.

Hemp products were widely used in the Middle East and Africa around 1000 A.D.[2] Cannabis most likely reached South America in the sixteenth century when African slaves brought cannabis seeds to Brazil. In the 1800s cannabis was used in medicine for its narcotic effect. In the second half of the nineteenth century, scientific articles in Europe and United States touted the therapeutic value of cannabis, but in the beginning of the twentieth century, medical use of cannabis was reduced significantly.[3] Today in the United States, cultivation of the hemp plant is illegal and marijuana is a controlled substance, but the abuse of marijuana is still widespread.

Cocaine occurs naturally as an alkaloid in the leaves of the coca plant (*Erythroxylon coca*). Native South Americans (in Peru, Bolivia, and Ecuador) used to chewed coca leaves in the past. The Incas, whose civilization lasted from 1200 A.D. to 1400 A.D., chewed coca leaves as a part of their religious ceremonies. In the mid-nineteenth century, cocaine became known to western civilizations, and after 1885 pharmaceutical companies started selling cocaine. Cocaine was used in local anesthesia and in many tonics designed for regaining strength and vigor. Extract of coca leaves was even used in the original formula for the drink Coca-Cola, but in the early twentieth century, the coca extract was removed from the formula and replaced by more caffeine.[2]

In 1912 the German company Mark synthesized the drug MDMA (3,4-methylenedioxymethamphetamine), although it never marketed it. In the 1960s and 1970s MDMA was used experimentally as an adjunct of psychotherapy until its abuse potential was recognized. Nicknamed "ecstasy" in the 1980s for the sense of euphoria it produces, MDMA has no known medicinal use. Unfortunately, the drug is widely abused worldwide, commonly sold at all-night dance parties (known as "raves"; see also Chapter 3). According to the World Health Organization (WHO), 8.5 million people abused ecstasy (both regular and occasional users) in 2004.[4]

Lysergic acid is a naturally occurring alkaloid found in the ergot fungus (*Claviceps purpurea*). Lysergic acid diethylamide, commonly known as LSD, is a potent hallucinogen. It was synthesized in 1938 at the Swiss pharmaceutical company Sandoz Laboratories by Albert Hoffman, who later discovered its hallucinogenic effect. LSD is abused throughout the world today.

 ## DRUG ABUSE IN THE UNITED STATES

A 2006 survey indicated that about 20.4 million Americans (8.3%) aged 12 or older were current illicit drug abusers, meaning they abused drugs during the month prior to the survey. The survey also showed that marijuana was the most common illicit drug abused (14.8 million people). In the same year, 2.4 million people abused cocaine, 528,000 people abused ecstasy, and 731,000 people abused methamphetamines. In addition, 7.0 million people took prescription medication nonmedically; among them, 5.2 million people abused pain relievers with no corresponding medical condition. The number of current heroin abusers increased from 136,000 in 2005 to 338,000 in 2006. **Table 1-1** summarizes the findings of the study.[5,6]

In 2006, 9.8% of adolescents aged 12 to 17 were abusing illicit drugs. The most commonly abused drug was marijuana (6.7%). In addition, 3.3 % of adolescents between the ages of 12 and 17 abused prescription medications, and 1.2% abused volatile substances. Rate of drug abuse was higher among young adults aged 18 to 25

Table 1-1 Estimated Numbers of People Using Commonly Abused Drugs in the United States in 2006	
Drug of Abuse	**Estimated Number of People (in millions)**
Marijuana	14.8
Prescription medications (nonmedical use)	7.0
Cocaine	2.4
Tranquilizers	1.8
Crack	0.7
Methamphetamine	0.7
MDMA (ecstasy)	0.5
Heroin	0.3
Oxycodone	0.1
LSD	0.1

Source: U.S. Department of Health and Human Services. *National Survey on Drug Use and Health.* Washington, DC: Government Printing Office; 2006.

(19.8%) than among youths aged 12 to 17 (3.3% abused drugs). Marijuana was again shown to be a major drug of abuse (16.3%). Among adults age 25 and older, 6.1% reported use of illicit drugs in the month prior to the survey. In this group, 4.2% abused marijuana, 2.2% used prescription-type drugs without any medical condition, and 0.8% abused cocaine, while only 0.1% abused hallucinogens and 0.2% abused inhalants.[6]

In general, males (10.5%) abuse drugs more than females (6.2%) among persons 12 years and older. Combined data from 2005 and 2006 showed that among pregnant women (ages 15 to 44), 4.0% reported abuse of illicit drugs in the month prior to the survey. Although only 5.9% of college graduates abuse drugs, compared with 8.6% of high school graduates and 9.2% of people who did not graduate from high school, college graduates are more likely to experiment with illicit drugs than adults who have not completed high school. College students aged 18 to 22 have lower current abuse of illicit drugs (19.2%) than people of the same age group (22.6%) who do not attend any college or are part-time students or in other grades. Among adults aged 18 or older, the rate of illicit drug use was higher among unemployed persons (18.5%) compared with persons who are employed full time (8.4%) or part time (9.4%). However, illicit drug use is relatively high in the criminal justice population compared with the general population in the United States. In 2006, 29.7% of people who were on parole or supervised release abused drugs. Among the 4.6 million people on probation at some time in 2006, 31.9% reported use of illicit drugs.[6]

Table 1-2	Percentages of People Aged 12 and Older Reporting Use of Illicit Drugs in the Previous Month
City	% of Population Abusing Drugs
Atlanta	8.3
Boston	8.5
Chicago	8.2
Dallas	6.5
Detroit	9.5
Houston	6.2
Los Angeles	8.2
Miami	8.2
New York	7.6
Philadelphia	9.1
Phoenix	7.6
San Francisco	12.7
Seattle	9.6
Washington, DC	6.5

Source: U.S. Department of Health and Human Services. National Survey on Drug Use and Health. Washington, DC: Government Printing Office; 2007.

DRUG ABUSE IN MAJOR U.S. CITIES

Among the 15 largest metropolitan statistical areas (big cities in the United States and surrounding areas, where 32.9% of the total U.S. population of 296 million lived in 2005), San Francisco has the highest percentage of illicit drug users (12.7%), followed by Detroit (9.6%). These percentages are higher than the percentage of illicit drug abuse (8.1%) in the general population. The rates of past-month illicit drug use were lower than the national average in Houston (6.2%), Dallas (6.5%), and Washington, DC (6.5%). Table 1-2 gives percentages of people abusing drugs in major cities of the United States.[7]

COMMONLY ABUSED DRUGS

According to surveys conducted by the U.S. Department of Health and Human Services (2002–2005), marijuana remains the most commonly abused drug in the United States.[5,6] Use of prescription medications for nonmedical purposes is also a serious public health issue. Cocaine abuse is widespread among the general population. In general, drugs that are commonly encountered in individuals in the United States can be classified under the following categories:

- *Cannabinoids:* marijuana, hashish
- *Stimulants:* amphetamines, methamphetamines, MDMA, cocaine
- *Narcotic analgesics and opiates:* opium, heroin, codeine, morphine, oxycodone, hydrocodone, meperidine, methadone, fentanyl and its analogs
- *Central nervous system depressants and tranquilizers:* barbiturates, diazepam, alprazolam, flunitrazepam and other

Table 1-3 Street Names of Common Drugs of Abuse in the United States	
Drug	**Street Name**
Marijuana	Ganja, herb, joint, pot, weed, dope, Mary Jane, skunk, reefer
Hashish	Hash, hemp oil, boom, chronic, gangster
Heroin	Brown sugar, dope, junk, white horse, smack, MDMA, ecstasy, XTX, X, Adam, peace, lover's speed
GHB	Liquid ecstasy, Georgia home boy, G, bodily harm
LSD	Acid, blotter, cubes
Cocaine	Coke, crack, rock, snow, candy, blow, bump, C
Fentanyl	China girl, dance fever, apache, tango and cash
α-methylfentanyl	China white
Morphine	Miss Emma, monkey, white stuff
Oxycodone	Oxy, OC, killer
Opium	Big O, black stuff, gum, hop
Amphetamine	Black beauty, hearts, speed, LA, truck drivers
Methamphetamine	Chalk, crystal, fire, glass, meth, ice, speed
Phencyclidine	Angel dust
Barbiturates	Barbs, red birds, yellow jacket
Benzodiazepines	Candy, sleeping pill, downers

benzodiazepines, methaqualone, gamma-hydroxybutyrate (GHB)

- *Anesthetics:* ketamine, phencyclidine
- *Hallucinogens:* LSD
- *Inhalants:* solvents, paint remover, gasoline, aerosol propellants, household gases such as butane and propane

The less frequently encountered agents are magic mushrooms (which contain mescaline), peyote cactus (psilocybin), and various designer drugs (see Chapter 3 and Chapter 13). Teenagers are more likely than adults to abuse solvents. In addition, drug abusers may also abuse various herbal products, such as jimson weed, and chew Khat leaves (known as Khat abuse) (see also Chapter 18). All agents with high abuse potential are treated as controlled substances in the United States, and their use is regulated by the Federal Drug Administration (FDA).

STREET NAMES OF COMMON DRUGS

Abused drugs are called by different names in the underground market and also among abusers. For example, in the United States common street names of the widely abused drug marijuana include "blunt" and "dope." Another drug that is sometimes encountered in date rape situations, GHB, is called "liquid ecstasy," "bodily harm," "easy lay," "Georgia home boy," and "G" by abusers who collect it from clandestine markets. **Table 1-3** gives street names of commonly abused drugs.

REGULATORY ISSUES

Governments in most parts of the world regulate drugs of abuse and related substances with high abuse potential. In the United States, the first federal laws passed for the purpose of controlling drugs were the 1906 District of Columbia Pharmacy Act and the 1906 Pure Food and Drug Act. In 1909 the Smoking Opium Exclusion Act was introduced, and in 1914 the Harrison Narcotic Act was passed. These regulations were created in response to the epidemic of opiate and cocaine abuse by immigrants in the United States. The Boggs Act of 1951 was introduced to sentence individuals found in violation of federal drug laws. The Daniel Act of 1956 established further sentencing guidelines for violators of federal drug laws. The Drug Abuse Control Act of 1956 provided guidelines for pharmaceutical industries for manufacturing and dispensing controlled substances. The Controlled Substances Act of 1970 regulated drugs that have medical benefits as well as prohibited the improper import, manufacture, distribution, and possession of controlled substances. The major focus of this law was the scheduling of drugs into five different classes based on abuse potential, harmfulness, and development of drug dependence as well as potential benefits when used for medical reasons.

Several amendments were later added to the Controlled Substances Act of 1970. In 1984 the Comprehensive Crime Control Act provided power to the attorney general and subsequently to DEA to classify a drug with high abuse potential as belonging to Schedule I prior to completion of formal review. Under this act, MDMA was classified as a Schedule I drug. The two other well-known amendments to the drug act are the Anti-Drug Abuse Acts of 1986 and 1988.[8]

CLASSIFICATION OF DRUGS AS CONTROLLED SUBSTANCES

Controlled substances are categorized in five groups depending on their medical need and abuse potential.[9]

- *Schedule I:* Drugs with high abuse potential and no known medical use. Heroin is a Schedule I drug.
- *Schedule II:* Drugs with currently accepted medical use but also a high abuse potential whose use may lead to drug dependency. Cocaine is a Schedule II drug.
- *Schedule III:* Drugs with a currently accepted medical use but also with a lower abuse potential than Schedule I and II drugs. Abuse of Schedule III drugs may cause moderate to low dependency. Anabolic steroids are classified as Schedule III drugs.
- *Schedule IV:* Drugs with current medical use but also low potential for abuse relative to Schedule I, II, and III drugs. Abuse of Schedule IV drugs may cause limited dependency relative to drugs classified in Schedule III. Diazepam is a Schedule IV drug.
- *Schedule V:* Drugs with a current medical use and a low potential for abuse compared with drugs in Schedule IV. Abuse of Schedule V drugs may lead to limited dependency relative to Schedule IV drugs. A cough mixture containing a low level of codeine is classified as a Schedule V drug.

Table 1-4 shows the classification of drugs of abuse as controlled substances.

Table 1-4	Commonly Abused Drugs Classified as "Controlled Substances" in the United States

Drug	Controlled Substance Category
Heroin	Schedule I
MDMA	Schedule I
5-methoxy-3,4-methyl-enedioxy-amphetamine	Schedule I
3,4,5-trimethoxy-amphetamine	Schedule I
GHB	Schedule I
Hashish	Schedule I
Marijuana	Schedule I
LSD	Schedule I
Mescaline	Schedule I
Peyote cactus (psilocybin and psilocin)	Schedule I
Cocaine	Schedule II
Fentanyl	Schedule II
Methadone	Schedule II
Oxycodone	Schedule II
Hydromorphone	Schedule II
Codeine	Schedule II
Amphetamine/ methamphetamine	Schedule II
Phencyclidine	Schedule II
Testosterone	Schedule III
Other anabolic steroids	Schedule III
Benzodiazepines	Schedule IV

ABUSE OF PRESCRIPTION MEDICATIONS

Abuse of prescription drugs is a serious public health concern worldwide. In 2006, out of an estimated 20.4 million Americans (8.3%) aged 12 or older who abused drugs, 7.0 million people abused prescription medications, while an estimated 14.8 million people abused marijuana.[6] Medications that belong to Schedule II to V are legally available with a prescription. People who abuse prescription drugs may obtain them illegally from underground markets, illegal Internet-based pharmacies, from friends or family members, or by "doctor shopping," the practice of going from one doctor to another claiming intense pain in order to get the same prescription from different physicians. Abusers may also attempt to mislead physicians to obtain prescription medications they do not need; however, the overwhelming majority of prescriptions by clinicians are done properly in the United States—fewer than 1% of physicians over-prescribe controlled substances.[10] Abusers of prescription medications may also use leftover medications from illness or injury, or they may visit Mexico, South America, and the Caribbean to obtain prescription medications. Some abusers even steal from others' medicine cabinets to obtain medications. Prescription medications are also sold illegally on streets; drug dealers may obtain these drugs from pharmacy or hospital theft, or from the illegal imports of these medications from other countries.[11]

The most commonly abused pain medications are oxycodone and hydrocodone with acetaminophen.[10] Other opiate analgesics are also abused, as well as various central nervous system depressants (such as benzodiazepines), central nervous system stimulants (such as phenmetrazine, dextroamphetamine), and medications used to treat attention deficit hyperactivity disorder (ADHD). The abuse of drugs used in treating ADHD is approximately 2% among the general population, but the rate is as high as 4.3% among young adults (age 18 to 25). Most individuals addicted to ADHD medication obtained this medication from friends and family members.[12] Arria et al studied the prevalence of nonmedical use of ADHD drugs among college students. Out of 1208 first-year college students aged 17 to 20, 218 (18.0%) were engaged in nonmedical use of prescription stimulants mostly for studying but also to "get high" or "party."[13] Benzodiazepines are also widely abused, especially among the elderly and individuals abusing opiates. Clinical studies suggest that use of benzodiazepines intensifies the abuse-related effects of opiates. In addition, people with a history of moderate to high alcohol abuse also tend to abuse benzodiazepines. In 2005, 34% of visits to emergency rooms due to nonmedical use of prescription medications involved use of sedatives or hypnotics. Moreover, the number of emergency room visits by individuals due to abuse of benzodiazepines was comparable to the number of emergency room visits due to abuse of opiates.[14] **Table 1-5** provides a list of commonly abused prescription medications.

Muscle relaxants such as carisoprodol (Soma) and drugs for treating erectile dysfunction like sildenafil (Viagra) are also abused, although to a lesser extent than benziodiazepine. Carisoprodol metabolizes to meprobamate, a Schedule IV drug that has a sedative and hypnotic effect. When ingested in high amounts, Carisoprodol can cause euphoria as well as impaired hand-eye coordination and balance. Sildenafil is abused by both men and women, and its abuse among individuals using MDMA is increasing because sildenafil can reverse the erectile dysfunction effect of ecstasy.[15]

ABUSE OF NONPRESCRIPTION MEDICATIONS

Dextromethorphan is present in many over-the-counter cough and cold medications (e.g., Robitussin DM, Vicks Formula 44). Although dextromethophan is safe and effective in the

Table 1-5	Commonly Abused Prescription Medications
Drug Class	**Commonly Abused Drugs**
Opiate analgesic	Oxycodone, Hydrocodone, Hydromorphone, morphine, codeine, Meperidine, methadone, propoxyphene
Barbiturates	Mephobarbital
Benzodiazepines	Diazepam, alprazolam, triazolam, lorazepam, clonazepam, chlordiazepoxide
Non-benzodiazepine hypnotic	Zolpidem, Zaleplon
Stimulants	Methylphenidate, phenmetrazine, dextro-amphetamine

recommended dosage, at higher dosages it can produce euphoria. Teenagers abuse dextromethorphan-containing products such as Coricidin HBP cough and cold medication (dextromethorphan hydrobromide 30 mg and chlorpheniramine malate 4 mg) in high doses in order to achieve a high-like state similar to the effect of LSD. From January 1 to October 1, 2000, the California Poison Control System reported that 65 out of 92 patients (71%) documented to have ingested high doses of Coricidin HBP had ingested the medication for abuse. Of these 65 patients, 58 (89%) of them were teenagers (aged 13 to 17). Street names for Coricidin include "poor man's PCP," "CCC," "red devils," "DXM," and "robo."[16] Other dextromethorphan-containing over-the-counter medications are also abused, such as cough syrup or capsules that contain guaifenesin, ephedrine, or pseudoephedrine. Dextromethorphan in high dosage (5 to 10 times the recommended dose) can cause psychosis, dependence, and physical withdrawal symptoms. At very high doses dextromethorphan can be life threatening. Diphenhydramine (Benadryl), an antihistamine that is often used as a sleep aid, is also abused. People with a genetic predisposition to addiction use diphenhydramine to get high or as a stimulant. People without an addictive genetic predisposition use this drug as a long-term hypnotic and sleeping aid. Other over-the-counter sleeping aids such as Sominex, Nytol, and Sleep-Eze are also abused because these drugs contain diphenhydramine and can produce hallucination, delirium, and confusion when taken in excessive amounts. Cyclizine, an over-the-counter antihistamine, is also abused because in high doses it produces a euphoric effect. Even the decongestant medications ephedrine and pseudoephe-drine are sometimes abused in order to prolong erection and sexual function.[16] The DEA has provided testimony to the U.S. Congress on the growing problem of misuse of medications. Joseph T. Rannazzisi, the deputy assistant administrator of the Office of Diversion Control, testified before the Subcommittee on Criminal Justice, Drug Policy, and Human Resources of the House Government Reform Committee on July 26, 2006.[10]

ADVERSE EFFECTS OF DRUGS OF ABUSE

Substance abuse in the workplace imposes a high cost on the employers due to lower productivity of workers, increased absenteeism, and more workplace accidents. Moreover, substance abuse treatment programs are responsible for a significant percentage of total health care spending in the United States. The substance abuse treatment cost in the United States increased from $9.3 billion in 1986 to $20.7 billion in 2003.[17] These high costs prompted many companies to implement workplace drug testing to deter employees from abusing drugs. Approximately 90% of Fortune 200 companies currently perform routine drug testing on their employees. Many companies have adopted "zero tolerance" policies regarding substance abuse. Studies have indicated that this testing deters employees from substance abuse, thus justifying implementation of workplace drug-testing programs.[18]

Alcohol and drug abuse are also associated with driving accidents and fatalities. A Consensus Development Panel in 1986 concluded that most drugs that affect the central nervous system have the potential to impair driving ability. Longo et al analyzed blood specimens from 2500 injured drivers and observed that overall, one-quarter of these drivers tested positive for drugs. Alcohol was the most frequently detected drug, followed by marijuana metabolite (THC-COOH), while benzodiazepines were detected at a lower rate. Male drivers were more likely to test positive for alcohol and marijuana, and female drivers were more likely to test positive for benzodiazepine.[19] Other studies also reported that after alcohol, cannabinoids are the most frequently found drugs detected in the blood of injured drivers.

Many reports in the literature describe fatality from accidental overdose of recreational drugs. Opiate overdose is a leading cause of death among drug abusers who inject drugs into their body (IUD). Over half of the deaths among heroin abusers are from overdose. Death from opioid overdose rarely occurs instantaneously; it usually takes place between one and three hours after overdose. Therefore, if a person with opiate overdose is brought to the hospital within a short period of time, life-saving measurements and therapy with the opiate antagonist naloxone (Narcan) can prevent death. One study found that 81% of heroin addicts are male, with a median age of 38. They typically have been abusing drugs over a median of 10 years and have witnessed a median of 6 overdoses in their course of drug abuse.[20] Although fatal overdose of heroin is usually encountered in IUD drug abusers, Rop et al reported an interesting case in which a person died from heroin ingestion. The urine showed the presence only of morphine at a very high level of 3650 ng/ml, but the blood showed the presence of heroin (109 ng/ml), heroin metabolite 6-acetylmorphine (168 ng/ml), and morphine (1140 ng/ml).[21]

Cocaine and opiate abuse are the leading causes of death among drug abusers. One survey of causes of fatal drug overdoses in New York City from 1990 to 1992 showed that cocaine, often with opiates and alcohol, accounted for almost three-fourths of the deaths, while opiates without cocaine caused the remaining overdoses. The highest rate of cocaine overdoses was observed among males, African Americans, and Latinos, but no racial difference was observed among individuals with opiate without cocaine overdose.[22] A study by Shah et al found that heroin, prescription opioids, cocaine, and alcohol/drug combinations together were responsible for 89% to 98% of accidental drug overdose fatalities between 1990 and 2005.[23] Except for drug couriers who swallow drug-containing packages ("body packers"), who usually die from massive overdoses of cocaine, death from accidental overdose of cocaine is usually not related to the concentration of cocaine in the blood. Most deaths from cocaine abuse occur after prolonged

drug abuse, which most likely initiates changes in tissue levels as well as in molecular and cellular levels.[24] Body packers that swallow or insert packets of drugs into their bodies for the purpose of evading custom officials are at higher risk of fatality from drug overdose due to rupture of the packages within the gastrointestinal tract. Body packers usually carry high-profit drugs such as heroin and cocaine. Koehler et al described a case of a body packer who died of cocaine overdose. Examination of the gastrointestinal system showed the presence of 3 plastic-wrapped balloons filled with white powder. A few ruptured balloons were also found in the stomach. The blood cocaine level was 4670 ng/ml.[25]

Although it occurs less frequently, fatality from overdose of drugs other than heroin, opiates, and cocaine has also been reported. Massive overdose from amphetamine or methamphetamine can also cause death. Usually methamphetamine is abused at a dose of 5 to 60 mg; the lethal dose is 200 mg or more.[26] Karch et al reported that blood concentrations of methamphetamine (2008 ng/ml vs 1780 ng/ml) and amphetamine (217 ng/ml vs 190 ng/ml) were indistinguishable in deaths for which methamphetamine was related to the cause of death and for which methamphetamine was not the primary cause of death.[27] Death caused by ingestion of GHB has also been reported. A 35-year-old male partying with friends ingested an unknown amount of wine and GHB. No alcohol or other drugs were detected in the body, but urine GHB concentration was 1665 μg/ml, while GHB concentrations in femoral and heart blood were 461 μg/ml and 276 μg/ml, respectively.[28] Tracqui et al reported a fatal case from overdose with sildenafil citrate (Viagra) for a 56-year-old male. The concentration of sildenafil in the postmortem blood was 6.27 μg/ml, at least 4 times the highest therapeutic level reported for sildenafil.[29]

 CONCLUSION

Drug abuse is a serious public health and public safety issue worldwide. Drug abuse not only reduces productivity at work but also is associated with driving accidents and accidental overdose from recreational drugs. Workplace drug testing deters employees from abusing drugs, thus justifying the extra cost to the companies for initiating and maintaining programs for the testing. Substance abuse rehabilitation programs also account for a significant portion of health care costs in the United States. Accidental heroin or cocaine overdose with or without alcohol are leading causes of deaths among drug abusers.

 REFERENCES

1. Norn S, Kruse PR, Kruse E. History of opium poppy and morphine. *Dan Medicinhist Arbog.* 2005;33:171–184.

2. Vetulani J. Drug addiction (Part I): psychoactive substances in the past and the present. *Pol J Pharmacol.* 2001;53:201–214.

3. Zuardi AW. History of cannabis as a medicine: a review. *Rev Bras Psiquiatr.* 2006;28: 153–157.

4. Karlsen SN, Spigset O, Slordal L. The dark side of ecstasy: neuropsychiatric symptoms after exposure to 3,4-methylenedioxymethamphetamine. *Basic Clin Pharmacol Toxiol.* 2008;102:15–24.

5. U.S. Department of Health and Human Services. *National Survey on Drug Use and Health.* Washington, DC: Government Printing Office; 2003. http://www.oas.samhsa.gov. Accessed November 4, 2008.

6. U.S. Department of Health and Human Services. *National Survey on Drug Use and Health.* Washington, DC: Government Printing Office; 2006. http://oas.samhsa.gov. Accessed November 4, 2008.

7. U.S. Department of Health and Human Services. *National Survey on Drug Use and Health.* (NSDUH Report) [Research findings from the SAMHSA 2002–2005 national surveys on drug use and health]. Washington, DC: Government Printing Office 2007. http://oas.samhsa.gov. Accessed November 4, 2008.

8. Courtwright DT. The controlled substances act: how a "big tent" reform became punitive drug law. *Drug Alcohol Depend.* 2004;75:9–15.

9. U.S. Drug Enforcement Administration. Schedules of Controlled Substances. http://www.usdoj.gov/dea/pubs/cas/812.htm. Accessed November 5, 2008.

10. Dekker AH. What is being done to address the new drug epidemic? *J Am Osteopath Assoc.* 2007;107(9 Suppl 5):E21–E26.

11. Inciardi JA, Surratt HL, Kurtz SP, Cicero TJ. Mechanism of prescription drug diversion among drug involved club and street based populations. *Pain Med.* 2007;8:171–183.

12. Novak SP, Kroutil LA, Williams RL, Van Brunt DL. The nonmedical use of prescription ADHD medications: result from a national Internet panel. *Subst Abuse Treat Prev Policy.* 2007;2:32 [open access journal].

13. Arria AM, Caldeira KM, O'Grady KE, et al. Nonmedical use of prescription stimulants among college students: association with attention deficit hyperactivity disorder and poly drug use. *Pharmacotherapy.* 2008;28: 159–169.

14. Licata SC, Rowlett JK. Abuse and dependence liability of benzodiazepine type drugs: GABA (A) receptor modulation and beyond. *Pharmacol Biochem Behav.* 2008;90:74–89.

15. Lessenger JE, Feinberg SD. Abuse of prescription and over the counter medications. *J Am Board Fam Med.* 2008;21:45–54.

16. Banerji S, Anderson IB. Abuse of Coricidin HBP cough and cold tablets: episodes recorded by a poison center. *Am J Health Syst Pharm.* 2001;58:1811–1814.

17. Mark TL, Levit KR, Vandivort-Warren R, et al. Trends in spending for substance abuse treatment, 1986-2003. *Heath Aff.* 2007;26: 1118–1128.

18. Carpenter CS. Workplace drug testing and worker drug use. *Heath Serv Res.* 2007;42: 795–810.

19. Longo MC, Hunter CE, Lokan RJ, et al. The prevalence of alcohol, cannabinoids, benzodiazepines, and stimulants amongst injured drivers and their role in drive the drug-positive group. *Accid Anal Prev.* 2000;32:613–622.

20. Sherman SG, Gann DS, Carlberg S, et al. A qualitative study of overdose responses among Chicago IUDs. *Harm Reduct J.* 2008;5:2 [Open access journal].

21. Rop PP, Fornaris M, Salmon T, et al. Concentrations of heroin, 06-monocaetylmorphine, and morphine in a lethal case following an oral heroin overdose. *J Anal Toxicol.* 2007;21:232–235.

22. Tardiff K, Marzuk PM, Leon AC et al. Accidental fatal drug overdoses in New York City: 1990–1992. *Am J Drug Alcohol Abuse.* 1996;22:135–146.

23. Shah NG, Lathrop SL, Reichard RR, Landen MG. Unintentional drug overdose trends in New Mexico, U.S.A., 1990–2005: combination of heroin, cocaine, prescription opioids and alcohol. *Addiction.* 2008;103:126–136.

24. Karch SB. Cocaine cardiovascular toxicity. *South Med J.* 2005;98:794–799.

25. Koehler SA, Ladham S, Rozin L, et al. The risk of body packing: a case of a fatal cocaine overdose. *Forensic Sci Int.* 2005;151: 81–84.

26. Sribanditmonogkol P, Chokjamsai M, Thampitak S. Methamphetamine overdose and fatality: two case reports. *J Med Assoc Thai.* 2000;83:1120–1123.

27. Karch SB, Stephens BG, Ho CH. Methamphetamine-related deaths in San Francisco: demographic, pathologic, and toxicologic findings. *J Forensic Sci.* 1999;44:259–268.

28. Mazarr-Proo S, Kerrigan S. Distribution of GHB in tissues and fluids following a fatal overdose. *J Anal Toxicol.* 2005;29:398–400.

29. Tracqui A, Miras A, Tabib A, Raul JS. Fatal overdosage with sildenafil citrate (Viagra): first report and review of literature. *Hum Exp Toxicol.* 2002;21:623–629.

CHAPTER 2

Pharmacology and Genetic Aspects of Abused Drugs

ABSTRACT

Drugs are metabolized, and several factors, including genetic ones, regulate disposition, metabolism, and excretion of drugs. Advances in human genetics have identified several genes that are associated with the addiction mechanism as well as the metabolism of abused drugs. Commonly abused drugs include amphetamine, methamphetamine, barbiturates, benzodiazepines, cocaine, opiates, methadone, phencyclidine (PCP), propoxyphene, and marijuana. In addition, designer drugs such as ecstasy (3,4-methylenedioxymethamphetamine), gamma-hydroxybutyrate (GHB), and various fentanyl derivatives (designer drugs) are also abused. This chapter summarizes pharmacologic and genetic aspects of commonly abused drugs.

Drug abuse is among the top three problems in the United States in terms of health care costs. Addiction to drugs and alcohol appears to arise from a number of factors, both genetic and environmental.

The chronic use of a drug despite negative consequences indicates that drug abuse is a psychiatric illness caused by the prolonged effects of a drug on the human brain.[1] The genetic vulnerability to drug addiction is supported by several familial, adoption, and twin studies,[2] although the complete gene variants involved are not understood and are an active area of investigation.

As discussed in Chapter 1, the most frequently abused drugs include various prescription opioid narcotic analgesics, propoxyphene, benzodiazepines, and barbiturates, as well as over-the-counter medications such as cold and cough medications. Genetic variation in regulation of enzymes in the liver plays an important role in the metabolism of these drugs.

In addition to the genetic factors, unique environmental factors may also play a role in determining the susceptibility of a person to drug addiction and relapse after successful detoxification. Behavior and stress contribute to the vulnerability of an individual to drug addiction.

THE ROLE OF DOPAMINE

Drugs of abuse exert their rewarding effect by activating a system that relies primarily on the neurotransmitter dopamine. The cell bodies that contain dopamine are found in an area in the middle of the brain called the ventral tegmental area. Drugs like cocaine, amphetamine, marijuana, nicotine, phencyclidine, and opiates increase extracellular concentrations of dopamine in this area, rewarding the user with pleasant effects. Imaging studies have shown that the reinforcing effects of abused drugs in humans depend not only on dopamine increase itself but also on the rate of dopamine increase, and more intense effects are observed with quickly rising dopamine levels. Interestingly, long-term drug abuse is associated with reduction in dopamine function.[3,4] Apart from the dopaminergic neurotransmission induced by addictive drugs, other neurotransmitters and pathways, including opioid, cholinergic, gamma-aminobutyric acid, nonadrenergic, serotonergic, and glutamatergic systems, are also involved in the neurobiologic process of drug addiction. In addition, studies have shown that intracellular mechanisms of signal transmission all play significant roles in the mechanism of addiction.[5]

GENETIC FACTORS RELATED TO DRUG ADDICTION

Genetic variation in the human genome is common. Most differences involve a single nucleotide variation, commonly called a single nucleotide polymorphism (SNP). The effect of genetic variations on determining vulnerability to drug addiction is still not clear. One study, known as the Harvard twin study of substance abuse, studied 8000 male twins who served in the U.S. military between 1965 and 1975. The study showed significant influence of genetic, shared environmental factors and unique environmental factors on patterns of addiction.[6] Some link between sensitivity of an individual to drug addiction and a person's genetic makeup has been established. Kendler et al studied 1196 male-male twin pairs, concluding that both genetic and shared environmental effects are risk factors for the abuse of cannabis, cocaine, hallucinogens, sedatives, stimulants, and opiates.[7]

The dopaminergic system plays an important role in the reward mechanism of the brain function. A decrease in dopamine function leads to abnormal drug- and alcohol-seeking behavior. A strong correlation has been demonstrated between a variant of the dopamine D_2 receptor gene and drug abuse, including cocaine abuse. Lower than normal density of dopamine receptors in brain tissue may lead to drug addiction. Using positron emission tomography (PET), Martinez et al demonstrated that cocaine-dependent subjects had a modest decrease in dopamine D_2 receptor availability.[8] Cocaine also directly blocks dopamine and serotonin transporters, thus blocking the reuptake of dopamine and serotonin in the releasing neurons. No association has been found between cocaine dependence and polymorphism in the serotonin transport gene. However, there is an association between Taq1 A and Taq1 B polymorphisms in the gene that codes for dopamine D_2 receptors and heavy use of stimulants.[9]

Dopamine D_2 and D_4 receptors play major roles in the reward effect of methamphetamine abuse. However, no association was observed in a Chinese male population between methamphetamine abuse and polymorphism of genes coding dopamine receptors.[10] One study found that genetic variation of the glycine transporter 1 gene

(*GLYT1*) may contribute to the vulnerability of methamphetamine dependence as well as methamphetamine-induced psychosis.[11] Using PET, Muncro et al observed a sex difference in release of dopamine in humans and concluded that the robust dopamine release in men compared with that in women could account for the increased vulnerability of men for use of methamphetamine or other stimulants.[12]

Although dopamine is the primary neurotransmitter of the reward pathway, serotonin, norepinephrine, gamma-aminobutyric acid (GABA) opioid, and cannabinoid receptors all modify dopamine metabolism and dopamine neurons. The μ-opioid receptor encoded by the *OPRM1* gene plays an important role in analgesic as well as addictive properties of opiate drugs. The analgesic effect of morphine depends on the amount of opioid receptors. More than 100 polymorphisms of the *OPRM1* gene have been described, and some of them are associated with tendency toward opiate addiction.[13] Specific haplotypes of the dopamine D_2 receptor gene are also associated with vulnerability to heroin dependence.[14]

The cannabinoid receptor CB1 is found in abundance in brain neurons, and CB2 and possibly CB3 are also present. CB1 plays an important role in regulating the behavioral effects of Δ^9-tetrahydrocannabinol (THC), the major psychoactive component of marijuana.[15] New evidence indicates that the gene that encodes the G-protein-coupled CB1 receptor might contribute to the individual differences in human vulnerability to addiction.[16]

METABOLISM OF ABUSED DRUGS

Most drugs are metabolized in the liver by what is known as cytochrome P450 mixed-function oxidase (CYP450), while CYP3A4 and CYP2D6, the two isoforms of cytochrome P450 mixed-function oxidase, are responsible for the metabolism of the majority of drugs in the liver. Extrahepatic organs such as kidneys, lungs, and liver may also express CYP450 enzymes. Genetic factors that determine the level of drug-metabolizing enzymes are certainly important for metabolism of certain drugs. Defective serum butyrylcholinesterase (also known as pseudocholinesterase) activity results in prolonged effects and the toxicity of the muscle relaxant succinylcholine in 1 out of 3500 patients. Polymorphism of gene-encoding CYP2D6 activity significantly affects the metabolism of tricyclic antidepressants and the response of a patient to therapy, as well as drug toxicity.[17] Genetic polymorphism of drug-metabolizing enzymes, N-acetyltransferase, and the enzymes CYP2D6 and CYP2C19 has significant clinical relevance, and genetic polymorphism of the CYP3A4 enzyme has also been described. The polymorphisms are expressed in two phenotypes: poor metabolizers that lack sufficient enzyme activity and extensive metabolizers. The prevalence of poor metabolizers varies significantly among individuals. If the metabolite of a drug is responsible for the pharmacologic response, a poor metabolizer may not show any response to the drug, or the user may experience drug toxicity. The ultra-metabolizers, who usually have duplicate genes, also do not respond to therapy because the drug is cleared too quickly from the body.

Variants of gene-encoding proteins involved in the metabolism of abused drugs play a role in vulnerability of an individual to drug addiction. Most opiates other than heroin and morphine are metabolized by cytochrome P450 enzymes. Codeine is metabolized to morphine by *CYP2D6*. Over 60 variants of the *CYP2D6* gene, which affects the analgesic response and abuse potential of drugs, have been described. Some of these variants increase the activity of *CYP2D6*, which increases the transformation of codeine to its more active metabolite, morphine, while other variants result in reduced enzyme activity. The activity of *CYP2D6* is reduced or absent in 7% of the Caucasian population, and these people do not respond to the analgesic effect of codeine.[18] Heroin is metabolized to 6-acetylmorphine in the body by plasma pseudocholinesterase (butyrylcholinesterase) and carboxylesterase 1 and then 6-acetylmorphine is further metabolized to morphine by carboxylesterase 2. Similarly, these enzymes are responsible for metabolism of cocaine. More recently, the activity of several human cholinesterase variants with cocaine has been reported. One variant of cholinesterase has 10-fold lower binding efficiency and catalytic activity for metabolizing cocaine.[19] In the Iranian population, 70% to 80% of people have an atypical mutation of butyrylcholinesterase, whereas in European and American populations only 4% of people carry this atypical allele. This atypical variant of butyrylcholinesterase is known to be associated with toxicity and prolonged apnea after administration of the muscle relaxants succinylcholine or mivacurium, and it is also thought to be associated with abnormal sensitivity to cocaine toxicity.[20] **Table 2-1** gives examples of some genes that are associated with addiction and pharmacogenomics.

AMPHETAMINE, METHAMPHETAMINE, AND SIMILAR DRUGS

Amphetamine and methamphetamine are derivatives of phenethylamine that are also called sympathomimetic amines. Both drugs act as stimulants. Amphetamine and

Table 2-1   Some Genes Associated with Addiction and Pharmacogenetics

Gene	Drug Involved
Butylcholinesterase	Cocaine
Cytochrome P450 family 2, subfamily A, polypeptide 6 (*CYP2D6*)	Codeine
Cytochrome P450 family 3, subfamily A, polypeptide 4 (*CYP3A4*)	Various drugs
Dopamine transporter	Opiates
Dopamine receptors D2, D3, and D4	Opiates, stimulants
Opioid receptor κ 1	Opiates
Opioid receptor μ 1	Opiates
Glycine transporter1 (*GLYT1*)	Methamphetamines

methamphetamine are optically active compounds, and it is the d-isomers of amphetamine and methamphetamine that are abused because of their more stimulatory effects compared with l-isomers. Both drugs can produce increased alertness, energy, self-confidence, and euphoria while decreasing fatigue and appetite. Both amphetamine and methamphetamine are used medically for treating attention deficit disorder, obesity, and narcolepsy and can be administered orally because of their good bioavailability. In addition, protein bindings of amphetamine and methamphetamine are low (less than 20%). Both amphetamine and methamphetamine are controlled substances and are classified as Schedule II drugs.

Hepatic and renal clearance contribute to the elimination of amphetamine and methamphetamine with an elimination half-life between 6 and 12 hours. Hepatic metabolism is extensive, but a significant part of both drugs is excreted unchanged in urine. Amphetamine and related compounds have a weak base, with pKa around 9.9, and have relatively low molecular weights. Therefore, amphetamine and related compounds can diffuse through cell membranes and lipid layers to tissues and biological matrices that have a pH lower than that of blood. In addition to urine and blood, amphetamine-like compounds can also be detected in alternative matrices such as sweat, saliva, hair, and nail.[21]

Other than being excreted unchanged in urine, the two major hepatic pathways of amphetamine metabolism are aromatic hydroxylation to para-hydroxyamphetamine and oxidative deamination to produce, finally, benzoic acid.[22] A small portion of the drug is also converted into norephedrine. Almost half of methamphetamine is excreted in urine unchanged, but methamphetamine is also metabolized to amphetamine. Therefore, amphetamine must be detected in the urine specimen of an individual who is abusing methamphetamine. **Table 2-2** lists major metabolites of amphetamine and methamphetamine.

Fatal poisoning from amphetamine and methamphetamine has been reported in the literature. In addition, methamphetamine abuse increases the length of hospital stay for minimally injured patients. It results in trauma center resource utilization disproportional to the severity of injury.[23]

MDMA (ecstasy) is a synthetic designer drug with structural similarity to methamphetamine. This drug is widely abused in all-night "rave" parties and for other recreational purposes. CYP2D6, an enzyme of the cytochrome P450 family, metabolizes MDMA to 3,4-methylenedioxyamphetamine

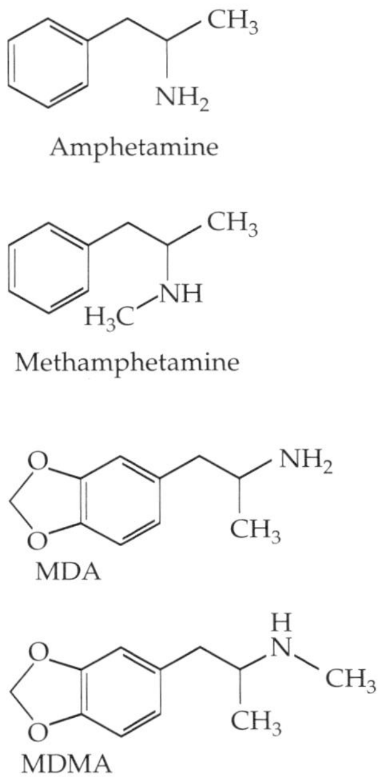

Figure 2-1. *Chemical Structures of Amphetamine, Methamphetamine, MDA, and MDMA*

(MDA), 4-hydroxy-3-methoxymethamphetamine, and 4-hydroxy-3-methoxyamphetamine. About 10% of the Caucasian population are genetically deficient for hepatic CYP2D6 activity, which puts them at risk of developing acute toxicity from moderate use of MDMA. Moreover, enzyme saturation causes a disproportionate increase in MDMA concentrations in plasma. Studies have indicated that small increases in MDMA dosage may translate into higher increases in MDMA plasma levels, causing MDMA toxicity even in individuals who are not deficient in CYP2D6 activity.[24] **Figure 2-1** gives the chemical structures of amphetamine and methamphetamine along with the designer drugs MDMA and MDA.

Table 2-2   Major Metabolites of Commonly Abused Drugs

Drug	Major Metabolite
Amphetamine	Amphetamine, norephedrine
Methamphetamine	Amphetamine, norephedrine
Barbiturates	
Secobarbital	3-hydroxysecobarbital, secodiol
Pentobarbital	3-hydroxy pentobarbital
Amobarbital	3-hydroxy amobarbital
Phenobarbital	Para-hydroxy phenobarbital[a]
Benzodiazepines	
Alprazolam	4-hydroxy alprazolam, α-hydroxy alprazolam
Diazepam	Oxazepam*, nordiazepam
Lorazepam	Conjugated with glucuronic acid
Oxazepam	Conjugated with glucuronic acid
Clonazepam	7-aminoclonazepam
Triazolam	4-hydroxy triazolam α-hydroxy triazolam
Cocaine	Benzoylecgonine, ecgonine methyl ester
Heroin	6-monoacetylmorphine, morphine[a]
Codeine	Morphine*
Morphine	Morphine 3-glucuronide
Hydromorphone	Hydromorphone
Hydrocodone	Hydromorphone
Oxycodone	Oxymorphone
Methadone	2-ethylidene-1, 5-dimethyl-3, 3-diphenyl pyrrolidine (EDDP) and 2-ethyl-5-methyl-3, 3-diphenylpyrrolidine (EMDP)
Phencyclidine	Various hydroxy metabolites
Propoxyphene	Norpropoxyphene
Tetrahydrocannabinol	11-nor-9-carboxy Δ^9-tetrahydrocannabinol[a] (THC-COOH)

a. Also excreted in urine as a conjugate of glucuronic acid.

BARBITURATES

Barbiturates are central nervous system (CNS) depressants and are used medically as sedative hypnotic drugs, as well as anesthetics and anticonvulsants. Barbituric acid, which was synthesized in 1864, is devoid of any pharmacologic activity. In the early 1900s barbital, the first barbituric acid derivative with pharmacologic activity was discovered. More than 2500 derivatives of barbituric acid have been synthesized, of which 50 were marketed. About 12 different barbiturates are used medically. Based on the duration of action, barbiturates are classified as ultra short acting, short acting, intermediate acting, and long acting. Long-acting barbiturates, such as phenobarbital (Luminal) and mephobarbital (Mebaral), are classified as Schedule IV drugs and are medically used as anticonvulsants and also for daytime sedation. The action of barbiturates may last up to 12 hours. These long-acting barbiturates are not abused because they produce little euphoria.

The ultra-short-acting barbiturates can produce anesthetic effects within minutes after intravenous administration. Thiopental (Pentothal), thiamyl (Surital), and methohexital (Brevital) are ultra-short-acting barbiturates that are used medically. Both thiopental and thiamyl are classified as Schedule III drugs. Other short- and intermediate-acting barbiturates that are also classified as Schedule III drugs include butalbital (Fiorinal), butabarbital (Butisol), talbutal (Lotusate), and aprobarbital (Alurate). After oral administration, the onset of action is within 15 to 40 minutes. The effects of these barbiturates may last up to 6 hours. These drugs are used for treating insomnia and may also be used to achieve preoperative sedation. Short- and intermediate-acting barbiturates that are classified as Schedule II drugs include amobarbital (Amytal), pentobarbital (Nembutal), and secobarbital (Seconal). Drug abusers usually prefer amobarbital, pentobarbital, and secobarbital. A combination of amobarbital and secobarbital (Tuinal) is also abused. Veterinarians use pentobarbital for anesthesia and euthanasia.[25] **Figure 2-2** lists the chemical structures of commonly abused barbiturates.

The γ-aminobutyric acid (GABA) system plays an important role in anxiety disorder. GABA, the major inhibitory neurotransmitter in the brain, activates various GABA receptors (GABA$_A$, GABA$_C$, and GABA$_B$). Barbiturates are activated through GABA-mediated inhibition of synaptic transmission. At low doses, barbiturates act as modulators of GABA receptors. At higher doses barbiturates act as GABA agonists. Barbiturates reduce anxiety at dosages close to those used

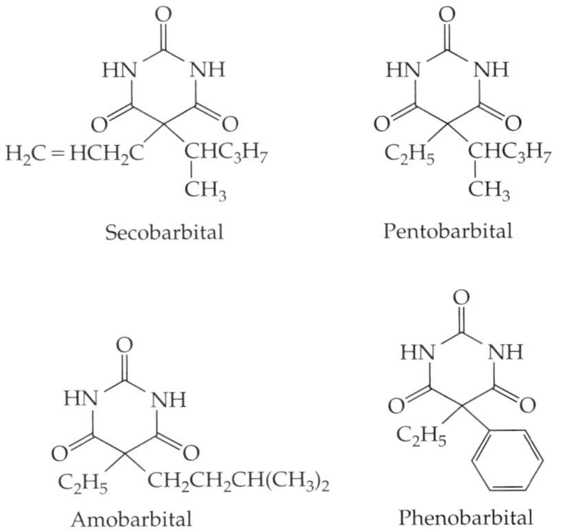

Figure 2-2. *Chemical Structures of Commonly Abused Barbiturates: Secobarbital, Pentobarbital, Amobarbital, and Phenobarbital*

to produce hypnotic effects; such dosages also affect motor skill and mood. Chronic use of barbiturates leads to dependence. Because barbiturates bind nonselectively with GABA receptors and have negative side effects, these drugs are usually replaced by benzodiazepines in treating anxiety disorders.[26]

Barbiturates are extensively metabolized to a number of different metabolites. Secobarbital is metabolized to 3-hydroxy-secobarbital, secodiol, and 5-(1-methylbutyl) barbituric acid. None of the metabolite has any pharmacologic activity. Pentobarbital is metabolized primarily to 3-hydroxypentobarbital, which is inactive. Another metabolite, N-hydroxypentobarbital, is present in much lower amounts in urine compared with 3-hydroxypentobarbital. A major metabolite of amobarbital is 3-hydroxy-amobarbital, which has some pharmacologic potency.[27] Table 2-2 gives major metabolites of commonly abused barbiturates.

BENZODIAZEPINES

Benzodiazepines are some of the most frequently prescribed drugs in the United States and are used as tranquilizers, muscle relaxants, anticonvulsants, and also to treat anxiety disorder. There are more than 50 different types of benzodiazepines, but only 15 members of these are marketed in the United States, which classifies them as Schedule IV drugs. The most commonly prescribed benzodiazepines in the United States are diazepam, temazepam, alprazolam, lorazepam, and clonazepam.

Benzodiazepines are CNS depressants that produce sedation in low dosage, act as anxiolytics in moderate dosage, and have hypnotic effects in high dosage. Short-acting benzodiazepines are generally prescribed to treat insomnia. These benzodiazepines include estazolam (ProSom), flurazepam (Dalmane), temazepam (Restoril), and triazolam (Halcion). These benzodiazepines have hypnotic effects. Another short-acting benzodiazepine, midazolam (Versed) is used in critical-care patients for sedation and also used prior to anesthesia. Benzodiazepines with a longer duration of action— for example, alprazolam (Xanax), chlordiazepoxide (Librium), clorazepate (Tranxene), diazepam (Valium), halazepam (Paxipam), lorazepam (Ativan), oxazepam (Serax), prazepam (Centrax), and quazepam (Doral)—are used for treating insomnia and anxiety disorders. Other benzodiazepines such as clonazepam (Klonopin), diazepam, and clorazepate are used as anticonvulsants. Zolpidem (Ambien) and zaleplon (Sonata) are benzodiazepine-like depressants of the CNS that are used in the short-term treatment of insomnia. Both of these drugs are classified as Schedule IV drugs and are benzodiazepine receptor antagonists.[28,29]

The anxiolytic effects of benzodiazepines are related to enhanced γ-aminobutyric acid (GABA) neurotransmission. Benzodiazepines bind selectively to the benzodiazepine/GABA receptor complex, thereby increasing the affinity of these receptors for γ-aminobutyric acid. When γ-aminobutyric acid binds to GABA receptors, the frequency of chloride channel openings is increased and the cells are hyperpolarized. As a result, cellular excitability decreases, producing the anxiolytic effect of benzodiazepines.[29] Two central benzodiazepine receptor subtypes (BZ1 and BZ2) and one peripheral benzodiazepine receptor have been identified. BZ1 receptors are found in the part of the brain responsible for sedation, while BZ2 receptors are concentrated in the area of the brain responsible for cognition, memory, and psychomotor action. Most benzodiazepines except quazepam bind nonselectively to both receptor subtypes, accounting for both hypnotic effect and the adverse effect of benzodiazepines. Long-term treatment with benzodiazepines results in tolerance and dependence in the patient.

Commonly abused benzodiazepines are diazepam (Valium), alprazolam (Xanax), chlordiazepoxide (Librium), lorazepam (Ativan), oxazepam (Serax), clonazepam (Klonopin), and triazolam (Halcion). Other benzodiazepines are also abused. In one study in Norway, the most common benzodiazepines detected in the blood of people driving under the influence of drugs included diazepam, oxazepam, clonazepam, nitrazepam, and alprazolam.[30] Because of the widespread abuse of different benzodiazepines, most commercially available immunoassays can detect a wide variety of benzodiazepines and their metabolites. **Figure 2-3** shows structures of commonly abused benzodiazepines.

The half-life of benzodiazepines varies widely depending on the particular drug. For example, chlordiazepoxide has a half-

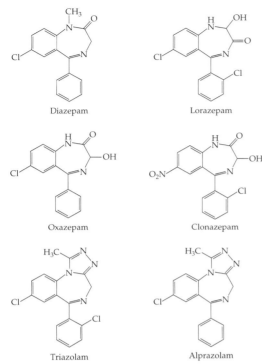

Figure 2-3. *Chemical Structures of Commonly Abused Benzodiazepines: Diazepam, Lorazepam, Oxazepam, Clonazepam, Triazolam, and Alprazolam*

life of 5 to 30 hours, while the half-lives of diazepam, oxazepam, clorazepate, and lorazepam are 20 to 50 hours, 5 to 20 hours, 30 to 60 hours, and 10 to 15 hours, respectively.[31] Alprazolam has an average half-life of 12 hours, while the average half-lives of estazolam, flurazepam, quazepam, temazepam, and zolpidem are 16 hours, 36 hours, 11 hours, 2.9 hours, and 2.3 hours, respectively.[29]

Benzodiazepines are extensively metabolized by liver enzymes and are excreted in the urine. Oxazepam, a common metabolite of both diazepam and temazepam, is an active metabolite. Oxazepam is conjugated and excreted in urine as oxazepam glucuronide.

Diazepam is also metabolized to the active metabolite nordiazepam. Clorazepate is metabolized to nordiazepam, and further metabolized to oxazepam. Chlordiazepoxide is metabolized to norchlordiazepoxide and demoxepam, which are both active metabolites. Demoxepam is further metabolized to nordiazepam, and nordiazepam is subsequently metabolized to oxazepam.

Alprazolam is metabolized to two hydroxylated metabolites: 4-hydroxy alprazolam and α-hydroxy alprazolam. Both metabolites are active, but the activities are lower than those of the parent drug. Therefore, clinical activity of alprazolam is mostly due to the parent compound.[32] The major metabolite of estazolam is 4-hydroxy estazolam, which is devoid of any biological activity. Both flurazepam and quazepam are slowly eliminated from the body to N-desalkyl-2-oxoquazepam. Temazepam is eliminated mainly by conjugation-producing temazepam glucuronide. A minor fraction of temazepam is metabolized to oxazepam, and then it is also conjugated in the liver. Triazolam undergoes extensive first-pass metabolism, thus reducing its bioavailability. Its half-life is 2 to 3 hours. Major hydroxy metabolites of triazolam are α-hydroxy triazolam and 4-hydroxy triazolam (29). Table 2-2 lists major metabolites of commonly abused benzodiazepines.

COCAINE ABUSE

Cocaine is extracted from the leaves of *Erythroxylon coca,* a shrub that grows in many parts of South America but primarily in Bolivia and Peru. Indigent people of South America, in the past, chewed the coca leaf for recreational purpose. Cocaine was first isolated from the coca leaf in 1855. Currently there is no prescription medication that contains cocaine. Cocaine is used only as a topical anesthetic in ear, nose, and throat surgery, in ophthalmologic procedures, or in skin suturing. A combination of tetracaine, adrenalin, and cocaine is also used for topical anesthesia. Medical use of cocaine may cause a positive urine test for cocaine up to 2 to 3 days after a procedure. The physician performing the procedure must always document such use of cocaine in the medical record of the patient. In the case of a positive drug test for cocaine, records of medical use of cocaine must be verified by a medical review officer (MRO) (see also Chapter 15). Cocaine is a Schedule II drug.

Cocaine promotes the transmission of dopamine, a neurotransmitter in the part of the brain associated with producing pleasure, called the mesolimbic reward pathway. Dopamine transporter is responsible for terminating synaptic transmission of dopamine by transporting it out of the synaptic cleft and putting dopamine back into the presynaptic terminal. Cocaine prevents this process by selectively binding to the dopamine transporter by prolonging the life of dopamine in the synaptic cleft, producing a pleasurable effect. Prolonged use of cocaine leads to dependence and addiction. From a medical perspective, cocaine addiction is a drug-induced disease of neuroplasticity in the brain circuit mediating normal reward learning. Addicts have uncontrolled urges to take the drug.[33] Repeated abuse of cocaine alters the brain chemistry, affecting dopamine, GABA, and glutamate regulation of pyramidal cell activity.[34]

Cocaine is abused in the form of hydrochloride salt, which can be snorted. Crack cocaine is a form of cocaine that has not been neutralized by acid to produce hydrochloride salt. Crack cocaine comes as rock crystal, which can be heated, and the resulting smoke can be inhaled for abuse.

The term "crack cocaine" comes from the cracking sound that is produced during heating.

Cocaine has a short half-life, and the body rapidly deactivates it by producing inactive metabolites. After intravenous cocaine administration of 0.2 mg/Kg in healthy volunteers, peak plasma concentration was achieved after 6.7 minutes (on average). The average elimination half-life of cocaine was 45.2 minutes in men, while in women the average plasma half-life of cocaine was 46.4 minutes. No significant difference in the pharmacokinetic parameter of cocaine was observed between men and women.[35] Benzoylecgonine and ecgonine methyl ester are the major urinary metabolites of cocaine. Cocaine is rapidly metabolized by plasma butyrylcholinesterase into ecgonine methyl ester. Benzoylecgonine probably arises spontaneously in plasma by hydrolysis of cocaine in vivo. A minute amount of unchanged cocaine can also be recovered in urine. Liver enzymes also metabolize a small amount of cocaine into norcocaine. Other minor metabolites of cocaine include p (para)-hydroxy-cocaine, m (meta)-hydroxy-cocaine, p-hydroxy-benzoylecgonine, and m-hydroxy-benzoylecgonine.[36] Table 2-2 lists major metabolites of cocaine.

Abuse of Cocaine and Alcohol: A Deadly Combination

Simultaneous abuse of cocaine and alcohol (ethanol) causes more toxicity than abuse of cocaine or alcohol alone. Such combined abuse leads to significant increases in morbidity and mortality. Controlled studies have shown substantial increases in cardiovascular response to the combination of cocaine and alcohol compared with cocaine alone. The combined effect of cocaine and alcohol in humans is related to the formation of cocaethylene, the active metabolite of cocaine with cocaine-like pharmacological properties. Cocaethylene is formed by the transesterification of benzoylecgonine in the presence of ethanol by liver carboxylesterase. In one controlled study, the authors reported significantly increased heart rates in subjects who received both cocaine and alcohol compared with subjects who received cocaine alone. Moreover, euphoria was greater in subjects with the cocaine-alcohol combination compared with subjects who received cocaine alone. Cocaine exposure was also greater in combination with cocaine and alcohol compared with cocaine alone, and the half-life of cocaethylene (average 156 minutes) was significantly longer than the half-life of cocaine.[37] **Figure 2-4** gives the chemical

structures of cocaine, benzoylecgonine, and cocaethylene.

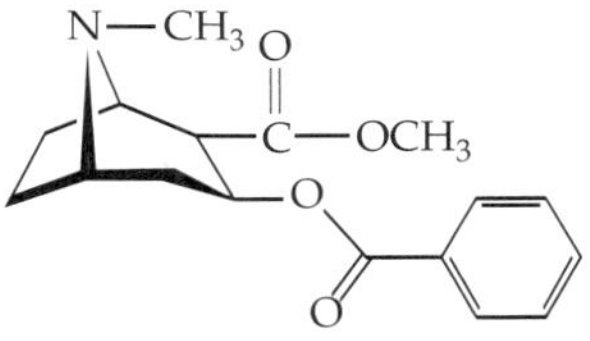

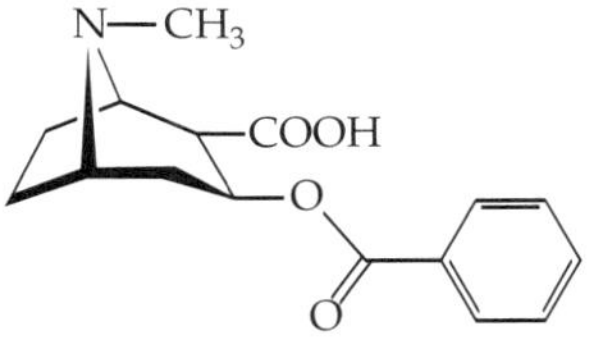

MARIJUANA

Δ^9-tetrahydrocannabinol (THC) is the most active component (out of over 60 related compounds identified) of marijuana, which is found in various parts of the cannabis plant (*Cannabis sativa*) including flowers, stem, and leaves. Marijuana is abused worldwide, mostly by smoking cigarettes containing marijuana. It is the most commonly abused drug in the Unites States as well as in the United Kingdom. The most potent form of marijuana, known as sinsemilla, is prepared from dried parts of mostly indoor-grown female plants. Marijuana usually consists of dried parts of plants grown outdoors. Hashish, a resin-like material is extracted from flowers and glandular trichomes. Hashish is usually sold as cakes that are dark brown to black in color. Hashish is usually more potent than marijuana because its THC content is higher. The highest amount of marijuana is found in sinsemilla, followed by hashish. In one report, the median THC content of sinsemilla was 13.9%, followed by 3.54% in hashish, while the median THC content of marijuana was 2.14%. However, cannabidiol, another component of the cannabis plant that antagonizes the effect of THC, was also found in small amounts in hashish, sinsemilla, and other marijuana preparations. People who consistently abuse marijuana, especially the preparation lacking antipsychotic cannabidiol, are at greater risk of developing schizophrenia-like psychosis.[38] THC exerts its effect by binding to specific cannabinoid receptors in the brain. Interestingly, both THC and opioids produce an analgesic effect through G-protein-coupled mechanisms that block propagation of neurotransmitters causing

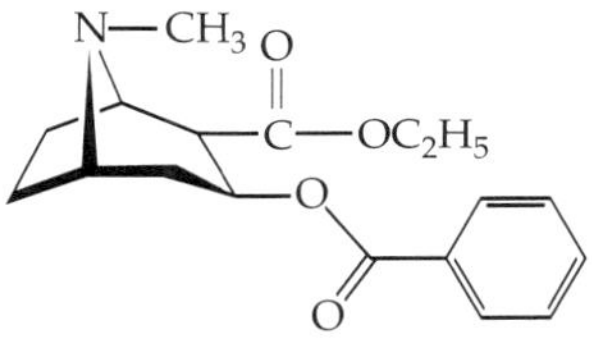

Figure 2-4. *Chemical Structures of Cocaine, Benzoylecgonine, and Cocaethylene*

pain in the brain and spinal cord. The analgesic effect of THC may also be due to interaction of THC with delta and kappa opioid receptors.[39]

A synthetic THC marketed under the brand name Marinol is a prescription medication available in 2.5-, 5-, or 10-mg dosages for stimulating appetite in patients with acquired immune deficiency syndrome (AIDS) and also for treating nausea and vomiting in cancer patients receiving chemotherapy. The peak level of marijuana in the blood appears faster after smoking marijuana than taking it orally. Pulmonary assimilation of inhaled THC produces a maximum plasma concentration within minutes, and psychotropic effects reach a maximum after 15 to 30 minutes and may last as long as 2 to 3 hours. Following oral administration, psychotropic effects start after 30 to 90 minutes, reach a maximum in 2 to 3 hours, and may last 4 to 12 hours. The most important acute adverse effects are anxiety and panic attacks with increased blood pressure and heart rate.[40] THC is rapidly oxidized by cytochrome P450 enzymes (mostly CYP3A4, CYP2C9, and CYP2C11) to 11-hydroxy Δ^9-tetrahydrocannabinol (11-OH-THC), an equipotent psychoactive metabolite, and also to 11-nor-9-carboxy Δ^9-tetrahydrocannabinol (THC-COOH), an inactive metabolite. Smaller quantities of other metabolites are also formed. After oral administration both THC and its active metabolite 11-OH-THC are found in blood in almost equal quantities, but after smoking marijuana or injecting it intravenously only THC and a small amount of active metabolite are able to be detected in the blood. The plasma half-life of THC after oral administration is approximately 30 hours, but after intravenous administration, the average plasma half-life is 23 hours.[41] The major urinary metabolite

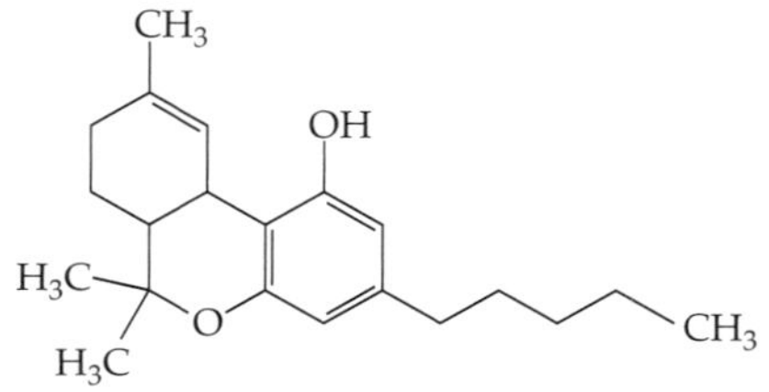

Tetrahydrocannabinol (THC)

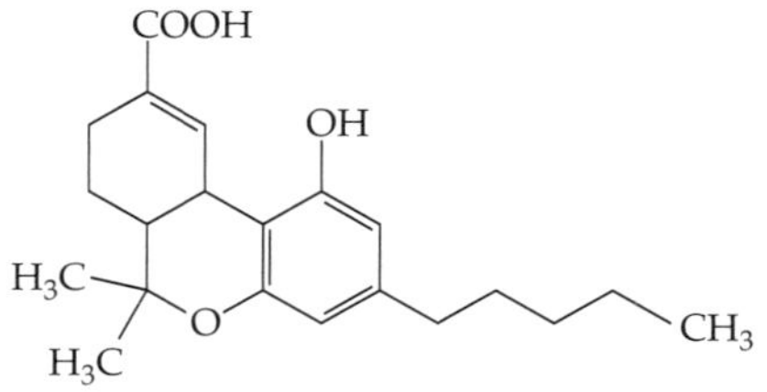

11-nor-9-carboxyΔ^9-tetrahydrocannabinol

Figure 2-5. *Chemical Structures of THC and TCH-COOH*

of THC is THC-COOH, which is found in urine in conjugated form. **Figure 2-5** gives the chemical structures of THC and its major metabolite.

OPIATES

Poppy plants (*P. somniferum* and other varieties) are annual plants that can grow almost anywhere. Opium is found in the latex (a milky fluid) collected from immature seed capsules of poppy plants 1 to 3 weeks after flowering by incision of green seed pods. More than 20 alkaloids have been isolated from *Papaverus somniferum*, out of which 3 alkaloids (morphine, codeine, and noscapine [antitussive]) are used in therapy. Another natural component, thebaine, is used for synthesis of oxycodone and the opiate antagonist naloxone. Several prescription medications for treating moderate to severe pain contain morphine, codeine, hydrocodone, oxycodone, or related opioids. Oxymorphone is the newest oral opioid used in treating moderate to severe persistent pain (see also Chapter 15). Heroin (diacetylmorphine) was synthesized in 1874. Heroin has no known medical use. Heroin is classified as a Schedule I drug, while morphine and codeine are both Schedule II drugs. **Figure 2-6** gives the chemical structures of opiates.

Morphine is available for administration in oral form, but its effect is usually diminished when given orally. Morphine is most effective as an intravenous injection. However, codeine, hydromorphone, and oxycodone can be administered orally. The major analgesic effect of codeine is due to its active metabolite, morphine. Heroin has little oral bioavailability because it is subjected to complete first-pass metabolism. The heroin abuser takes this drug by injection.

Heroin is metabolized to 6-acetylmorphine and then morphine by hydrolysis of ester linkage by pseudocholinesterase in serum and also in the liver by human carboxylesterase-1 and carboxylesterase-2. A small part of morphine (less than 5%) is normorphine, but the majority of morphine is excreted in urine as morphine-3-glucuronide. This metabolite is formed by conjugation in the liver by the action of the liver enzyme uridine diphosphate glucuronosyltransferase. Codeine is metabolized to morphine in the liver mostly by CYP2D6.[19] Hydromorphone is also excreted in urine, mostly in conjugated form, but a small part of free hydromorphone can also be recovered in urine. Oxycodone is metabolized to oxymorphone, which is then conjugated in the liver. Another metabolite of oxycodone is the relatively inactive noroxycodone. Table 2-2 lists the major metabolites of opiates.

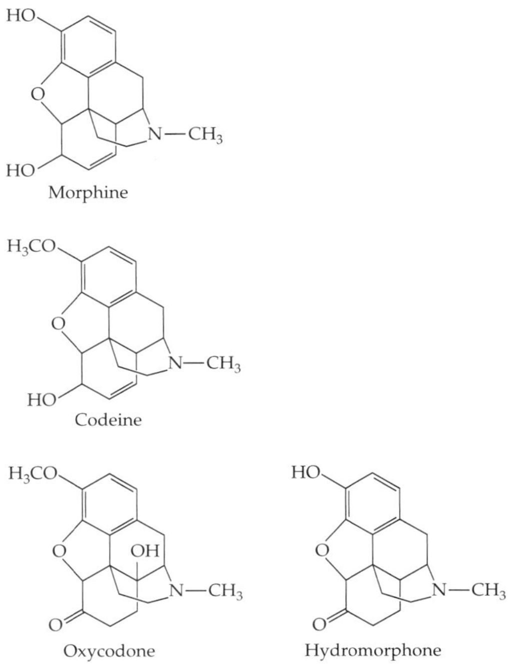

Figure 2-6. *Chemical Structures of Morphine, Codeine, Oxycodone, and Hydromorphone*

METHADONE

Methadone is a synthetic opiate widely used for the treatment of heroin and opiate dependency. Methadone is also an effective analgesic, especially for neuropathic pain management. Methadone is available as a racemic mixture, but most of its activity is due to the R-isomer. Methadone binds to the μ-opiate receptor and thus exerts its pharmacological effect. In addition, methadone also acts as an agonist of N-methyl-D-aspartate receptors, which may increase the effectiveness of methadone in treating neuropathic pain. The oral bioavailability of methadone is 60% to 70%. Methadone is strongly bound to serum proteins, mostly

α_1-acid glycoprotein. For treatment of heroin and opiate dependency, methadone can be administered orally once a day, but for pain management more frequent dosing is needed. The elimination half-life of methadone is 15 to 55 hours, but the analgesic effect lasts only for 4 to 6 hours. Methadone is mostly metabolized by cytochrome P 450 enzymes in the liver, especially by CYP3A4 but also to a lesser extent by CYP2D6. Methadone is also metabolized in the intestines. The methadone half-life may be prolonged in approximately 10% of the Caucasian population, who tend to be poor metabolizers and have low CYP2D6 activity.[42] Two major pharmacologically inactive urinary metabolites of methadone are 2-ethylidene-1,5-dimethyl-3,3-diphenylpyrrolidine (EDDP) and 2-ethyl-5-methyl-3,3-diphenylpyrrolidine (EMDP). Although methadone has been used clinically for more than 35 years for treating heroin addiction, higher dosage is needed for pain management. There are reports of ventricular arrhythmia in patients when higher dosages of methadone are used, indicating the need for screening of patients using ECG prior to administration of methadone. There may be an association between methadone use and torsade de pointes in patients.[43] Unfortunately, methadone is also abused, especially in combination with other illicit drugs.

PROPOXYPHENE

Propoxyphene, which is structurally similar to methadone and binds to opiate receptors, is administered orally for treating mild to moderate pain and was approved by the Federal Drug Administration in 1957. Propoxyphene exists as an optical isomer where d-propoxyphene has analgesic activity and is used in pain management, while the l-isomer is devoid of analgesic activity and is used medically as an antitussive agent (Novrad). Propoxyphene (65 mg of hydrochloride salt is equivalent to 100 mg napsylate salt) is used alone or in combination with acetaminophen for pain control. Propoxyphene has approximately 33% to 50% of the potency of codeine. After oral administration, peak plasma concentrations of propoxyphene can be observed after 2 hours and the average plasma half-life is 15 hours. Propoxyphene is metabolized by liver enzymes, mainly by CYP2D6, to norpropoxyphene. Propoxyphene is both a substrate and an inhibitor of CYP2D6 and has pharmacokinetically important drug interactions with drugs that are metabolized via CYP2D6. Norpropoxyphene has a substantially longer half-life than propoxyphene, and this metabolite tends to accumulate in plasma of patients with renal impairment. Norpropoxyphene is an active metabolite that has local anesthetic effects similar to those of lidocaine. However, norpropoxyphene has more cardiac toxicity than propoxyphene and can initiate pulmonary edema, apnea, cardiac arrest, and death. Propoxyphene should not be prescribed to patients who are suicidal or prone to addiction. Moreover, this drug should be prescribed with extreme caution to patients taking antidepressants or tranquilizers, or who abuse alcohol. Prolonged use of this drug may cause dependence. Unfortunately, due to the euphoric effect of propoxyphene, this drug is also abused.[44] **Figure 2-7** gives the chemical structures of methadone and propoxyphene.

PHENCYCLIDINE

Phencyclidine (PCP) was developed in the 1950s as a human anesthetic but was discontinued soon thereafter due to serious psychological side effects. In contrast to

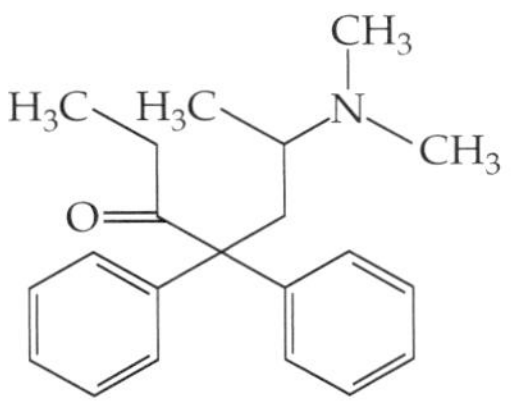

Methadone

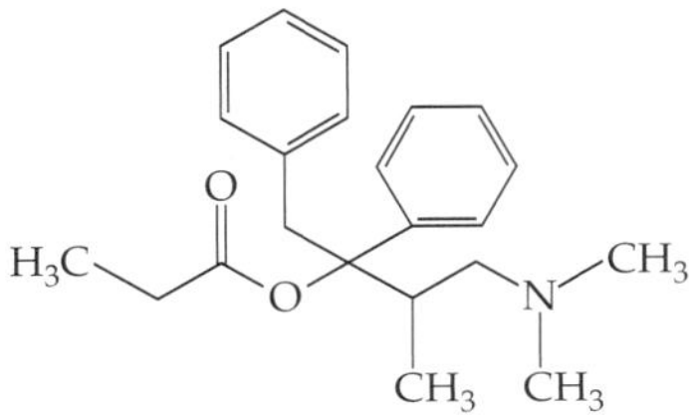

Propoxyphene

Figure 2-7. *Chemical Structures of Methadone and Propoxyphene*

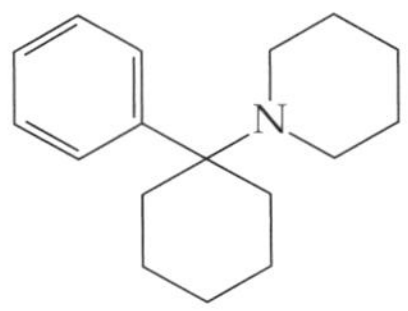

Phencyclidine

Figure 2-8. *Chemical Structures of Phencyclidine*

(1-phenylcyclohexyl)-4-hydroxypiperidine, and 5-(1-phenylcyclohexylamino) pentanoic acid. The elimination half-life of PCP varies significantly in humans (7–57 hours; average 17 hours).[46] Because there is no medical use for PCP, positive urine drug-testing results can only be due to PCP abuse.

METHAQUALONE AND GLUTETHIMIDE

Methaqualone is a sedative hypnotic drug with pharmacological effects similar to those of barbiturates such as pentobarbital. This drug has chemical resemblance to barbiturates but was originally synthesized as an antimalarial agent. Methaqualone was introduced in 1954 in the United States, but due to its high abuse potential it was discontinued in 1984 and classified as a Schedule I drug with no known medical use. In the 1960s and 1970s methaqualone was a popular street drug in the United States.[47,48] Although oral abuse of methaqualone is decreasing in Western countries, the practice of smoking methaqualone is a serious public health issue in South Africa (where it is known as Mandrax), other parts of Africa, and India.[49]

Glutethimide was introduced in the United States in 1954 as a safe alternative to barbiturates. However, this drug also has a high abuse potential and became widely abused in the United States. In 1991 glutethimide was classified as a Schedule II

amphetamine-induced psychosis, PCP-induced psychosis incorporates both positive (hallucination, paranoia) and negative (emotional withdrawal, motor retardation) effects. In sub-micromolar concentrations, PCP interacts with a specific binding site (PCP receptor) of an N-methyl-D-aspartate (NMDA)–type excitatory receptor. Binding of PCP to this receptor induced noncompetitive inhibition of NMDA receptor-mediated neurotransmission. Use of PCP produces a range of symptoms that are remarkably similar to those in patients suffering from schizophrenia. Endogenous dysfunction of NMDA receptor-mediated neurotransmission by PCP might contribute to the pathogenesis of schizophrenia.[45] **Figure 2-8** shows the chemical structure of phencyclidine.

Phencyclidine undergoes extensive metabolism by liver cytochrome P450 enzymes (especially CYP3A4) into several hydroxy metabolites, including cis-1-(1-phenyl-4-hydroxycyclohexyl) piperidine, trans-1-(1-phenyl-4-hydroxycyclohexyl) piperidine, 1-

drug with little medical use.[47] Abuse of oral combination of glutethimide and codeine, commonly referred to as "sets," was on the rise in the 1970s and 1980s in the United States. The glutethimide/codeine combination produces a euphoric effect comparable to that of heroin, but it is longer in duration. This effect may be related to the induction of liver enzymes, most likely CYP2D6, which metabolize codeine to its more active metabolite, morphine. Glutethimide may also inhibit conjugation of morphine to form the inactive metabolite morphine 3-glucuronide. In animal models, a single dose of glutethimide and codeine results in much higher concentrations of morphine and lower than expected concentrations of morphine 3-glucuronide, indicating that glutethimide potentiates and prolongs the effects of codeine by pharmacokinetic interactions.[50] Havier and Lin reported 16 medical examiner cases related to abuse of a combination of codeine and glutethimide. The average postmortem blood levels of codeine and glutethimide were 0.62 mg/L and 4.07 mg/L, respectively. The corresponding concentrations of codeine and glutethimide in urine were 38.06 mg/L and 12.68 mg/L, respectively.[51] **Figure 2-9** shows the chemical structures of methaqualone and glutethimide.

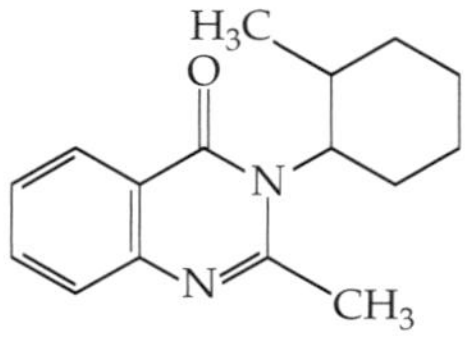

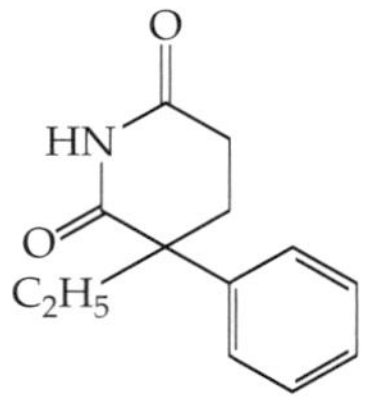

Figure 2-9. *Chemical Structures of Methaqualone and Glutethimide*

tors, such as opiate receptors, play an important role in the addiction mechanism of these abused drugs. Understanding metabolism and disposition of these abused drugs is important to interpret results of drug testing.

CONCLUSION

Drug abuse is a psychiatric illness governed by a complex pattern of genetic and environmental factors. Marijuana, amphetamine, cocaine, barbiturates, benzodiazepines, opiates, methadone, propoxyphene, and phencyclidine, along with LSD and designer drugs, are abused in the United States. Most of these drugs act by activating the neurotransmitter dopamine, although specific recep-

REFERENCES

1. Hyman SE, Malenka RC. Addiction and the brain: the neurobiology of compulsion and its persistence. *Nat Rev Neurosci.* 2001;2: 695–703.

2. Duaux E, Krebs MO, Loo H, Poirier MF. Genetic vulnerability to drug abuse. *Eur Psychiatry.* 2000;15:109–114.

3. Adinoff B. Neurobiologic process in drug reward and addiction. *Harv Rev Psychiatry.* 2004;12:305–320.

4. Volkow ND, Fowler JS, Wang GJ, et al. Dopamine in drug abuse and addiction: results of imaging studies and treatment implications. *Arch Neurol.* 2007;64: 1575–1579.

5. Tsai SJ. Increased central brain-derived neurotropic factor activity could be a risk factor for substance abuse: implications for treatment. *Med Hypothesis.* 2007;68: 410–414.

6. Tsuang MT, Bar JL, Harley RM, Lyons MJ. The Harvard twin study of substance abuse: what we have learned. *Harv Rev Psychiatry.* 2001;9:267–279.

7. Kendler KS, Jacobson KC, Prescott CA, Neale MC. Specificity of genetic and environmental risk factors for use and abuse/dependence of cannabis, cocaine, hallucinogens, sedatives, stimulates and opiates in male twins. *Am J Psychiatry.* 2003;160:687–695.

8. Martinez D, Broff A, Foltin RW, et al. Cocaine dependence and D$_2$ receptor availability in functional subdivisions of striatum: relationship with cocaine seeking behavior. *Neuropsychophramacology.* 2004;29:1190–1202.

9. Persico AM, Bird G, Gabbay FH, Uhl GR. D2 dopamine receptor gene Taq A1 and B1 restriction fragment length polymorphism: enhances frequencies in psychostimulant preferring polysubstance abusers. *Bio Psychiatry.* 1996;40:776–784.

10. Tsai SJ, Chenh CY, Shu LR, Yang CY. No association for D2 and D4 dopamine receptor polymorphism and methamphetamine abuse in Chinese males. *Psychiatr Genet.* 2002;12:29–33.

11. Morita Y, Ujike T, Tanaka Y, et al. The glycine transporter 1 gene (GLYT1) is associated with methamphetamine use disorder. *Am J Genet B Neuropsychiatr Genet.* 2008;147:54–59.

12. Muncro CA, McCaul ME, Wong DF, et al. Sex difference in striatal dopamine release in healthy adults. *Biol Psychiatry.* 2006;59:966–974.

13. Ikeda K, Ide S, Han W, et al. How individual sensitivity to opiates can be predicted by gene analysis. *Trends Pharmacol Sci.* 2005;26:311–317.

14. Xu K, Lichtermann D, Lipsky RH, et al. Association between specific haplotypes of D$_2$ dopamine receptor gene with vulnerability to heroin dependence in 2 distinct populations. *Arch Gen Psychiatry.* 2004;61: 597–606.

15. Cooper ZD, Haney M. Cannabis reinforcement and dependence: role of cannabinoid CB1 receptor. *Addict Biol.* 2008;13(2): 188–195.

16. Zhang PW, Ishiguro H, Ohtsuki T, et al. Human cannabinoid receptor 1:5′ exon, candidate regulatory regions, polymorphism, haplotypes, and association with polysubstance abuse. *Mol Psychiatry.* 2004;10:916–931.

17. Oscarson M. Pharmacogenomics of drug metabolizing enzymes: importance of personalized metabolism. *Clin Chem Lab Med.* 2003;41:573–580.

18. Sindrup SH, Brøsen K. The pharmacogenetics of codeine hypoalgesia. *Pharmacogenetics.* 1995;5:335–246.

19. Kreek MJ, Bart G, Lilly C, et al. Pharmacogenetics and human molecular genetics of opiate and cocaine addictions and their treatments. *Pharmacol Rev.* 2005;57:1–26.

20. Vahdat-Mashhadian N, Hassanzadeh MK, Hosseini J, Saffaresharag AA. Ethnic difference in the frequency of distribution of serum cholinesterase activity in Iranian population. *Can J Physiol Pharmacol.* 2004;82:326–330.

21. de la Torre R, Farre M, Navarro M, et al. Clinical pharmacokinetics of amphetamine and related substances: monitoring in conventional and nonconventional matrices. *Clin Pharmacokinetic.* 2004;43:157–185.

22. Green CE, LaValley SE, Tyson CA. Comparison of amphetamine metabolism using isolated hepatocytes from five species including human. *J Pharamacol Exp Ther.* 1986;237:931–936.

23. Tominaga GT, Garcia G, Dzierba A, Wong J. Toll of methamphetamine on the trauma system. *Arch Surg.* 2004;139:844–847.

24. de la Torre R, Farre M. Ortuno J, et al. Nonlinear pharmacokinetics of MDMA ("ecstasy") in humans. *Br J Clin Pharmacol.* 2000;49:104–109.

25. U.S. Drug Enforcement Administration. Barbiturates. http://www.usdoj.gov/dea/concern/barbiturates.html. Accessed November 13, 2008.

26. Nemeroff CB. The role of GABA in the pathophysiology and treatment of anxiety disorders. *Psychopharmacol Bull.* 2003;37: 133–146.

27. Freudenthal RI, Carroll FI. Metabolism of certain commonly used barbiturates. *Drug Metab Rev.* 1973;2:265–278.

28. U.S. Drug Enforcement Administration. Benzodiazepines. http://www.usdoj.gov/dea/concern/benzodiazepines.html. Accessed October 22, 2008.

29. Wang JS, Devane CL. Pharmacokinetics and drug interactions of the sedative hypnotics. *Psychopharmacol Bull.* 2003;37: 10–29.

30. Skurtveit S, Abotnes B, Christophersen AS. Drugged drivers in Norway with benzodiazepine detection. *Forensic Sci Int.* 2002;125:75–82.

31. Shader RI, Greenblatt DJ. Clinical implications of benzodiazepine pharmacokinetics. *Am J Psychiatry.* 1977;134:652–656.

32. Greenblatt DJ, von Moltke LL, Harmatz JS, Ciraulo DA. Alprazolam pharmacokinetics: metabolism and plasma levels: clinical implications. *J Clin Psychiatry.* 1993(54 Suppl): 4–11.

33. Kalivas PW. Neurobiology of cocaine addiction: implications for new pharmacotherapy. *Am J Addict.* 2007;16:71–78.

34. Steketee JD. Cortical mechanism of cocaine sensitization. *Crit Rev Neurobiol.* 2005;17:69–86.

35. Mendelson JH, Mello NK, Sholar MB, et al. Cocaine pharmacokinetics in men and women during the follicular and luteal phase of the menstrual cycle. *Neuropsychopharmacology.* 1999;21:294–303.

36. Kolbrich EA, Barnes AJ, Gorelick DA, Boyd SJ. Major and minor metabolites of cocaine in human plasma following controlled subcutaneous cocaine administration. *J Anal Toxicol.* 2006;30(8):501–510.

37. McCance-Katz FF, Kosten TR, Jatlow P. Concurrent use of cocaine and alcohol is more potent and potentially more toxic than use of either alone: a multiple dose study. *Biol Psychiatry.* 1998;44:250–259.

38. Potter DJ, Clark P, Brown MB. Potency of Δ^9 THC and other cannabinoids in cannabis in England in 2005: Implications for psychoactivity and pharmacology. *J Forensic Sci.* 2008;53:90–94.

39. Cichewicz DL. Synergistic interactions between cannabinoid and opioid analgesics. *Life Sci.* 2004;74:1317–1324.

40. Grotenhermen F. Pharmacokinetics and pharmacodynamics of cannabinoids. *Clin Pharmacokinet.* 2003;42:327–360.

41. Wall ME, Perez-Reyes M. The metabolism of Δ^9-tetrahydrocannabinol and related cannabinoids in man. *J Clin Pharmacol.* 1981;21(8-9 Suppl):178S–189S.

42. Brown P, Kraus C, Fleming M, Reddy S. Methadone: applied pharmacology and use as adjunctive treatment in chronic pain. *Postgrad Med J.* 2004;80:654–659.

43. Iskandar SB, Abi-Saleh BS, Mechleb BK, Fahrig SA. Methadone and torsade de pointes: case report and review of the literature. *Tenn Med.* 2007;100:35–37.

44. Barkin EL, Barkin SJ, Barkin DS. Propoxyphene (dextropropoxyphene): a critical review of a weak analgesic that should remain in antiquity. *Am J Ther.* 2006;13:534–542.

45. Javitt DC, Zukin SR. Recent advances in the phencyclidine model of schizophrenia. *Am J Psychiatry.* 1991;148:1301–1308.

46. Laurenzana LM, Owens SM. Metabolism of phencyclidine by human liver microsomes. *Drug Metab Dispos.* 1997;25:557–563.

47. U.S. Drug Enforcement Administration. Glutethimide and Methaqualone. http://www.usdoj.gov/dea/concern/glutethimidep.html. Accessed October 22, 2008.

48. Ionescu-Pioggia M, Bird M, Orzack MH, et al. Methaqualone. *Int Clin Psychopharmacol.* 1988;3:97–109.

49. McCarthy G, Myers B, Siegfried N. Treatment of methaqualone dependence in adults. *Cochrane Database Syst Rev.* 2005;18:CD004146.

50. Popa D, Loghin F, Imre S, Curea E. The study of codeine-glutethimide pharmacokinetics. *J Pharm Biomed Anal.* 2003;32:866–877.

51. Havier RG, Lin R. Deaths as a result of a combination of codeine and glutethimide. *J Forensic Sci.* 1985;30:563–566.

CHAPTER 3

Designer Drugs: A New Challenge

ABSTRACT

Designer drugs are analogs of known drugs. They are produced by minor modification of the structure of an existing drug to produce a new compound that has similar pharmacologic actions. Well-known designer drugs are derivatives of fentanyl, amphetamine, and methamphetamine analogs such as 3,4-methylenedioxyamphetamine (MDA), phenylethylamine-based compounds, tryptamine-based hallucinogens, phencyclidine analogs, and gamma-hydroxybutyric acid (GHB) analogs. Because designer drugs are widely abused, in 1986 the Controlled Substance Act of the United States was amended to include designer drugs in order to make it illegal to manufacturer, possess, or sell chemicals that are similar in structure and pharmacologic properties to Schedule I or Schedule II drugs. Abuse of these designer drugs may cause severe toxicity and even death. Several designer drugs—for example, MDA—can be detected and confirmed by urine testing, although not all designer drugs are detected by even the most comprehensive workplace drug-testing programs. Date rape drugs like GHBA do not cross-react with any commercially available screening assay and may be easily missed unless the abuse of such an agent is suspected and special sophisticated techniques, like gas chromatography mass spectrometry (GC/MS), are applied for analysis.

Designer drugs were initially produced by underground laboratories in order to bypass the legal consequences of manufacturing and selling illicit drugs. In 1986 the U.S. Controlled Substances Act was amended to include designer drugs. Other countries also passed laws to ban the manufacture and sale of designer drugs. There are many classes of designer drugs, which are created by the structural modification of controlled substances. Common types of designer drugs are amphetamine analogs, opiate analogs (including fentanyl derivatives), piperazine analogs, tryptamine-based hallucinogens, phencyclidine analogs, and gamma-hydroxybutyric acid (GHB) analogs. Several of these drugs are known as "rave party" drugs, so called because they are abused by younger people attending parties or rock concerts. These drugs include 3,4-methylenedioxymethamphetamine (MDMA, "ecstasy"), methampheta-

Table 3-1 Common Designer Drugs and Their Street Names		
Designer Drug	**Analog of Drug**	**Common Street Name(s)**
MDMA	Methamphetamine	Ecstasy, XTC, Adam
MDEA	Amphetamine	Eve
2-CB	Phenylethylamine	Venus, Bromo, XTC, Erox, Nexus
Pentazocine and tripelennamine	IV use substitute for heroin	Ts, Blues
α-methylfentanyl	Fentanyl	China White
GHB	Endogenous substance	Liquid ecstasy, G, Nitro
GBL	GHB	Blue nitro, GH Revitalizer
1,4-BD	GHB	Weight belt
Flunitrazepam	Drug legal in Europe	Roofies, R 2, Forget-me-pill

mine, various hallucinogens, ketamine, and a variety of other drugs. Drugs like GHB and flunitrazepam (Rohypnol) are also used at rave parties and involved in date rapes. For a list of common designer drugs, see **Table 3-1**.

Although designer drugs such as MDMA and MDA have significant cross-reactivity with amphetamine-screening assays, many designer drugs are fentanyl analogs, meperidine analogs, or GHB analogs, which escape detection by routine drugs-of-abuse testing. Inability to detect a drug is particularly frustrating in medical situations in which it is essential to identify a drug causing an overdose, or in legal situations involving assault and or rape. More sophisticated techniques, such as gas chromatography combined with mass spectrometry and liquid chromatography combined with tandem mass spectrometry, are required to detect such designer drugs in blood, urine, or other biologic structures like hair and nail. Unfortunately, clinical laboratories in many small hospitals do not have the equipment necessary to analyze such specimens, and in cases of suspected overdose, specimens need to be sent to a reference laboratory or a university-based hospital laboratory.

DESIGNER DRUGS AS AMPHETAMINE ANALOGS

One of the most well known and probably most abused designer drugs is MDMA, commonly known as "ecstasy," which was synthesized in 1914 by a chemist at the Merck company in Germany to be marketed for appetite control. There was very little interest in this drug until the 1970s, when widespread abuse of MDMA was observed in the United States. MDMA's close relative, MDA, was first synthesized in 1910. After 1986 a large number of amphetamine analogs were synthesized by underground laboratories to produce more potent drugs for abuse. Common examples of these designer drugs are 3,4-methylene-dioxy-N-ethylamphetamine (MDEA), 2,5-dimethoxy-4-methylamphetamine (DOM), and 2,5-dimethoxy-4-methylthioamphetamine (DOT).[1] In addition, a chlorinated analog of MDMA has been detected in the urine of a drug abuser.[2] Bossong et al also described two other ecstasy-like substances: 3,4-methylenedioxymethcathinone (methylone) and meta-chlorophenylpiperazine (mCPPP). Methylone is the main ingredient of liquid designer drugs that appeared in the underground market in the Netherlands.[3] Para-methoxyamphetamine (PMA), para-methoxymethamphetamine (PMMA), and 4-methylthioamphetamine (4-MTA) are also used at rave parties.

MDMA is metabolized to MDA and a variety of other compounds, including 4-hydroxy-3-methoxymethamphetamine (major metabolite), 3,4 dihydroxy-metham-phetamine, and 3-hydroxy-4-methoxymethamphetamine. 4-hydroxy-3-methoxymethamphetamine is excreted in urine as conjugated with glucuronide or sulfate. MDMA along with its metabolites can be determined in human urine by gas chromatography/mass spectrometry (GC/MS). Shima et al recently described a sensitive technique using liquid chromatography combined with electron spray ionization mass spectrometry to detect major metabolites of MDMA in human urine.[4]

Recent abuse of MDMA or MDA can be detected by a urine drug screen using amphetamine immunoassays. Various commercially available immunoassays for screening of amphetamine or methamphetamine in urine specimens, such as the fluorescence polarization immunoassay (FPIA amphetamine/methamphetamine II; Abbott Laboratories, Abbott Park, IL, the enzyme multiplied immunoassay technique (EMIT II Plus amphetamine assay, the EMIT II Plus monoclonal amphetamine/methamphetamine assay; Dade Behring, now Siemens, Deerfield, IL), and the kinetic interaction of microparticles in solution (KIMS) system (standard protocol and MDMA protocol; ONLINE DAT immunoassays; Roche, Indi-anapolis, IN) are all able to detect MDMA and related drugs in urine. The sensitivities are 93% to 100% for detection of MDMA by these immunoassays.[5] Hsu et al compared performance evaluations of eight commercially available immunoassays for detection of MDMA in urine and concluded that the CEDIA amphetamine/ecstasy assay (Microgenics Corporation, Fremont, CA) can best predict the concentration of MDMA and methamphetamine in urine and is also capable of detecting low concentrations of MDMA in urine.[6] In addition, several point-of-care on-site drug-testing devices are also capable of detecting MDMA in urine.[7]

Although the number of deaths from abuse of MDMA is relatively small compared with other drugs of abuse, fatality from MDMA abuse has been reported. Klys et al described a fatal case of MDMA abuse in a 22-year-old man with a history of drug abuse. Using liquid chromatography combined with atmospheric pressure chemical ionization tandem mass spectrometry, the authors confirmed the presence of MDMA (1.42 mg/L) and its metabolite 3,4-methylenedioxamphetamine (MDA; 0.17 mg/L) in his blood. The presence of MDMA in the hair also confirmed the history of drug abuse.[8] High serum MDMA concentrations correlated with coma, hyperpyrexia, cardiovascular complications, acidosis, and hyperkalemia. Greene et al reported a series of seven patients who ingested ecstasy in a nightclub and presented with various symptoms of MDMA toxicity. One patient died within an hour of hospital admission, and another patient died after four days of fulminant hepatic failure. Another patient recovered after spending 12 days in the intensive care unit. Significant concentrations of MDMA were found in serum of all 7 patients.[9]

DESIGNER DRUGS DERIVED FROM PHENYLETHYLAMINE

Phenylethylamine itself is not abused because it is rapidly metabolized after ingestion, but a number of drugs derived from phenylethylamine are abused as designer drugs. These drugs have amphetamine-like effects because amphetamine itself is a phenylethylamine derivative. Therefore, these designer drugs are broadly classified as amphetamine-like designer drugs. Designer drugs derived from phenylethylamine include 4-bromo-2,5-dimethoxy-b-phenylethylamine (2C-B), 2,5-dimethoxy-4 ethylthio-b-phenylethylamine (2C-T-2), 2,5-dimethoxy-4 propylthio-b-phenylethylamine (2C-T-7), 2,5-dimethoxy-4-iodo-b-phenylethylamine (2C-I), and related drugs that are also abused. The drugs belonging to the 2C series are among the most potent drugs and are selective serotonin 5-HT$_2$ receptors. These designer drugs are also toxic, and fatality from using 2C-T-7 has been reported. These designer drugs are metabolized in the liver.[10]

FENTANYL AND FENTANYL ANALOGS

Fentanyl is a widely used synthetic narcotic analgesic that is approximately 75 to 100 times more potent than morphine. Several analogs of fentanyl, such as sufentanil, alfentanil, lofentanil, and remifentanil, have been synthesized by pharmaceutical companies and are used clinically. In the United States, fentanyl is currently classified as a Schedule II drug. Injection of 50 to 100 mg of fentanyl produces rapid analgesic effect and unconsciousness. Therefore, it is widely used as an anesthetic. Fentanyl is also available as lozenges and transdermal patches (Duragesic) for pain management. Oral transmucosal fentanyl citrate (Actiq) is a relatively new formulation in which fentanyl is incorporated into a sweetened matrix to produce fentanyl lozenge. This lozenge can be allowed to dissolve in the mouth (which takes approximately 15 minutes) for rapid absorption of fentanyl through the mucosa. Fentanyl lozenges are used for control of breakthrough pain in cancer patients and also for control of severe pain. Fentanyl lozenges come in a variety of dosage forms, delivering 200, 400, 600, 800, 1200, or 1600 µg of fentanyl citrate. Peak fentanyl concentration in blood is observed within 20 to 40 minutes, with the bioavailability of fentanyl approximately 50%. The peak concentrations vary from 0.31 to 2.51 ng/ml, depending on the dosage of fentanyl. The therapeutic range of fentanyl is considered 1 to 3 ng/ml in serum, and the toxicity of fentanyl is similar to opiate toxicity.[11]

The Duragesic patches deliver 25, 50, 75, or 100 µg of fentanyl per hour through the transdermal route. The patch provides a continuous systemic delivery of fentanyl for the intended application duration of 72 hours. Fentanyl patches should only be given to patients who are tolerant of opioid therapy. Fentanyl is rapidly metabolized by the liver to norfentanyl and other inactive metabolites. The plasma half-life varies between 1.5 and 6 hours.[12] Abuse of transdermal patches can even cause death. Coopman et al reported a case in which a 78-year-old woman with a history of cancer died and external examination found 10 patches on her body. The fentanyl concentration in the right femoral blood was 21.3 ng/ml, while the blood fentanyl concentration collected from the left femoral artery was 20.9 ng/ml. The urine fentanyl concentration was 282.9 ng/ml, and the concentration of norfentanyl was 121.2 ng/ml. The stomach content of fentanyl was 688.2 ng/ml. After transdermal application, 3% to 4% of fentanyl is secreted to stomach content. The analgesic serum concentration ranges from 0.2 to 1.2 ng/ml, while risk of hypoventilation develops at serum fentanyl levels over 2 ng/ml.[13] In 2000 Anderson and Muto reported their experience of investigating 25 deaths over the past 3 years in Los Angeles County that involved Duragesic patches. Of these deaths, 15 were accidental, 5 natural, 3 suicidal, and 2 undetermined. The concentration of fentanyl in heart blood ranged from 1.8 to 139 ng/ml, femoral blood ranged from 3.1 to 43 ng/ml, and the urinary concentration of fentanyl ranged from 2.9 to 895 ng/ml.[14] After application of a patch, the absorption of fentanyl from the skin starts immediately. Removing the patch after overdose may not reverse the toxicity because the drug is already in the circulation.

Fentanyl is also abused by intravenous injection. An overdose from fentanyl can cause coma, and the person may stop breathing. Death from fentanyl overdose is common. Martin et al reported that 54 deaths in Ontario, Canada, from 2002 to 2004 were related to fentanyl. In their study, the mean fentanyl concentration in blood was 25 ng/ml (3.0–383 ng/ml).[15] Fentanyl is also abused in combination with other drugs such as cocaine, methadone, and morphine. Fentanyl gained international attention in October 2002 when Russian authorities pumped an aerosol version of fentanyl into a theater in Moscow where Chechen separatists had taken 800 people hostage. The gas was pumped inside the theater to put both rebels and their hostages to sleep. Unfortunately, 129 hostages and 41 terrorists died from breathing the aerosols containing fentanyl.[16]

ILLICIT DRUGS THAT ARE FENTANYL ANALOGS

The designer drug "China White," an analog of fentanyl, appeared in the underground market of California in 1979. The active ingredient of China White is α-methylfentanyl, a very potent analog of fentanyl. Abuse of China White caused over 100 deaths in California. Gillespie et al determined postmortem blood, bile, and liver concentrations of α-methylfentanyl in a drug overdose victim. The blood concentration of α-methylfentanyl was 3.1 ng/ml, bile concentration was 6.4 ng/ml, and the level in the liver was 78 ng per gm of liver tissue.[17]

In 1984 another illicit designer drug, 3-methylfentanyl, appeared as a street drug in California. This drug was also related to fatal drug overdose. In 1988, 3-methylfentanyl was identified in 16 fatal overdose cases in Allegheny County in Pennsylvania. In addition to 3-methylfentanyl, morphine was detected in the blood of five individuals, and cocaine was detected in the blood of three people.[18] Ojanpera et al also described three fatal poisoning cases involving 3-methylfentanyl. The mean blood level of 3-methylfentanyl was 0.5 μg/ml (range: 0.3 to 0.9 ng/ml). The blood fentanyl levels were measured using a specific tandem mass spectrometric technique.[19]

Regular opiate screening assays are unable to detect either fentanyl or its analogs in urine. These compounds do not have cross-reactivity against the antibodies specific for morphine that are usually detected by immunoassays designed for screening of opiates in urine. The concentrations of fentanyl and its analogs can be measured in serum, urine, and other biological matrices using GC/MS or liquid chromatography combined with tandem mass spectrometry.[12,13]

OXYCODONE: USE AND ABUSE

Oxycodone is a semisynthetic opiate, derived from thebaine, which is used for management of severe pain, including pain due to cancer. Oxycodone is a strong analgesic opiate, like morphine, but has high oral bioavailability (42% to 87%). Oxycodone is metabolized by the liver mainly to noroxycodone and also to oxymorphone (a minor metabolite).[20] Pain control can be achieved within an hour after oral ingestion of an oxycodone tablet, and the pain control may last for 12 hours. The plasma half-life of oxycodone is 3 to 5 hours. Oxycodone is also available in controlled release form (OxyContin) containing 10, 20, 40, or 80 mg oxycodone. The tablet must be taken orally without chewing or breaking the tablet.[21]

Oxycodone is widely abused by breaking controlled release tablets for rapid onset of action. The commonly abused drugs in combination with oxycodone include benzodiazepines, cocaine, alcohol, other opiates, and marijuana. Cone et al evaluated 1014 fatality cases involving oxycodone. Many of these deaths involved use of other drugs along with oxycodone. The mean blood concentration of oxycodone was 1.64 μg/ml in cases involving a single drug, while the mean oxycodone concentration was 0.71 μg/ml when other drugs were also involved in the overdose.[22] Wolf et al reported 172 deaths involving oxycodone in Palm Beach County, Florida. The authors reported that 18 deaths were due to oxycodone toxicity alone, 117 due to combined drug toxicity, 23 due to trauma, 9 due to natural causes, and 5 due to another drug use. The mean oxycodone concentration in blood was 0.69 μg/ml in cases involving mainly oxycodone toxicity, compared with oxycodone concentration of 0.087 μg/ml in cases in which deaths were due to natural causes. The authors further observed that benzodiazepine was involved in 96 cases, making it the most common co-toxicant. The most common benzodiazepine abused was alprazolam. Cocaine was detected in 41 cases.[23]

Oxycodone has minimal cross-reactivity with the opiate screening assays utilized in drugs-of-abuse testing. However, specific immunoassays for screening of oxycodone in urine specimens are commercially available from several different vendors. Confirmation of the presence of oxycodone in urine or other biological matrices requires a more sophisticated technique such as GC/MS.

ABUSE OF MEPERIDINE AND ITS ANALOGS

Introduced in 1931, meperidine (Demerol) is a synthetic narcotic analgesic with a much lower potency than morphine. It is available both for injection and for oral use, supplied as hydrochloride salt. The average peak plasma concentration of meperidine in 4 subjects who ingested 100 mg dose orally was 170 ng/ml at 1.3 hours. The average half-life was 4.4 hours.[24] Shih et al compared serum concentrations of meperidine after oral and intramuscular delivery of the drug. The mean meperidine concentration was 118 ng/ml one hour after oral ingestion of 150 mg tablets. The mean concentration of meperidine one hour after a 100-mg intramuscular injection was 377 ng/ml.[25] Meperidine metabolizes to normeperidine, which has a longer half-life than meperidine and is also active. The neurotoxicity of meperidine manifests in patients with renal impairment. Jiraki reported a case of lethal effect of meperidine in a patient with renal failure who abused meperidine.[26]

Meperidine and several of its analogs are abused. One of its analogs, MPPP (1-methyl-4-phenyl-4-propionoxypiperdine), is a common designer drug. An impurity found in some illicitly synthesized MPPP preparation that was identified as 1-methyl-4-phenyl-1,2,3,6-tetrahydropyridine (MPTP) caused permanent parkinsonism in a number of intravenous drug abusers. Opiate activity is found only in MPPP, which is a potent μ-type antagonist.[27] Meperidine and its analogs have very poor cross-reactivity with the opiate screening assay for drugs of abuse and if present in urine can not be detected by routine urine screening. A more sophisticated technique, such as GC/MS, needs to be applied to determine the presence of such drugs in blood, urine, or other biological matrices.

ABUSE OF GHB AND ITS ANALOGS

Gamma-hydroxybutyrate (GHB) is an endogenous constituent of mammalian brain and is a metabolite of gamma-hydroxybutyric acid (GHBA). Gamma-hydroxybutyrate is present in nanomolar concentration in the brain and acts as a neurotransmitter. Until 1990 it was sold in health food stores as a food supplement and became popular among athletes as an alternative to steroids. It was believed that GHB helped an individual to build muscle mass without exercise. Sixteen cases of adverse effects due to GHB-containing health products were reported to the San Francisco Bay Area Regional Poison Control Center from June 1990 to October 1990. Use of GHB caused coma in 4 patients and tonic-clonic seizure in two patients for dosage ranging from one-fourth of a teaspoon to 4 tablespoons.[28] The U.S. Federal Drug Administration banned the over-the-counter sale of GHB in November 1990. In March 2000 GHB was classified as a Schedule I controlled substance in the United States. A 25-mg/kg oral dose caused dizziness in adult subjects, producing an average plasma concentration of 80 μg/ml. Blood GHB concentration over 260 μg/ml caused deep sleep, levels of 156 to 260 μg/ml caused moderate sleep, and levels of 52 to 156 μg/ml caused light sleep.[29] In lower doses GHB produces euphoria.

Abuse of GHB is widespread throughout the world, and because GHB can make an individual unconscious, it is widely used in drug-induced sexual assaults. Because the criminal penalties associated with manufacturing and possession of GHB are stringent, several analogs of GHB have appeared in underground markets. Although sale of GHB and its analogs for human consumption is against the law in the United States, several GHB analogs are commercially available as industrial solvents and are used in the manufacture of plastic and other products. GHB analogs that can be found as street drugs include gamma-butyrolactone (GBL), 1,4-butanediol (1,4-BD), gamma-hydroxyvaleric acid (GHV), and gamma-valerolactone (GVL).

Gamma-butyrolactone and BD are converted endogenously after abuse into GHB and exert similar effects of GHB abuse. However, neither GBL nor 1,4-BD directly binds to GHB receptors (GABA receptors). In contrast, GHV binds directly to GHB receptors and has an effect similar to that of GHB. However, GVL does not metabolize to GHB. It is a precursor of GHV and also can be found as a street drug. GVL like GHB produces sedation, catalepsy, and ataxia but requires a larger dose than GHB to produce similar effects. A larger dose of GHV can be lethal.[30] There is no antidote for treating GHB overdose. Management is mostly supportive, with emphasis on airway management.

Usually a dosage of 20 to 30 mg/kg of GHB causes sleep, and doses of 50 mg/kg or higher produces an anesthetic effect. The typical dose of GHB in cases of abuse is over 35 mg/kg. Both GHB and its analog 1,4-BD have a short half-life in humans. Thai et al studied the pharmacology of 1,4-BD in humans and observed that 1,4-BD is quickly absorbed and cleared, with a maximum plasma concentration achieved at an average of 24 minutes after ingestion. The elimination half-life is 39.3 minutes on average. 1,4-DB is also extensively converted into GHB endogenously, and the average half-life of GHB is 32.3 minutes.[31] Because GHB has no distinct taste, it can be slipped into a drink and has been used in date rape situations. Gamma-hydroxybutyrate is also produced endogenously. Abuse of GHB is associated with high morbidity and mortality rates.

The concentration of GHB in blood should not exceed 50 µg/ml, and in urine it should not exceed 10 µg/ml because of the endogenous production of GHB. However, Kintz et al demonstrated that in 71 subjects in whom cause of death was not related to GHB abuse, the concentrations of GHB in heart blood ranged from 0.4 to 409 mg/L. Although in most cases observed GHB concentrations ranged from 10 to 40 mg/L, in 14 cases the concentration of GHB exceeded the 50 mg/L cutoff.[32] Yeatman and Reid studied the urinary concentrations of endogenous GHB in 55 volunteers and observed that the endogenous urinary concentrations of GHB ranged from 0.9 to 3.5 mg/L, with a mean urinary concentration of 1.56 mg/L. They concluded that the suggested 10-mg/L cutoff value for endogenous GHB concentration in forensic analysis is justified.[33]

As expected, concentrations of GHB in blood and urine in subjects who had died from GHB overdose are significantly higher than the suggested cutoff values in blood and urine owing to the endogenous production of GHB. In one report the concentrations of GHB in blood of 8 patients who had died from GHB overdose ranged from 77 mg/L to 370 mg/L.[34] Another report showed that the femoral blood and urinary concentrations of GHB in a fatal overdose were 2937 mg/L and 33,727 mg/L, respectively. These values seem to be the highest reported concentrations of GHB in fatal overdose.[35] Because GHB is cleared from both blood and urine relatively rapidly compared with other drugs, testing of a hair specimen is useful to document exposure of a victim to GHB during sexual assault. Kintz et al documented the presence of GHB in hair after a single exposure and demonstrated that hair analysis is useful to document use of GHB during a sexual assault.[36]

Currently, there is no immunoassay for routine screening of GHB in urine or any other biological matrix. Therefore, GHB will not be detected by routine drugs-of-abuse testing protocol. In the case of suspected overdose of GHB, a more sophisticated analytical technique such as GC/MS should be employed for determination of GHB concentrations in blood or urine. Several big laboratories and national reference laboratories offer the testing of GHB in blood and urine. Moreover, most forensic toxicology laboratories in the medical examiners' or coroners' offices offer GHB testing. In cases of suspected GHB, overdose specimens can be sent to these laboratories for analysis.

DATE RAPE DRUG: ROHYPNOL

Flunitrazepam (Rohypnol) is a benzodiazepine that is not currently available in the United States, although it is used medically in Europe and other parts of the world. Flunitrazepam can cause rapid sedation and is used in date rape situations. A single 1- or 2-mg dose of flunitrazepam can produce significant sedative effects, and this drug is more potent than diazepam. The effects of flunitrazepam can last up to 12 hours. Like other benzodiazepines, prolonged use of flunitrazepam can cause dependence and withdrawal symptoms if the use of the drug is suddenly stopped.[37]

The liver metabolizes flunitrazepam into 7-aminoflunitrazepam (major metabolite) and also to a lesser extent into desmethylflunitrazepam and 3-hydroxyflunitrazepam. Benzodiazepine screening tests detect the presence of flunitrazepam and its metabolites in urine because flunitrazepam and its metabolites cross-react with the antibody used in the screening assays. The confirmation of flunitrazepam and its metabolites in urine should be carried out by using GC/MS. Usually the concentration of flunitrazepam is very low in urine, but the concentration of 7-amino flunitrazepam is relatively higher. Jourdil et al reported that the concentration of 7-aminoflunitrazepam in the urine of 5 abusers ranged from 455 to 844 ng/ml, while the concentrations of the parent drug flunitrazepam ranged from "none detected" to 4.8 ng/ml. The authors used liquid chromatography combined with electrospray ionization mass spectrometry for the determination of blood and urinary concentrations of flunitrazepam and its metabolites.[38]

CONCLUSION

Drugs such as MDMA, GHB, Rohypnol, and ketamine are used at all-night "rave" parties, and therefore these drugs are often called "club drugs." GHB, Rohypnol, and ketamine are also used for making a victim unconscious before a sexual assault. These drugs pose a challenge to health care providers because several designer drugs escape detection in routine toxicological analysis. Currently, a relatively small number of laboratories in the United States offer tests for GHB, ketamine, and other designer drugs. It is important for health care providers to be aware of these drugs so that in the case of a suspected drug overdose or sexual assault where a urine toxicology screen is negative, proper steps can be taken to send specimens to an appropriate reference laboratory for further testing.

REFERENCES

1. Christophersen AS. Amphetamine designer drugs—an overview and epidemiology. *Toxicology Lett*. 2000;112-113:127–131.

2. Maresove V, Hampl J, Chundela Z, et al. The identification of a chlorinated MDMA. *J Anal Toxicol*. 2005;29:353–358.

3. Bossong MG, Van Dijk JP, Niesink RJ. Methylone and mCPP, two new drugs of abuse. *Addict Biol*. 2005;10:321–323.

4. Shima N, Kamata H, Katagi M, et al. Direct determination of glucuronide and sulfate of 4-hydroxy-3-methoxymethamphetamine, the main metabolite of MDMA in urine. *J Chromatogr B Analyt Technol Biomed Life Sci*. 2007;857:123–129.

5. Verstraete AG, Heyden FV. Comparison of the sensitivity and specificity of six immunoassays for the detection of amphetamines in urine. *J Anal Toxicol*. 2005;29:359–364.

6. Hsu J, Liu C, Liu CP, et al. Performance characteristics of selected immunoassays for preliminary test of 3,4-methylene-dioxymethamphetamine, methamphetamine, and related drugs in urine specimens. *J Anal Toxicol.* 2003;27:471–478.

7. Crouch DJ, Hersch RK, Cook RF, et al. A field evaluation of five on-site drug testing devices. *J Anal Toxicol.* 2002;26:493–499.

8. Klys M, Rojek S, Wozniak K, Rzepecka-Wozniak E. Fatality due to use of a designer drug MDMA (Ecstasy). *Leg Med (Tokyo).* 2007;9:185–191.

9. Greene SL, Dargan PI, O'Connor N, et al. Multiple toxicity from 3,4-methylene-dioxymethamphetamine (ecstasy). *Am J Emerg Med.* 2003;21:121–124.

10. Theobald DS, Fehn S, Maurer HH. New designer drug 2,5-dimethoxy-4propylthio-b-phenylethylamine (2C-T-7): studies on its metabolism and toxicological determination in rat urine using gas chromatography/mass spectrometry. *J Mass Spectrom.* 2005;40:105–116.

11. Mystakidou K, Katsouda E, Parpa E, et al. Oral transmucosal fentanyl citrate: overview of pharmacological and clinical characteristics. *Drug Deliv.* 2006;13:269–276.

12. Poklis A, Backer R. Urine concentrations of fentanyl and norfentanyl during application of Duragesic transdermal patches. *J Anal Toxicol.* 2004;28:422–425.

13. Coopman V, Cordonnier J, Pien K, Van Varenbergh D. LC/MS/MS analysis of fentanyl and norfentanyl in a fatality due to application of multiple Duragesic transdermal therapeutic system. *Forensic Sci Int.* 2007;167:223–227.

14. Anderson DT, Mutto JJ. Duragesic transdermal patch: postmortem tissue distribution of fentanyl in 25 cases. *J Anal Toxicol.* 2000;24:627–634.

15. Martin TL, Woodall KL, McLellan BA. Fentanyl-related deaths in Ontario, Canada: toxicological findings and circumstances of death in 112 cases (2002-2004). *J Anal Toxicol.* 2006;30:603–610.

16. Donahoe J. The Moscow hostage crisis: an analysis of Chechen terrorist goals. *Strategic Insights.* 2003;2(5).

17. Gillespie TJ, Gandolfi AUJ, Davis TP, Morano RA. Identification and quantification of alpha-methylfentanyl in post mortem specimens. *J Anal Toxicol.* 1982;6:139–142.

18. Hibbs J, Perper J, Winek CL. An outbreak of designer drug-related deaths in Pennsylvania. *JAMA.* 1991;265:1011–1013.

19. Ojanpera I, Gergov M, Rasanen I, et al. Blood levels of 3-methylfentanyl in 3 fetal poisoning cases. *Am J Forensic Sci.* 2006;27:328–331.

20. Riley J, Eisenberg E, Muller-Schwefe G, et al. Oxycodone: a review of its use in the management of pain. *Curr Med Res Opin.* 2008;24:175–192.

21. Ordonez Gallego A, Gonzalez Baron M, Espinosa Arranz E. Oxycodone: a pharmacological and clinical review. *Clin Trans Oncol.* 2007;9:298–307.

22. Cone EJ, Fant RV, Rohay JM, et al. Oxycodone involvement in drug abuse death: II. Evidence of toxic multiple drug-drug interactions. *J Anal Toxicol.* 2004;28:217–225.

23. Wolf BC, Lavezzi WA, Sullivan LM, Flannagan LM. One hundred seventy two deaths involving the use of oxycodone in Palm Beach County. *J Forensic Sci.* 2005;50:192–195.

24. Baselt RC, Cravey RC. Meperidine. In: *Disposition of Toxic Drugs and Chemicals in Man.* Foster City, CA: Chemical Toxicology Institute; 1995:450–453.

25. Shih AP, Robinson K, Au WY. Determination of therapeutic serum concentrations of oral and parenteral meperidine by liquid chromatography. *Eur J Clin Pharmacol.* 1976;22:451–456.

26. Jiraki L. Lethal effect of normeperidine. *Am J Forensic Med Pathol.* 1992;13:42–43.

27. Johannessen JN, Markey SP. Assessment of the opiate properties of two constituents of a toxic illicit drug mixture. *Drug Alcohol Depend.* 1984;13:367–374.

28. Dyer JE. Gamma-hydroxybutyrate: a health food product producing coma and seizure like activity. *Am J Emerg Med*. 1991;9: 321–324.

29. Baselt RC, Cravey RC. Gamma-hydroxybutyrate. In *Disposition of Toxic Drugs and Chemicals in Man*. Foster City, CA: Chemical Toxicology; 1995:348–349.

30. Carter LP, Chen W, Wu H, et al. Comparison of the behavioral effects of gamma-hydroxybutyric acid (GHB) and its 4-methyl substituted analog, gamma-hydroxyvaleric acid (GHV). *Drug Alcohol Depend*. 2005;78:91–99.

31. Thai D, Dyer JE, Jacob P, Haller CA. Clinical pharmacology of 1,4-butanediol and gamma-hydroxybutyrate after oral 1,4-butanediol administration to healthy volunteers. *Clin Pharmacol Ther*. 2007;81: 178–184.

32. Kintz, P, Villain V, Cirimele V, Ludes B. GHB in postmortem toxicology: discrimination between endogenous productions from exposure using multiple specimens. *Forensic Sci Int*. 2004;143:177–181.

33. Yeatmen DT, Reid K. A study of urinary endogenous gamma-hydroxybutyrate (GHB) level. *J Anal Toxicol*. 2003;27:40–42.

34. Caldicott DG, Chow FY, Burns BJ, Felgate PD et al. fatalities associated with the use of gamma-hydroxybutyrate and its analogs in Australia. *Med J Aust*. 2004;181:310–313.

35. Kintz P, Villain M, Pelissier AL, Cirimele V et al. Unusually high concentrations in fatal GHB case. *J Anal Toxicol*. 2005;29:582–585.

36. Kintz P, Cirimele V, Jamey C, Ludes B. Testing for GHB in hair by GC/MS after single exposure: application to document sexual assault. *J Forensic Sci*. 2003;48: 195–200.

37. Gahlinger PM. Club drug: MDMA, gamma-hydroxybutyric acid (GHB), rohypnol and ketamine. *Am Fam Physician*. 2004;69:2619–2626.

38. Jourdil N, Bessard J, Vincent F, et al. Automated solid phase extraction and liquid chromatography-electrospray ionization mass spectrometry for the determination of flunitrazepam and its metabolites in human urine and plasma samples. *J Chromatogr B Analyt Technol Biomed Life Sci*. 2003;788:207–219.

CHAPTER 4

Evolution of Pre-Employment and Workplace Drug Testing

ABSTRACT

The drug-testing program in its present form began in 1986 when President Ronald Reagan issued Executive Order 12564 requiring federal agencies to conduct drug testing for federal personnel employed in sensitive positions. In 1988 the U.S. Congress passed the Drug-Free Workplace Act. Initially, the National Institute on Drug Abuse (NIDA) was given the responsibility to initiate programs for achieving drug-free workplaces. In 1992 NIDA was transferred from the Alcohol, Drug Abuse, and Mental Health Administration (ADAMHA) to the National Institutes of Health (NIH), which is a part of the Department of Health and Human Services (DHHS). In 1992 the ADAMHA was reorganized, and the agency was renamed the Substance Abuse and Mental Health Services Administration (SAMHSA). Currently, SAMHSA, an agency within the DHHS, is the lead agency for improving access to quality substance abuse prevention, addiction treatment, and mental health services in the United States. In addition, SAMHSA certifies laboratories that perform drugs-of-abuse testing and publishes testing guidelines.

Drug abuse is a serious public health issue worldwide. In 1996 heroin addiction in the United States was associated with social, economic, medical, and public health costs estimated at $22 billion. In addition, 200,000 heroin addicts (about 24% to 36% of all heroin addicts) pass through the correctional system each year, placing an additional cost burden on society.[1] The cost associated with public substance abuse treatment programs increased from $9.3 billion in 1986 to $20.7 billion in 2003.[2] The estimated total cost of drug abuse in the United States increased 5.3% annually from $107.5 billion in 1992 to $180.9 billion in 2002. In 2002 loss of productivity related to drug abuse was estimated at $128.6 billion, which was also a significant increase from an estimated cost of $77.4 billion in 1992. Another major contributor to the cost of drug abuse is the expenditure associated with criminal justice system activities associated with drugs of abuse.[3] SAMHSA reported that in 2006 approximately 74.9%

of illicit drug users over 18 years of age were employed.[4]

In the workplace, drug abuse is associated with absenteeism, sleeping on the job, interpersonal problems, dishonesty, and poor performance. Moreover, alcohol and drug abuse are also associated with hangover, impaired coordination, and inability to respond to hazards, which result in workplace injury to the user and other innocent victims. In the 1970s drinking and abusing drugs were accepted as a part of life of workers. For example, in 1978 about 32% of railroad workers were reported to be drunk at least once upon returning to duty. Some of the nation's earliest employee assistance programs were started in the transportation industry to help workers with substance abuse and mental health problems. Drug abuse in the workplace eventually prompted initiation of the concept of a drug-free workplace and federally mandated random workplace drug testing.[5,6]

EXECUTIVE ORDER OF PRESIDENT REAGAN

On September 15, 1986, President Ronald Reagan issued Executive Order 12564 directing all federal employees involved in law enforcement, national security, protection of life and property, public health and safety, as well as other functions requiring a high degree of public trust to be subjected to mandatory drug testing. This order has little significance for private employers. Following this executive order the DHHS developed guidelines and protocols for drugs of abuse testing. The overall testing process under mandatory drug-testing guidelines consists of proper collection of specimen, initiation of chain of custody, and finally analysis of specimen (screening and confirmation by GC/MS) by a

SAMHSA–certified laboratory. The screening by immunoassay should be performed using Federal Drug Administration–approved methods. The test should be confirmed by a second technique, preferably by GC/MS.

IMPORTANT LAWS AND REGULATIONS

Several laws and regulations are important in understanding workplace drug-testing policies. The executive order by President Reagan was directed toward federal employees working in sensitive positions that involve national security and safety. However, government agencies were also allowed to test applicants to and employees in nonsensitive positions if there was a suspicion of drug usage or there was an accident. The important laws and documents regarding employment drug testing in the United States are:

- National Labor Relations Act (1935)
- Title VII of the Civil Rights Act (1964)
- Drug-Free Workplace Act (1988)
- Omnibus Transportation Employee Testing Act (1991)
- Americans With Disabilities Act (1990)
- Family and Medical Leave Act (1993)
- Department of Defense regulations
- Department of Transportation regulations
- State drug-testing laws
- State workers' compensation laws

Title VII of the Civil Rights Act of 1964 applies to all private employers with 15 or more employees. This act prohibits discrimination against applicants based on race, sex, religion, or national origin. Therefore, during pre-employment drug testing and workplace drug testing employees should not be treated differently based on race, sex, religion, or national origin. The Americans With Disabilities Act also applies to all employers with 15 or more employees. This law prohibits an employer from discriminating against a qualified individual based on disability. This law also allows an employer to adopt a drug-free workplace policy, and a person who is abusing drugs or alcohol is not considered a "disabled person" under this act. However, this act also prohibits an employer from discriminating against a person who has a prior history of drug abuse or who is enrolled in a substance abuse rehabilitation program. In addition, an employee has no obligation to inform the employer that he or she is receiving a prescription medication such as codeine or hydrocodone under medical advice. Discrimination against such an employee is also prohibited.

Employers with more than 50 employees must comply with the Family and Medical Leave Act of 1993, which allows an employee who has worked for an employer for at least one year to take an unpaid leave of absence up to 12 weeks for dealing with a serious health problem, including a substance abuse problem. Any retaliation against that employee is prohibited by this law.

The federal Drug-Free Workplace Act of 1988 requires any organization receiving a federal contract worth $100,000 or more to establish a drug-free workplace policy. This law also is applicable to all organizations receiving a federal grant of any size, and all such organizations must maintain a drug-free workplace policy in order to continually receive federal grants. Although formal drug testing is not required by the law, at a minimum the organization must do the following:

- Prepare and distribute a formal drug-free workplace policy.
- Establish a drug-free awareness program.
- Ensure that all employees working on the federal contract understand their personal reporting obligation.
- Notify the federal contacting agency of any covered violation.
- Take direct action against an employee convicted of a workplace drug violation.
- Maintain an ongoing good-faith effort to meet all the requirements of the act throughout the life of the contract.

This law is not applicable to subcontractors of federal grants.

In 1991 the U.S. Congress passed the Omnibus Transportation Employee Testing Act, which requires drug and alcohol testing of safety-sensitive employees working in aviation, trucking, railroads, mass transits, pipeline, and other transportation industries. The U.S. Department of Transportation publishes rules on who must conduct drug testing, what procedures to use, and when such testing should be done. These regulations are applicable to roughly 12.1 million people and encompassed in 49 Code of Federal Regulations (CFR), Part 40. The Office of Drug and Alcohol Policy and Compliance (ODAPC) publishes, implements, and provides authoritative interpretations of these results. The federal agencies covered under this law are:

- Federal Aviation Administration
- Federal Highway Administration
- Federal Railroad Administration
- U.S. Coast Guard
- Urban mass transit administrations
- Research and special program administration

The core requirements of these drug-testing programs are:

1. All employers in the transportation industry are required to test safety-sensitive employees at certain key points of their professional career.

2. All employers in the transportation industry are required to have a program of random drug testing in place.

3. All drug testing conducted under the act must be carried out by a laboratory certified by SAMHSA.

4. All drug testing conducted under this act must test for five different classes of drugs (marijuana, cocaine, opiates, amphetamine, and phencyclidine).

5. All alcohol testing of employees must strictly adhere to the Department of Transportation's policies and procedures.

6. All positive tests must be reviewed by a trained medical review officer (MRO).

7. All employees, whether in safety sensitive positions or not, must receive drug and alcohol awareness training and education.

8. All supervisors must receive at least 2 hours of training in substance abuse detection, documentation, and intervention.

9. Any employee who is determined to have a substance abuse problem must be referred by the employer to a trained substance abuse professional.

The Department of Defense has developed its own regulations for contractors working in the national security arena (Section 48 CFR 252, 223-7004). Under these regulations defense contractors must maintain a drug-free workplace that includes a comprehensive employee assistance program, provision for self-referral, and supervisory referrals for drug testing, supervisory training on detecting and responding to illegal drug use, and a carefully controlled and monitored employee drug-testing policy. The Department of Energy, the National Aeronautics and Space Administration, and the Nuclear Regulatory Commission all have drug testing requirements for safety-sensitive contractors.

Employers implementing drug-free workplace policies and workplace drug-testing programs affecting unionized workers must be aware of the National Labor Relations Act. The employer must negotiate with the union to determine when the testing will be conducted and what penalties a worker might face in the event of a failed drug test.

Many states have their own drug laws in addition to federal laws and regulations. In general, three types of state legislation may affect workplace drug-testing policies:

- State and local laws regulating drug testing

- State workers' compensation law

- State unemployment insurance law

In the interest of promoting a safe work environment, some states offer employers discounts on their workers' compensation insurance premium. In addition, many states deny workers' compensation when injuries are determined to be related to substance abuse. Some states also deny unemployment benefits to people who were fired because of positive drug-test results or evidence of drug abuse.

WHEN SHOULD DRUG TESTING BE CONDUCTED?

Drug testing prior to employment is the most common type of workplace drug testing. Most Fortune 500 companies have implemented workplace drug-testing policies in order to achieve a drug-free work environment. In general, a person undergoing pre-employment drug testing has few legal rights. In cases of failed drug testing, employment is usually denied. Drug testing is not foolproof, however. For example, testing positive for opiates may be caused by poppy seed–containing food rather than drug abuse. Although SAMHSA has established a cutoff level of 2000 ng/ml in order to avoid a false-positive opiate test result, a private employer may have a cutoff level of 300 ng/ml. It is difficult for a potential employee to challenge the positive results of drug testing in a court of law by filing a lawsuit against the company or the laboratory that performed the urine drug testing (see also Chapter 16). Drug testing is also allowed in the following situations, especially for employees who are working in safety-sensitive positions:

- As part of an annual physical
- Prior to a promotion
- After a workplace accident
- As a follow-up to treatment for drug abuse
- Prior to returning to duty
- At random, unannounced times

Usually five drug classes are tested for, including amphetamine and methamphetamine, cocaine, marijuana, opiates, and phencyclidine (see Chapter 5 for details). An employer may also test for additional drugs such as benzodiazepines, barbiturates, and propoxyphene.

THE ROLE OF SAMHSA IN WORKPLACE DRUG TESTING

A research facility that opened in 1935 in Lexington, Kentucky, became the Addiction Research Center in 1948. This organization became the National Institute of Drug Abuse (NIDA) in 1974 and was established as a part of the Alcohol, Drug Abuse, and Mental Health Administration (ADAMHA) as the lead federal agency conducting research on substance abuse. The NIDA drug abuse information and treatment referral hotline was initiated in 1986, and NIDA became the lead agency to implement the drug-free federal workplace program as mandated by Ronald Reagan. In 1992 ADAMHA ceased to exist, and all of its major programs were moved to different agencies. NIDA was transferred to the National Institutes of Health (NIH), which is part of the DHHS. The new agency was the Substance Abuse and Mental Health Services Administration (SAMHSA), an operational division of the DHHS. The division of workplace programs in SAMHSA administers and directs the National Laboratory Certification Program (NLCP), which oversees laboratories conducting drug testing following the guidelines for federal workplace drug-testing programs. These mandatory guidelines were first published in the *Federal Register* on April 11, 1988 (53 CFR 11970) and have since been revised in the *Federal Register* on June 9, 1994 (59 CFR 29908), and also on September 30, 1997 (62 CFR 51118). Another notice was issued on

April 13, 2004 (*Federal Register,* vol. 69, no. 71). The intent of these guidelines is to ensure proper specimen collection, validity of urine specimens (check for specific gravity, temperature, pH, creatinine, and also test for adulterants), and also proper interpretation of test results by a qualified medically trained and licensed physician (the MRO).The majority of drug tests are performed using urine specimens. All urine specimens must be collected under chain of custody to document the integrity and security of the specimen from the point of collection until receipt by the laboratory.

On April 13, 2004, a proposal was published in the *Federal Register* by the DHHS to establish drug tests for alternative biological matrices. The proposal had the following key areas:

1. Scientific and technical guidelines for the testing of hair, sweat, and oral fluid specimens in addition to urine specimens

2. The requirement to test each specimen for 3,4-methylenedioxy-methamphetamine (MDMA), 3,4-methylenedioxy-ethylamphetamine (MDEA), and 3,4-methylenedioxyamphetamine (MDA)

3. Scientific and technical guidelines to test urine and oral fluid at the site of collection

4. Requirements of certification of initial test facilities

5. Requirements for collectors, individuals performing on-site testing, and MROs

This proposal had a 90-day period for the public to comment. More than 2000 comments were included in the final guideline. The guidelines also published proposed cutoff concentrations for testing of hair, sweat, and oral fluid.[7]

 SAMHSA–CERTIFIED LABORATORIES

Because the NLCP was transferred from NIDA to SAMHSA in 1992, a certified drug-testing laboratory can not be called a NIDA-certified laboratory. It should be called a SAMHSA–certified laboratory. These laboratories maintain a very high standard of quality control, quality assurance, and laboratory practice and are regularly inspected to ensure their high standard of performance. Laboratories must meet special requirements and standards in order to be SAMHSA certified. Each certified laboratory receives blind specimens from the agency quarterly for purposes of proficiency testing. The list of SAMHSA–certified laboratories is regularly updated in the *Federal Register*. The current list of certified laboratories is published during the first week of each month (see **Table 4-1**).

 CURRENT STATUS OF WORKPLACE DRUG TESTING IN THE UNITED STATES

The anticipated effect of workplace drug testing is to deter employees from abusing drugs and to prevent workplace accidents as well as improve productivity. Workplace drug testing was virtually nonexistent in the 1980s, and now there is a widespread acceptance of drug-testing programs by employers. Federal drug-testing programs applied to 1.8 million employees in 2005. Testing is conducted prior to employment, following workplace accidents, when drug use is suspected, as follow-up to treatment, and randomly and voluntarily.[7] Private employers also embrace the practice of pre-employment and workplace drug testing in order to achieve a drug-free workplace. Workplace drug testing deters employees

Table 4-1 SAMHSA-Certified Laboratories in Various States

State	Laboratory
Arkansas	Baptist Medical Center, Toxicology Laboratory, Little Rock
Arizona	Southwest Laboratories, Phoenix
California	National Toxicological Laboratories, Bakersfield
	Pacific Toxicological Laboratories, Chatsworth
	Laboratory Corporation of America, San Diego
	Pharmatech, San Diego
	Quest Diagnostics, Van Nuys
Florida	Diagnostic Services, Fort Myers
	Toxicology Testing Services, Miami
Georgia	Quest Diagnostics, Atlanta
	Doctors Laboratory, Valdosta
Indiana	South Bend Medical Foundation, South Bend
Kansas	Clinical Reference Laboratory, Lenexa
	LabOne/Quest Diagnostics, Lenexa
Louisiana	Kroll Laboratory Specialists, Gretna
Maryland	Army Forensic Drug-Testing Laboratory, Fort Meade (for military use)
Michigan	Sparrow Health System, Toxicology Testing Center, Lansing
Minnesota	Veteran Affairs Medical Center, Forensic Toxicology Laboratory,
Minneapolis	MedTox, St. Paul
Mississippi	ElSohly Laboratories, Oxford
	Laboratory Corporation of America, Southaven
Missouri	Toxicology and Drug Monitoring Laboratory, University of Missouri Hospital and Clinics, Columbia
New Jersey	Laboratory Corporation of America, Raritan
New Mexico	S.E.D. Medical Laboratories, Albuquerque
New York	ACM Medical Laboratory, Rochester
North Carolina	Laboratory Corporation of America, Research Triangle Park
Oklahoma	St. Anthony Hospital, Toxicology Laboratory, Oklahoma City
Oregon	Oregon Medical Laboratories, Springfield
	Legacy MetroLab, Portland
Pennsylvania	Quest Diagnostics, Norristown
	DrugScan, Warminster
Tennessee	Advanced Toxicology Network, Memphis
	Aegis Sciences, Nashville
Texas	One Source Toxicology Laboratory, Pasadena
	Laboratory Corporation of America, Houston
Virginia	Kroll Laboratory Specialists, Richmond
Washington	Pathology Associates Medical Laboratories, Spokane
	Laboratory Corporation of America, Seattle
Wisconsin	ACL Laboratories, West Allis

Source: SAMHSA. Division of Workplace Programs. http://www.samhsa.gov/DrugTesting/Level_1_1Pages/ CertifiedLabs.aspx. Accessed November 13, 2008.

from abusing drugs, as reflected by the *Drug Testing Index* newsletter published by Quest Diagnostics, a reputable national reference laboratory performing workplace drug testing. According to the *Drug Testing Index* published on March 12, 2008, among the combined U.S. workforces only 3.8% of the drug tests have positive results in 2007, compared with 13.6% in 1988. In addition, amphetamine, methamphetamine, and cocaine abuse by U.S. workers is also in decline.[8]

Over 80% of the large employers in the United States use some form of workplace drug testing. One report demonstrated that medical expenditures would be minimized if 42% of employees in a calendar quarter were tested for drugs. The same report also found that on average each employee should be tested 1.68 times per year.[9] Implementation of a drug-screening program in the automotive company General Motors resulted in a 50% reduction in workplace injury.[10] Gerber et al assess the impact of drug testing within the construction industry and conclude that companies with drug-testing programs experienced a 51% reduction in injury incident rates within two years of implementing drug-testing programs.[11] Miller et al studied the effectiveness of peer-based workplace substance abuse prevention coupled with random testing in the transportation industry and concluded that such a program was associated with a one-third reduction in injury rates, avoiding an estimated cost of $48 million to the employer in 1999. The peer-based program cost $35 per employee, and drug testing cost another $35 per employee in 1999, but the company avoided an estimated $1850 in employer injury cost per employee, corresponding to

a benefit-to-cost ratio of 26 to 1.[5] These findings along with those of other reports justify the costs associated with implementation of workplace drug-testing programs.

 CONCLUSION

In the past two decades workplace drug-testing has evolved from being almost nonexistent to a standard practice embraced by most of the large employers in the United States and also in many European countries, Australia, and New Zealand. The benefits of workplace drug-testing justify the cost involved in implementing such procedures. Apart from reducing workplace incidents and injuries, a drug-free workplace culture contributes to the productivity and general well-being of employees. Currently, there are 39 SAMHSA-certified laboratories in the United States and 3 in Canada that perform the majority of workplace drug tests. The Army Forensic Drug-Testing Laboratory in Maryland does not perform test for clients outside the U.S. military.

In addition to SAMHSA-certified laboratories, many hospital-based clinical laboratories perform drugs-of-abuse testing, but the majority of such tests are for medical purposes and may not be used for criminal prosecution if an individual tests positive for the presence of an illicit drug. Coroners' and medical examiners' offices also have accredited forensic toxicology laboratories where drug tests are routinely performed to investigate unnatural deaths. Such results can be used for legal purposes for prosecuting an individual. State and federal governments have their own crime laboratories, and the results can be used legally for prosecution.

REFERENCES

1. Boutwell AE, Nijhawan A, Zaller N, Rich JD. Arrested on heroin: a national opportunity. *J Opiod Manag.* 2007;3:328–332.

2. Mark TL, Levit LR, Vandivort-Warren R, et al. Trends in spending for substance abuse treatment, 1986–2003. *Health Aff.* 2007;26: 1118–1128.

3. Office of National Drug Control Policy. The Economic Cost of Drug Abuse in the United States, 1992–2002. http://www. whitehousedrugpolicy.gov/publications/ economic_costs/economic_costs.pd Accessed October 22, 2008.

4. U.S. Department of Health and Human Services, Substance Abuse and Mental Health Services Administration, Office of Applied Studies. *Results from the 2006 National Survey on Drug Use and Health Findings.* http://www.oas.samhsa.gov/ NSDUH/2K6NSDUH/2K6results.cfm. Accessed October 22, 2008.

5. Miller TR, Zaloshnja E, Spicer RS. Effectiveness and benefit-cost of peer based workplace substance abuse prevention coupled with random testing. *Accid Anal Prev.* 2007;39:565–573.

6. Drug-Free Workplace. Drug-Free Workplace Kit. http://www.drugfreeworkplace. gov/WPWorkit/legal.html. Accessed October 22, 2008.

7. Bush D. The U.S. mandatory guidelines for federal workplace drug-testing programs: current status and future considerations. *Forensic Sci Int.* 2008;174:111–119.

8. Quest Diagnostics. Use of methamphetamine among U.S. workers and job applicants drops 22 percent in 2007 and cocaine use slows dramatically. *Drug Testing Index* [electronic newsletter]; published March 12, 2008. http://www.questdiagnostics.com/ employersolutions/dti/2008_03/dti_index. html. Accessed October 22, 2008.

9. Ozminkowski RJ, Mark TL, Goetzel RZ, et al. Relationship between urinalysis testing for substance use, medical expenditure and the occurrence of injuries at a large manufacturing firm. *Am J Drug Alcohol Abuse.* 2003;29:151–167.

10. MacDonald S, Wells S. The impact and effectiveness of drug-testing programs in the workplace. In: MacDonald S, Roman P, eds. *Research Advances in Alcohol and Drug Problems.* Vol. 11, *Drug Testing in the Workplace.* New York: Plenum Press; 1994.

11. Gerber JK, Yacoubian GS Jr. An assessment of drug testing within the construction industry. *J Drug Educ.* 2002;32:53–68.

CHAPTER 5

Testing of SAMHSA and Non-SAMHSA Drugs

ABSTRACT

The Substance Abuse and Mental Health Services Administration (SAMHSA) mandatory guidelines for drugs-of-abuse testing require tests for amphetamines, cocaine, opiates, marijuana, and phencyclidine. If an initial urine screening indicates drug levels above the required cutoffs, confirmatory tests using gas chromatography mass spectrometry (GC/MS) will be conducted. Drug tests are intended to identify regular abusers of illicit drugs. Most workplace drug tests (over 90%) use urine specimens because they are noninvasive. In addition, each drug class has a longer detection window in urine compared with blood. Even so, the majority of illicit drugs can be detected only for few days to a week after last use. Hair testing can identify drug abuse up to three months prior to specimen collection, so it is much more useful for identifying a pattern of drug abuse. In addition to drug tests required by SAMHSA, private employers may use tests to look for the presence of various benzodiazepines, barbiturates, and designer drugs such as 3,4-methylenedioxymeth-amphetamine (MDMA) and 3,4-methylenedioxyamphetamine (MDA).

Many large employers in the United States, European countries, Australia, New Zealand, and other countries worldwide now commonly conduct pre-employment and workplace drug testing. The objective of workplace drug testing is to deter employees from drug abuse, thus reducing workplace accidents and improving productivity. In addition, cost benefit analysis clearly demonstrates the advantages of promoting a drug-free workplace and implementing some form of employee drug-testing program. In addition to commonly abused drugs,

many prescription medications, designer drugs, and other substances such as magic mushroom, peyote cactus, solvent, household gases, and solvents are also abused. A drug-testing program is geared toward identifying employees who are using common illicit drugs, which account for the majority of drugs abused in the United States. As discussed in Chapter 1, the most common illicit drug abused in the United States is marijuana, followed by cocaine, amphetamines, and heroin. SAMHSA requires testing for all of these drugs.

A negative test result for urine drug testing does not indicate that an individual never used drugs. It indicates only that the person has not abused any drug recently or used a drug in such a low quantity that it did not produce enough drug metabolite in the urine for the person to show positive results. Again, workplace drug-testing programs are intended to deter employees from abusing drugs, and past history of drug abuse is not a concern. Obviously, a person who has never experimented with any illicit drug should test negative in workplace drug testing unless the individual has eaten poppy seed–containing food or hemp-containing food or is taking a prescription medication that contains a controlled substance.

SAMHSA–MANDATED DRUG TESTS

The federal government requires testing for the presence of five drugs and their metabolites in the urine including amphetamines, cocaine, opiates, marijuana, and phencyclidine. The mandatory guidelines also dictate the cutoff concentrations of various drugs and metabolites both at the screening and confirmation steps. If the concentration of a particular drug or metabolite is below the cutoff, the drug testing is reported as negative. **Table 5-1** lists the cutoff concentrations in both screening and confirmation steps of drug tests.

The federal guidelines were first published in April 1988, and the major focus of the drug-testing program was urine specimens. An initial immunoassay screen should be performed using FDA-approved commercially available immunoassay kits and the proper instrumentation following manufacturer's recommendations. If the immunoassay screen is negative, no further testing is required, but every positive screening result must be confirmed by a rigorous second analytic technique, preferably GC/MS. No additional drug tests should be conducted unless authorized by the law.[1]

Amphetamines

In drugs-of-abuse testing either the parent drug or its metabolite is targeted for detection in the body, depending on the drug type. For example, after use of amphetamine, amphetamine is excreted unchanged in the urine along with other metabolites, and for urine drug testing amphetamine is targeted with a cutoff concentration of 1000 ng/ml. After ingestion of methamphetamine, a part of methamphetamine is metabolized to amphetamine, and both methamphetamine and amphetamine are detected in urine. The guideline requires that if methamphetamine is confirmed by GC/MS, amphetamine must be present in the specimen at a concentration of 200 ng/ml or higher in order to report the drug test as positive for methamphetamine. From a physiological point of view, after methamphetamine use, both amphetamine and methamphetamine must be present in the urine. In addition, in the 1990s it was reported that by increasing the injector port temperature (done as a confirmation step during GC/MS), pseudoephedrine, a common active ingredient in many over-the-counter cold medications, can be thermally degraded to methamphetamine and may cause a false-positive test for methamphetamine. However, no amphetamine can be generated by this process (see also Chapter 14 and Chapter 18). Therefore, detection of amphetamine in a urine specimen ensures that methamphetamine indeed is the source of amphetamine.

Table 5-1   Cutoff Concentrations Mandated by Federal Drug-Testing Programs[a]

Drug or Drug Class	Immunoassay (ng/ml)	GC/MS Confirmation (ng/ml)	
Amphetamines	1000	Amphetamine	500
Methamphetamine	500[b]		
Cannabinoids	50	THC-COOH[c]	15
Cocaine metabolites	300	Benzoylecgonine	150
Opiates	2000	Morphine	2000
Codeine	2000		
6-acetylmorphine	10[d]		
Phencyclidine	25	Phencyclidine	25

a. DHHS, SAMHSA. *Federal Register*. 1988;53:11970; *Federal Register*. 1994;59:29908; *Federal Register*. 1997;62:51118. Department of Transportation (DOT). *Federal Register*. 2000;65:79462.
b. Amphetamine must be present at levels $\geq$ 200 ng/ml.
c. THC-COOH, 11-nor-Δ^9-tetrahydrocannabinol-9-carboxylic acid.
d. Test for 6-acetylmorphine performed when morphine concentration is >2000 ng/ml.

Source: Dasgupta A. *Handbook of Drugs Monitoring Methods: Therapeutics and Drugs of Abuse.* New York: Humana Press; 2008. Reprinted with kind permission of Springer Science + Business Media.

Typical amphetamine abuse produces urine concentration of amphetamine and methamphetamine well over the cutoff concentration of 1000 ng/ml. Occupational exposure to such a drug does not produce a high enough concentration of amphetamine or methamphetamine in urine to test positive by urine drug testing. A study of personnel handling up to 500 gm of methamphetamine during assembly of training aids for drug detection dogs reported a maximum urinary concentration of methamphetamine of 262 ng/ml ($n = 101$). The mean methamphetamine concentration as measured by GC/MS was 48 ng/ml.[2]

Cocaine

Cocaine is metabolized to benzoylecgonine and ecgonine methyl ester. The major urinary metabolite is benzoylecgonine, which is inactive. In urine drugs-of-abuse testing, cocaine is detected and confirmed as benzoylecgonine if present at a concentration of 300 ng/ml or higher. A typical administration of cocaine by intranasal route, which is the usual route of abuse, typically produces a maximum urinary concentration of benzoylecgonine at a level of 15,611 ng/ml. This average level of maximum benzoylecgonine in urine was observed 5.6 hours after intranasal administration of cocaine in 6 subjects at a dosage of 25 mg of cocaine per subject, representing a typical dosage of cocaine.[3] However, use of cocaine as a local anesthetic during ear, nose, or throat surgery or use of cocaine as an ophthalmic drop also produces positive results for cocaine in urine using the cutoff of 300 ng/ml (see Chapter 15). Urine analysis of laboratory personnel training cocaine-sniffing dogs for the military may show detectable levels of benzoylecgonine in urine specimens. In one study using urine specimens collected from drug chemists, document examiners, evidence custodians, and one secretary, benzoylecgonine was detected in 88 out of 233 specimens. Two urine specimens showed benzoylecgonine levels of 138 ng/ml and 460 ng/ml, respectively. Using the cutoff confirmation of 100 ng/ml as mandated by the Department of Defense, both specimens tested positive for cocaine. Under the SAMHSA guidelines, the urine specimen containing 460 ng/ml of benzoylecgonine should be considered positive.[4] Passive inhalation of cocaine smoke results in urinary benzoylecgonine concentration well below the screening cutoff concentration of 300 ng/ml. In one study, 6 male volunteers were exposed to cocaine smoke for 1 hour in an unventilated room (the cocaine smoke was produced by 100 or 200 mg freebase cocaine heated at 200°C). Urine samples from this group showed peak urinary concentration of benzoylecgonine ranging from 2 to 123 ng/ml.[5]

Marijuana (Cannabinoid)

The major active component of cannabinoid (marijuana, hashish) is Δ^9-tetrahydrocannabinol (THC), which is metabolized to 11-nor-9-carboxy Δ^9-tetrahydrocannabinol (THC-COOH). The cutoff concentration of this major metabolite is 50 ng/ml, while for confirmatory purposes the corresponding cutoff concentration is 15 ng/ml. Passive inhalation of marijuana should not produce enough concentration of THC-COOH in urine to produce a positive result in drug testing, but in abusers this cutoff concentration is easily reached in urine (see also Chapter 12).

Bioavailability of THC is approximately 30% after smoking but 4% to 12% after oral use. The major metabolite of marijuana (THC-COOH) may be detected in urine for several weeks.[6] The urinary concentration of THC-COOH in marijuana abusers varies widely, but it is usually between 78.7 ng/ml and 2634 ng/ml (average 1153 ng/ml), according to one published report.[7] Therefore, most abusers should test positive using the screening cutoff of 50 ng/ml.

Opiates

The original cutoff of concentration for opiates for the screening was 300 ng/ml. Most immunoassays for opiates utilize an antibody that recognizes morphine in urine. Morphine-3-glucuronide is the major metabolite after use of codeine, morphine, or heroin (which is usually injected). However, in the 1990s several reports were published indicating that eating poppy seed–containing food resulted in a positive urine test for opiates. Moreover, observed concentrations of both morphine and codeine were well above the cutoff concentration of 300 ng/ml. To circumvent this problem, the DHHS increased the screening cutoff of opiate immunoassays from 300 ng/ml to 2000 ng/ml in 1998. Heroin is metabolized to 6-acetylmorphine (also called 6-monoacetylmorphine), which is then metabolized further to morphine and is excreted in urine as a glucuronide conjugate. The presence of 6-acetylmorphine can be detected only up to 24 hours after heroin abuse, but morphine is present in urine for up to 3 days. The mandatory guideline requires testing for 6-acetylmorphine by GC/MS in urine using a cutoff concentration of 10 ng/ml.

Morphine-3-glucuronide, codeine, and 6-acetylmorphine have high cross-reactivity with morphine antibody and if present in urine produce positive opiate screening results. Most opiate immunoassays have poor cross-reactivity with oxycodone and relatively low cross-reactivity with hydro-morphone and hydrocodone. If these compounds are present in high amounts in a urine specimen, it may test positive for opiates. Specific immunoassays are used for detecting the presence of oxycodone in urine because the pain medicine oxycodone is also widely abused. Several synthetic opioids are not metabolized to morphine and codeine. These drugs include:

- Buprenorphine
- Fentanyl
- Hydrocodone
- Meperidine
- Methadone
- Oxycodone
- Oxymorphone

Therefore, abuse of any of these drugs can not be detected by opiate screening assays.

Phencyclidine

Propoxyphene (PCP) is abused by snorting, smoking, intravenous injection, and also by being taken orally. Propoxyphene is absorbed into the circulation after intake by any one of these routes. Propoxyphene is metabolized by the liver to various hydroxylated metabolites, but a portion of PCP is also excreted unchanged in urine. Tests for PCP target the unchanged drug for detection both in immunoassay screens as well as in GC/MS confirmatory tests. The cutoff concentration for both screening and confirmation is 25 ng/ml.

Detection Windows of Drugs in SAMSHA-Mandated Tests

A drug or its metabolites can usually be detected in urine only for a limited time after last abuse. For example, cocaine can only be detected 2 to 3 days after use, but propoxyphene can be detected for up to 30 days. Most PCP is excreted within the first 9 days following use, and then the urinary excretion of PCP and its metabolites is reduced significantly. The mean detection window of PCP in urine is 14 days after last use.[8] Marijuana metabolites can only be detected for up to 3 days after a single use. In a chronic abuser, however, the metabolite may accumulate in the body and cause a positive test for up to 30 days.[9,10] After a single administration, benzoylecgonine may be detected for up to 2 days in urine, but after repeated use it may be present as long as 4 days.[11] Amphetamine and methamphetamine can be detected in urine up to 2 days after last use.[12] **Table 5-2** lists the detection windows for drugs in urine for which SAMHSA mandates testing.

Table 5-2	Windows of Detection for Drugs in Urine for Which SAMHSA Mandates Testing

Drug	Detection Window in Urine
Amphetamine	2 days
Methamphetamine	2 days
Cocaine (as benzoylecgonine)	2 days after single use, 4 days after repeated use
Morphine	2–3 days
Codeine	2 days
Heroin (as morphine)	2 days
Phencyclidine	14 days
Marijuana (as 11-nor-Δ^9-tetrahydrocannabinol-9-carboxylic acid)	2–3 days after single use, 30 days in chronic abuser

ROLE OF THE MEDICAL REVIEW OFFICER IN SAMHSA-MANDATED DRUG TESTING

Approximately 20 million employees are screened each year in the United States for illicit drugs. Drug-testing programs in the United States can be classified as mandatory or nonmandatory. In the first category an employer (for example, the Department of Transportation) is required by federal regulation to test employees. In the second category, employers choose to test for their own reasons. Private employers have instituted employee drug testing in order to create a drug-free workplace. Drug-testing programs have formalized the role of a specialist physician called a medical review officer (MRO) who is responsible for final review of results in workplace drug-testing programs. The MRO must be a licensed physician (MD or DO) and must have detailed knowledge of alternative medical explanations for a positive drug-testing result (e.g., interference, use of prescription drugs), knowledge about substance abuse and controlled substances, as well as familiarity with laboratory testing methods, including issues of specimen adulterations and causes of invalid test results. The MRO serves as the common point of contact between all parties involved in drug testing, including the donor, the collector, the laboratory, and the designated representative of the federal test agency (if applicable). The MRO may be an employee or contractor of a federal agency, but the MRO must not be an employee or agent of or have any financial interest in the laboratory performing the drug testing. In addition, the MRO must not get any financial benefit from having an agency use any specific drug-testing laboratory.[13] The MRO is an integral part of a drug-testing program and can determine the cause of positive results in drug testing and counsel the employee. A laboratory is required to submit a drug-testing result to the MRO within five working days of receiving the specimen. The result must be certified by the laboratory's certifying scientist.

TESTING FOR NON-SAMHSA DRUGS

Other than the five SAMHSA-mandated drug classes, a few other abused drugs are routinely tested for in workplace drug-testing programs. These drug classes include barbiturates and benzodiazepines. Depending on the program, other drugs such as methadone, oxycodone, propoxyphene, and methaqualone may also be included in the drug testing menu. Commercially available immunoassays are available for screening of these drugs, but for confirmation GC/MS is still the gold standard. **Table 5-3** gives the cutoff concentrations of immunoassays for screening of these drugs in urine.

Table 5-3	Cutoff Concentrations of Non-SAMHSA–Mandated Drugs

Drug or Drug Class	Immunoassay Cutoff Level
Barbiturates	200 ng/ml
Benzodiazepines	200 ng/ml
Methadone	300 ng/ml
Methaqualone	300 ng/ml
Propoxyphene	300 ng/ml
Oxycodone	100 or 300 ng/ml

Barbiturates

Barbiturates can be short acting or long acting. Although numerous different barbiturate derivatives have been synthesized, only a dozen such drugs are used medically. Interestingly, barbituric acid has no pharmacologic activity. Commonly abused barbiturates are secobarbital, pentobarbital, and amobarbital. These are the common barbitals targeted for confirmation if the barbiturate screening assay is positive. The usual cutoff concentration of immunoassays for screening of urine specimens is 200 ng/ml, and the same cutoff is usually used for GC/MS confirmation. Many commercially available immunoassays for barbiturates utilize antibodies against secobarbital.

Benzodiazepines

Many benzodiazepines are used in clinical practice, although not all are approved for medical use in the United States. The benzodiazepines that are commonly abused include diazepam, lorazepam, oxazepam, clonazepam, and triazolam. Gas chromatography/mass spectrometry is used to confirm the presence of any of these drugs after a positive screening test for benzodiazepines. Flunitrazepam (Rohypnol) is a benzodiazepine that is not legally available in the United States. However, it is found on the clandestine market and is widely abused in the United States; it is also associated with date rape situations. One of the major metabolites of flunitrazepam is 7-aminoflunitrazepam, which cross-reacts with antibodies used in the benzodiazepine screening assays. For example, cross-reactivity of 7-aminoflunitrazepam with an EMIT (enzyme multiplied immunoassay technique) Plus assay is 67.8%, and the corresponding cross-reactivity with a CEDIA (cloned enzyme donor immunoassay)

assay is 99%. Unfortunately, low concentrations of flunitrazepam and its major metabolite 7-aminoflunitrazepam may cause an immunoassay for benzodiazepine to fail to detect the presence of flunitrazepam in urine. Immunoassays are commercially available for detecting flunitrazepam. For example, Cozart Bioscience Ltd. (Oxfordshire, UK) markets a specific enzyme-linked immunosorbent assay for screening of flunitrazepam in urine.[14] One report recommended lowering the cutoff concentration of the EMIT assay for benzodiazepine from 300 ng/ml to 60 ng/ml to detect the presence of flunitrazepam and its metabolite 7-aminoflunitrazepam in urine specimens. Positive specimens should be further analyzed by gas chromatography.[15] Most toxicology laboratories performing workplace drug testing also have the capability of confirming the presence of flunitrazepam and its metabolite in urine using GC/MS.

Methadone

Methadone is metabolized to two pharmacologically inactive urinary metabolites, 2-ethylidene-1,5-dimethyl-3,3-diphenylpyrrolidine (EDDP) and 2-ethyl-5-methyl-3,3-diphenylpyrrolidine (EMDP). Both methadone and EDDP are usually found in urine in significant amounts, while the concentration of EDMP is relatively low. Cheng et al reported that urinary methadone concentration varied from 78 ng/ml to 9547 ng/ml (median: 1031 ng/ml) and EDDP concentration varied from 77 ng/ml to 9547 ng/ml (median: 6734 ng/ml) in 21 urine specimens collected from patients undergoing methadone maintenance therapy. The concentrations of EMDP were below the detection limit of the GC/MS assay.[16] Commercially available immunoassays for screening of methadone in urine have antibodies directed toward either methadone or EDDP. However, an immunoassay designed for detecting the presence of methadone in urine may have a low cross-reactivity with EDDP. Preston et al demonstrated that 2% of urine specimens collected from patients who had taken methadone tested negative for methadone, while all specimens tested positive for EDDP.[17]

Oxycodone

Most immunoassays for opiates have poor cross-reactivity with oxycodone, a widely abused prescription pain medicine. However, immunoassays are commercially available for screening of oxycodone in urine specimens. For example, the EMIT opiate assay can detect morphine, morphine-3-glucuronide, and codeine but is also capable of detecting hydrocodone at a concentration of 247 ng/ml and hydromorphone at a concentration of 498 ng/ml. However, for oxycodone the threshold concentration is 2550 ng/ml. When 437 urine specimens collected from 105 patients on methadone maintenance therapy were tested by an EMIT opiate assay using a cutoff of 300 ng/ml, only 20 specimens containing oxycodone tested positive. When the authors used a specific oxycodone test strip, 83 specimens tested positive for oxycodone. The oxycodone test strip used in this study is a lateral flow chromatographic immunoassay capable of detecting oxycodone in urine if present at a concentration of 100 ng/ml (TMS Labs Urine-1 card; ACON Laboratories, San Diego, CA).[18] The DRI Oxycodone assay (Microgenics Corporation, Fremont, CA) is a homogenous immunoassay that can selectively identify urine specimens containing oxycodone at a concentration of 100 ng/ml or higher. This assay has no cross-reactivity with codeine, morphine, hydrocodone, and hydromorphone. Backer et al reported that out of 1523 urine specimens collected from pain management patients, 435 specimens tested positive for oxycodone. The GC/MS analysis confirmed the presence of oxycodone or oxymorphone in 433 specimens at a concentration of 100 ng/ml and higher. In addition to oxycodone and oxymorphone, morphine, hydromorphone, hydrocodone, and codeine were detected in 189 specimens.[19]

Propoxyphene

Propoxyphene is used for treating mild to moderate pain, but this drug is also abused. Both propoxyphene and its metabolite norpropoxyphene can be recovered in urine. Most propoxyphene immunoassays utilize antibodies that can recognize the presence of propoxyphene in urine if present at a concentration of 300 ng/ml or higher. The cross-reactivity of the antibody with norpropoxyphene may vary widely among different immunoassays. McNally et al concluded that the OnLine DAT Propoxyphene Plus assay (Roche Diagnostics, Indianapolis, IN) has better sensitivity than the EMIT propoxyphene assay for detecting propoxyphene in urine because the antibody used in the OnLine assay has 77% cross-reactivity with norpropoxyphene, while the EMIT assay has only 7% cross-reactivity with norpropoxyphene.[20] Another report indicates that diphenhydramine (the over-the-counter medication Benadryl) interferes with the EMIT propoxyphene immunoassay.[21] Confirmation of the presence of propoxyphene in urine should be carried out by GC/MS, and the assay should be able to determine the concentrations of both propoxyphene and norpropoxyphene.

Methaqualone

Methaqualone is metabolized to 2'-hydroxy and 3'-hydroxy, which are then conjugated and excreted in urine as glucuronide. Brenner et al reported that both the Roche OnLine methaqualone immunoassay and the EMIT II—first introduced by Syva in San Jose, CA—methaqualone immunoassay have high cross-reactivity toward both 2- and 3-hydroxy metabolites of methaqualone as well as their conjugated form and are useful for screening of methaqualone in urine specimens. When volunteers received 200 mg of methaqualone, both immunoassays showed greater than 600 ng/ml of drug after the second void, and all urine specimens tested highly positive (at a 300 ng/ml cutoff) after 72 hours. When the specimens were analyzed by GC/MS without hydrolysis of glucuronide conjugates, low levels of methaqualone and metabolites were detected. However, when urine specimens were hydrolyzed with beta-glucuronidase and analyzed again by GC/MS, high concentrations of metabolites were found. Therefore, the authors recommend hydrolysis of the urine specimen prior to GC/MS analysis.[22]

Detection Windows of Non-SAMHSA Drugs

The window of detection of short-acting barbiturates such as pentobarbital in urine is one day, while a long-acting barbiturate like phenobarbital has a detection window of one month. Oxycodone may be detected in urine 2 to 4 days after use, while methaqualone can be detected up to 3 days.[12,2] **Table 5-4** summarizes the window of detection of common non-SAMHSA–mandated drugs.

Table 5- 4	Window of Detection of Non-SAMHSA-Mandated Tests for Drugs in Urine

Drug or Drug Class	Detection Window in Urine
Barbiturates	
Short acting (e.g., pentobarbital, secobarbital)	1 day
Long acting (phenobarbital)	21 days
Benzodiazepines	
Short acting (e.g., alprazolam, lorazepam)	3 days
Long acting (diazepam)	30 days
Methadone	3 days
Methaqualone	3 days
Oxycodone	2–4 days
Propoxyphene	6 hours–2 days

 ## COLLECTION OF URINE SPECIMENS

In the military, where the urine collection process is supervised, the chances of receiving adulterated specimen are reduced. In pre-employment screening, however, where direct supervision of specimen collection is not practiced, a drug user may attempt to escape detection by adulterating specimens to avoid the unwanted consequences of failing a drug test. Several precautions are taken by the personnel at the collection site to avoid such adulteration of submitted specimens. They may ask the donor to remove outer garments (such as a coat or jacket) that may contain concealed adulterating substances. Personal belongings like purses or briefcases will stay with the collector, but the donor may retain his or her wallet. The collector also will direct the donor to empty his or her pockets and display the items to ensure that no item is present that could be used to adulterate the specimen.

Shy Bladder Syndrome

"Shy bladder syndrome" is defined as the inability to produce a urine specimen on demand. Occasionally a person is unable to provide a specimen upon arrival at the collection site because he or she has urinated recently. In such cases, the collector gives the donor a reasonable amount of liquid to drink over a period of time (not to exceed 3 hours). Medically unsupported claims of anxiety or dehydration are not considered valid reasons for not providing a urine sample. If after a sufficient period of time the donor is still unable to provide a urine specimen, the donor will be considered as "refusing to test."[13]

CHAIN OF CUSTODY

After collection of the urine specimen, the name of the donor and related information (e.g., if the donor is taking any prescription medicine) are written on the form, and the specimen is sealed in the presence of the donor with the donor's initials. The date and time of collection is documented on the form, and then the collector initiates the "chain of custody" process. The chain of custody form documents who is in possession of the specimen and when (the date and time a person is in possession of the specimen must be documented on the chain of custody form), thus ensuring that the specimen is secure and its integrity is maintained from the time of collection to final deposition of the specimen. If the specimen can not be hand-delivered to the laboratory or requires shipping to a different location, it must be shipped by a certified courier and the process must be documented. The laboratory personnel who receive and process the specimen must verify that the seal of the specimen is intact and the chain of custody document is complete. The laboratory performing the drug testing must be in a secure area with access limited to authorized personnel. All visitors to the secure area must be escorted and their visits must be documented. Maintaining a chain of custody is vital in case of legal challenge

CONCLUSION

Drug testing in the workplace has become widespread in the past two decades. Urine drug screen is the most common method of drug testing because it is noninvasive. Moreover, specimens can be easily screened rapidly using automated analyzers and commercially available immunoassays. The federally mandated drug-testing protocol requires testing for five drug classes: amphetamine, cocaine, opiates, marijuana, and phencyclidine. However, other abused drugs, such as barbiturates, benzodiazepines, oxycodone, and propoxyphene, may also be tested for by private employers in pre-employment and workplace drug-testing programs. Positive screening results must be confirmed by using GC/MS. Workplace drug testing is intended for identifying regular abusers of drugs. After last use, most drugs may be detected for a few days in urine. Phencyclidine may be detected for up to two weeks.

REFERENCES

1. Bush D. The U.S. mandatory guidelines for federal workplace drug-testing programs: current status and future considerations. *Forensic Sci Int.* 2008;174:111–119.

2. Stout PR, Horn CK, Klette KL, Given J. Occupational exposure to methamphetamine in workers preparing training AIDS for drug detection dogs. *J Anal Toxicol.* 2006;30:551–553.

3. Cone EJ, Tsadik A, Oyler J, Darwin WD. Cocaine metabolism and urinary excretion after different routes of administration. *Ther Drug Monit.* 1998;20:556–560.

4. Gehlhausen JM, Klette KL, Given J. Urine analysis of laboratory personnel preparing cocaine training for a military working dog program. *J Anal Toxicol.* 2001;25:637–640.

5. Cone EJ, Yousefnejad D, Hillsgrove MJ, Holicky B et al. Passive inhalation of cocaine. *J Anal Toxicol.* 1995;19:399–411.

6. McGilveray IJ. Pharmacokinetics of cannabinoids. *Pain Res Manag.* 2005;10(A):15A–22A.

7. Fraser AD, Worth D. Urinary excretion of 11-nor-9-carboxy-Δ^9-tetrahydrocannaninol and 11-hydroxy-delta9-THC: cannabinoid metabolites to creatinine ratio stuffy IV. *Forensic Sci Int.* 2004;143:147–152.

8. Simpson GM, Khajawall AM, Alatorre E, Staples ER. Urinary phencyclidine excretion in chronic abuser. *J Toxicol Clin Toxicol.* 1982;19:1051–1059.

9. Dackis CA, Pottash AJC, Annitto W, Gold MS. Persistence of marijuana level after supervised abstinence. *Am J Psychiatry.* 1982;139:1196–1198.

10. Huestis MA, Mitchell JM, Cone EJ. Detection time of marijuana metabolite in urine by immunoassays and GC-MS. *J Anal Toxicol.* 1995;19:443–449.

11. Huestis MA, Darwin WD, Shimoura E., Lalani SA et al. Cocaine and metabolites urinary excretion after controlled smoke administration. *J Anal Toxicol.* 2007;31:462–468.

12. Moeller KE, Lee KC, Kissack JC. Urine drug screen: practical guides for clinicians. *Mayo Clin Proc.* 2008;83:66–76.

13. U.S. Department of Heath and Human Services, Substance Abuse and Mental Health Services Administration. Medical Review Officer Manual for Federal Agency Workplace Drug-Testing Programs. [Effective November 1, 2004.] http://www.workplace.samhsa.gov/DrugTesting/Level_1_Pages/HHS%20MRO%20Manual%20(Effective%20November%201,%202004).aspx. Accessed October 22, 2008.

14. Improved screen and confirmation test of 7-aminoflunitrazepam in urine specimens for monitoring flunitrazepam (Rohypnol) in urine. *J Anal Toxicol.* 2002;26:411–418.

15. Morland H, Smith-Kielland A. Urinary screening of flunitrazepam: applicability of emit immunoassay [Letter to the Editor]. *Clin Chem.* 1997;43:1245–1256.

16. Cheng PS, Lee CH, Liu C, Chen CS. Simultaneous determination of ketamine, tramadol, methadone, and their metabolites in urine by gas chromatography-mass spectrometry. *J Anal Toxicol.* 2008;32:253–259.

17. Preston LP, Epstein DH, Davoudzadeh D, Husetis MA. Methadone and metabolite concentrations in patients maintained on methadone. *J Anal Toxicol.* 2003;24:530–535.

18. Dunn KE, Sigmon SC, McGee MR, Heil SH, Higgins ST. Evaluation of ongoing oxycodone abuse among methadone maintained patients. *J Subst Abuse Treat.* 2008;21 [E-pub ahead of print].

19. Backer RC, Monforte JR, Poklis A. Evaluation of the DRI oxycodone immunoassay for the detection of oxycodone in urine. *J Anal Toxicol.* 2005;29:675–677.

20. McNally AJ, Pilcher I, Wu R, Salamone SJ et al. Evaluation of the online immunoassay for propoxyphene: comparison to EMIT II and GC-MS. *J Anal Toxicol.* 1996;20:537–540.

21. Schneider S, Wennig R. Interference of diphenhydramine with the EMIT II immunoassay for propoxyphene. *J Anal Toxicol.* 1999;23:637–638.

22. Brenner C, Hui R, Passarelli J, Wu R et al. Comparison of methaqualone excretion patterns using Abuscreen ONLINE and EMIT II immunoassay and GC/MS. *Forensic Sci Int.* 1996;79:31–41.

CHAPTER 6

Legal Issues

ABSTRACT

Many abused drugs are classified as controlled substances in the United States. Unlawful possession of such controlled substances is a serious offense, and depending on the amount of the controlled substance found in the possession of a person, the consequence may be a fine or a jail term. In many companies a new job is offered conditional upon passing a pre-employment drug test. In many states workers' compensation may be withheld if a job-related accident was caused by impairment of the worker due to drug or alcohol abuse. Moreover, if a person is fired from a job because of drug abuse, unemployment benefits will not be granted. In the criminal setting a positive drug test has more serious consequences because it may be considered a parole violation, and the offender may end up in jail again. Similarly, driving under the influence of a drug has serious legal consequences.

Abuse of drugs is a serious problem in society, and such abuse may cause legal problems. For example, all states in the United States punish a driver with a blood alcohol level at or above a certain limit (in most states this limit is a blood or serum alcohol at or over 0.08% or 80 mg/dl). An individual who fails a pre-employment drug test may simply not be hired, but someone who fails a drug test while on parole may be given more jail time. There are both state and federal laws that deal with illegal possession of controlled substances. Many states deny workers' compensation if the injured person had drugs in his or her system during an accident as evidenced by a confirmed positive drug-testing result reported by a certified laboratory. Many states also deny unemployment benefits for someone who is fired as a result of a positive drug test. However, a few states do not allow an employer to fire an employee based on a first-time positive result in workplace drug testing.[1]

MEDICAL DRUG TESTING VERSUS WORKPLACE DRUG TESTING

In workplace drug testing employees are aware of the testing and have access to written policy regarding it and the consequences of a failed test. Federal regulations also mandate specific procedures for collection and chain of custody to ensure the integrity of a specimen. In addition, there are requirements for confirming a positive immunoassay screening procedure using the sophisticated technique of GC/MS to safeguard accuracy of test results. A licensed physician with training and knowledge in workplace drug testing (the medical review officer, MRO) also reviews the results to ensure that there is no alternative medical explanation for positive test results.

In contrast, in medical drug testing there is no requirement for informed consent by the patient. Physicians sometimes order drug testing without a patient's consent, but such results can be used for medical purpose only. Moreover, no chain of custody is maintained, and in some laboratories immunoassay positive specimens are not confirmed by GC/MS.[2]

In medical drug tests, immunoassays are routinely used to screen urine specimens for the presence of drugs. The drugs most commonly tested for are amphetamines, cocaine, barbiturates, benzodiazepines, opiates, phencyclidine, propoxyphene, methadone, and cannabinoids. Immunoassays are subject to interferences. For example, over-the-counter cold medications can produce false-positive amphetamine screens, and positive opiate test results can be caused by eating poppy seed–containing foods (see also Chapters 12, 14, and 15). Positive immunoassay screening results without confirmation by GC/MS in a medical drug test may be inaccurate. A positive drug screen can be problematic for a patient, especially when the patient is not aware that drug testing was even performed. When a patient enrolls in a substance abuse program, consent is obtained for drug testing during the course of treatment. In contrast, when a patient undergoes treatments in a clinic or in a hospital, only a general consent for testing and treatment is obtained without any specific consent for drug testing.[2] Many states now require physicians to report positive drug tests for pregnant women or newborns to the appropriate law enforcement authority. In 2001 the U.S. Supreme Court ruled that conducting drug testing on pregnant women without consent and passing the result to police was a violation of a patient's rights.[3] In the case considered, the Medical University of South Carolina had initiated a policy with the local police department that stated that a pregnant woman who tested positive for cocaine should be prosecuted unless she successfully completed a drug treatment program. If she tested positive at the time of delivery she should be arrested immediately and prosecuted for child neglect. Patients were unaware of the drug testing and did not provide consent. Under that policy, which was valid until 1994, 253 women tested positive for cocaine, 30 were arrested, and 2 women served prison sentences. Ten of the women who were arrested sued the state for violation of their constitutional Fourth Amendment right to privacy and demanded monetary compensation. Finally, the Supreme Court overruled the state court's decision and decided in favor of the women, stating that drug testing without consent was a violation of their Fourth Amendment rights [*Ferguson v. City of Charleston* 121 Ct.1281 (2001)].[3,4] However, the Supreme Court did rule that drug testing with patient consent is constitutional.[3]

Another thing to consider is that although the intent of medical drug testing is to make a proper diagnosis or to convince a patient to enroll in a substance abuse treatment program, patients may also feel betrayed if they learn that they were tested for drugs without their consent, and the physician–patient relationship is weakened.[2]

WORKERS' COMPENSATION

Drug abuse costs U.S. industry and the public an estimated $100 billion a year, and as a result most U.S. employers embrace workplace drug testing.[5] Federally mandated drug testing is required by contractors and all recipients of federal grants in addition to selected groups of federal employees. Although there is no specific federal law demanding drug-testing programs by private employers, many states have drug-free workplace acts, and some states even provide discounts to employers on premiums for workers' compensation if they adopt a workplace drug-testing program. In mid-1980s, the College of American Pathologists initiated the Forensic Urine Drug Testing Accreditation Program. This program was directed to workplace drug-testing programs performed by nonfederal employers. Although this program is separate from the federally mandated drug program, it follows many of the same guidelines for workplace drug testing.[6]

The ideal workplace drug-testing program is cost effective, follows state or federal guidelines, can withstand potential legal challenge, and is accepted by employees. A drug-free workplace can be achieved by building employee consensus, having a detailed policy describing the drug testing and the consequences of failing a drug test, contracting a certified laboratory to get quality test results, having an MRO to review all positive results, and referring employees who test positive to employee assistance programs with a possibility of referral to an addiction treatment center.

Usually the employer pays for the workplace drug testing. In the event an employee fails a drug test and requests reanalysis of the specimen by another certified laboratory, the employee may have to pay the additional cost. Some technical issues are associated with retesting of specimens. The concentration of a drug or metabolite may be reduced on storage. Metabolite of marijuana 11-nor-9-carboxy Δ^9-tetrahydrocannabinol (THC-COOH) tends to get absorbed into the plastic container containing the specimen. One study showed that average losses of concentration of THC-COOH may be more than 5% per day of storage either because of the decreased solubility of THC-COOH or because the metabolite was absorbed into the plastic container.[7] Romberg and Past observed that the concentration of benzoylecgonine (a metabolite of cocaine) declined by an average of 19% upon storage for several months.[8]

In many states an employee is not eligible for workers' compensation if an accident was drug related. However, in a few states an employee may receive reduced workers' compensation pay in cases where an accident was due to drug or alcohol abuse (**Table 6-1**).

In addition, states such as Alaska, Arizona, Idaho, and Utah provide a legal shield against an employer-related drug-testing lawsuit if the drug testing is conducted under the state drug laws.[9] Some states provide discounts on workers' compensation premiums if an employer is committed to a drug-free workplace environment and has a workplace drug-testing policy (**Table 6-2**).

Table 6-1	Workers' Compensation When a Positive Drug Test Is Involved
State	**Workers' Compensation**
Colorado	Workers' compensation reduced by 50%
Idaho	Workers' compensation reduced by 50%
Missouri	Workers' compensation reduced by 50%
Wisconsin	Benefit reduced by 15%, but may not exceed $15,000
All other states	Workers' compensation denied

Table 6-2	Discount of Workers' Compensation Premium for Instituting a Drug-Free Workplace
State	**Discount on Premium**
Alabama	5%
Arkansas	5%
Florida	5%
Georgia	7.5%
Hawaii	5%
Idaho	5%
Kentucky	Employers certified by Office of Mine Safety and Licensing eligible for discount
Mississippi	5%
Ohio	Varies
South Carolina	5%
Tennessee	5%
Virginia	5%
Wyoming	10%

UNEMPLOYMENT COMPENSATION

In most states an employee is ineligible for unemployment compensation if the individual is fired from a job because of a positive workplace drug test. However, in some states, such as Minnesota, an individual can not be fired from a job because of a first-time positive result in workplace drug testing.[9] In most cases, depending on the employer, first-time offenders are often referred to an employee assistance program or substance abuse program for rehabilitation. However, employers usually choose to fire employees who have repeated positive drug testing. Over the past two decades most large companies have established workplace drug-testing programs. In general, these large companies have resources like in-house attorneys to write drug-testing policy, funds for medical resources, and funds for drug testing by a certified laboratory. Small employers do not have such resources, and sometimes unemployed drug abusers target such small companies for employment. The U.S.

Small Business Administration is now beginning to provide funding and assistance for small companies to develop workplace drug-testing programs.[10]

DRUG TESTING ON ALTERNATIVE SPECIMENS

Currently, drug testing on alternative specimens such as hair, sweat, and oral fluid are gaining widespread acceptance. On April 13, 2004, the Department of Health and Human Services published a notice in the *Federal Register* proposing to establish scientific and technical guidelines for testing of hair, sweat, and oral fluid for the presence of drugs of abuse. In addition, instrument requirements for such testing, guidelines for collection of such alternative specimens, and guidelines for MROs were also described. This notice was open for public comment for 90 days, and more than 200 separate comments were included. The proposed guidelines also described validity tests that should be performed on alternative specimens to ensure specimen integrity.[11]

A point-of-care testing device performs a test on a specimen at the collection site. Although most point-of-care devices for testing urine specimens are approved by the U.S. Federal Drug Administration (FDA), only a few oral fluid testing devices have FDA clearance.[10] Testing of a hair specimen is a complex process requiring digestion of hair for liberating drugs trapped in the hair matrix. Therefore, hair specimens must be transported to a certified laboratory for analysis.

Currently, the legal admissibility of oral fluid testing is not well established. Only a few countries, including the United States, have statutes that specifically mention use of alternative matrices for drug testing. The testing must be performed using FDA-approved devices or conducted by a certified laboratory using proper guidelines. Although there are no specific cases addressing the evidentiary weight of saliva as a matrix for drug testing, there are many cases in which the use of saliva as a diagnostic specimen has been accepted by courts as evidence. Based on the demonstrated accuracy and reliability of test methods and regulatory development, oral fluid testing should be able to withstand legal challenge.[12]

STATE AND FEDERAL DRUG LAWS

Possession of controlled substances is against the law. Both state and federal penalties may apply for such illegal possession. Congress passes all legislation relating to drug abuse prevention and control, balancing the need for various drugs with medical purposes with the desire to restrict those that have abuse potential. The penalties for manufacturing, distributing, or possession with intent to distribute a controlled substance can be found at 21 U.S.C. § 841 *et seq.* The punishments vary and are based on the amount of a controlled substance found in possession and the category of the controlled substance (Schedules I to IV). The greater the quantity, the stiffer the punishment range. For example, the penalty for possession with intent to distribute 1 kilogram or more of heroin, 5 kilograms or more of cocaine, 50 grams or more of crack cocaine, 100 grams or more of PCP, 10 grams or more of LSD, 50 grams or more of methamphetamine, or 1000 kilograms or more of marijuana, which are all Schedule 1 drugs, is imprisonment for ten years to life. In contrast, for a controlled substance listed in Schedule V, the possible jail term is not more than one year. Finally, a civil penalty not to exceed $10,000 may be imposed for possession of small amounts of controlled substances for personal use.

CONCLUSION

Drug-testing laboratories certified by SAMHSA currently perform testing on approximately 75,000 specimens every day, and many private employers may contract other laboratories for workplace drug testing. Approximately 30 million to 40 million U.S. workers and job applicants are tested annually.[10] Most companies in the United State conduct some form of workplace drug testing. Workers' compensation is usually denied for incidents caused by abuse of drugs or alcohol by the employee at the time of an accident, as evidenced by a positive drug test. In addition, most states deny unemployment compensation for employees who are fired from a job because of drug-related problems. Unlawful possession of controlled substances is against the law, and violators may be prosecuted. Testing of alternative specimens such as hair, skin, and oral fluid is gaining acceptance in workplace drug testing.

REFERENCES

1. Reynolds JL, McGovern PM, Kochevar L, et al. Minnesota workplace drug testing: analysis of policy and procedure. *AAOHN J*. 1991;39:523–533.

2. Warner EA, Walker RM, Friedmann PD. Should informed consent be required for laboratory testing for drugs of abuse in medical settings? *Am J Med*. 2003;115: 54–58.

3. Annas GJ. Testing pregnant women for cocaine-physicians as police investigators. *N Eng J Med*. 2001;344:1729–1732.

4. Foley EM. Drug screening and criminal prosecution of pregnant women. *J Obstet Gynecol Neonatal Nurs*. 2002;31:133–137.

5. Montoya ID, Elwood WN. Fostering a drug free workplace. *Health Care Superv*. 1995;14: 1–13.

6. Cone EJ. Legal workplace and treatment drug-testing program with alternate biological matrix on a global scale. *Forensic Sci Int*. 2001;121:7–15.

7. Goldings Farga S, Diaz-Flores Estevez J, Dia Romero C. Stability of cannabinoids in three storage conditions. *Ann Clin Lab Sci*. 1998;28:160–162.

8. Romberg RW, Past MR. Reanalysis of forensic urine specimen containing benzoylecgonine and THC-COOH. *J Forensic Sci*. 1994;39:479–485.

9. U.S. Department of Labor, Office of the Assistant Secretary for Policy. Working Partners for an Alcohol- and Drug-Free Workplace. https://www.dol.gov/workingpartners/welcome.html. Accessed October 22, 2008.

10. Walsh JM. New technology and new initiatives in U.S. workplace testing. *Forensic Sci Int*. 2008;174:120-124.

11. Bush DM. The U.S. mandatory guidelines for federal workplace drug-testing program: current status and future considerations. *Forensic Sci Int*. 2008;174:111–119.

12. Kadehjian L. Legal issues in oral fluid testing. *Forensic Sci Int*. 2005;150:151–160.

CHAPTER 7

Methodologies for Drugs-of-Abuse Testing

ABSTRACT

Urine is the most common specimen used for workplace drug testing. The first step in analysis is the screening of urine specimens for the presence of various abused drugs. If a specimen tests positive for the presence of any drug, then the second step is to confirm the presence of that particular drug or drugs using a specific analytical technique such as GC/MS. The immunoassay screening of urine specimens can be easily achieved by using commercially available immunoassay and automated analyzers. However, the GC/MS confirmation step is more cumbersome and requires extraction of a specific drug or drug class from the urine matrix either by using a specific extraction solvent or by using solid-phase extraction column and the proper organic extract solvent. After extraction for a drug or metabolite that is relatively polar, an additional step is required in which the polar molecule is chemically modified to a volatile nonpolar molecule (a process known as derivatization) prior to analysis by GC/MS.

In toxicology laboratories, urine specimens are screened for the presence of a drug using commercially available immunoassays and automated analyzers. For this purpose many urine specimens can be put in a batch and analyzed in a single run. Automated analyzers have high output and are capable of analyzing hundreds of specimens in an hour. Immunoassays are available commercially for a number of drugs or drug classes, including amphetamines, barbiturates, benzodiazepines, cocaine (as benzoylecgonine, its major metabolite), marijuana (cannabinoid, as its major metabolite 11-nor-9-carboxy Δ^9-tetrahydrocannabinol, THC-COOH) methadone, opiates, oxycodone, propoxyphene, phencyclidine, lysergic acid diethylamide (LSD), and methaqualone. These immunoassays use various cutoff concentrations that are either mandated by SAMHSA (which mandates tests for amphetamine, cocaine, marijuana metabolite, opiates, and phencyclidine) or generally acceptable to the scientific community. The cutoff concentrations vary widely. For example, the immunoassay cutoff level for screening of amphetamines is 1000 ng/ml, while the immunoassay cutoff for screening phencyclidine is 25 ng/ml.

A major limitation of the immunoassays is the cross-reactivity of a variety of structurally related compounds with the antibody utilized in the assay, thus producing false-positive results. Interference of components of over-the-counter cold medications with amphetamine immunoassays has been documented extensively. Because of this limitation, it is preferable to confirm positive immunoassay screening results by using a specific analytical technique such as gas chromatography/mass spectrometry (GC/MS). In fact, for workplace drug testing, confirmation of an initial positive screening result by GC/MS is mandatory. For medical drug testing involving trauma patients or patients visiting emergency rooms with suspected drug overdose, initial screening results may not be confirmed by GC/MS. One of the reasons for this is the high level of technical expertise required for performing confirmation tests using GC/MS, coupled with the high cost of purchasing GC/MS and the cost associated with maintenance of the instrument. Therefore, many small and medium-sized hospital laboratories do not have the capability to confirm a positive screening test result. A false-positive screening test result may jeopardize the patient/physician relationship. Moreover, interpreting urine drug-testing result is complex. Reisfield et al observed that family physicians who order urine drug testing to monitor their patients on chronic opioid therapy are not proficient in interpreting test results. The authors recommended that physicians work closely with laboratory professionals when ordering and interpreting urine drug tests.[1]

 IMMUNOASSAYS FOR DRUGS-OF-ABUSE TESTING: BASIC PRINCIPLES

In addition to immunoassays designed for analysis of urine specimens using automated analyzers, immunoassays are available for drug testing in urine and oral fluid at the point of collection. The immunoassay-based devices for analysis of specimens at the collection site are termed "point-of-care" testing techniques and are discussed in Chapter 8. One major advantage of immunoassays that can be used for analysis of many urine specimens in one run is the direct reporting of results to the Laboratory Information System (LIS) through the interface of the analyzer with the LIS after results are reviewed and approved by technologists.

The heart of the immunoassay design is the antibody that can recognize a drug molecule or a series of related drug molecules (in the same class of drug) or metabolites in urine specimens. In order to generate the antibody, the target analyte is conjugated to a large protein (for example, albumin), and then the conjugate is injected into an animal (rabbit, goat, sheep, etc). Then the serum of the animal is tested at regular intervals, and when the desired immunoreactivity against the analyte is observed, the animal is bled and specific antibodies are purified from the blood and used to develop an immunoassay. This type of antibody is called a polyclonal antibody. In order to generate more specific monoclonal antibody against an analyte, lymphocytes secreting a specific clone can be fused with cancer cell lines that are grown in vivo or in vitro to produce a very specific single clone of the target antibody. Both polyclonal and monoclonal antibodies are used in immunoassays designed for drugs-of-abuse testing. **Table 7-1** gives the

Table 7-1 Commercially Available Immunoassays for Urinary Screening of Abused Drugs and Cutoff Concentrations	
Drug	**Cutoff Concentration**
Amphetamine/ methamphetamine	1000 ng/ml
3,4-methylenedioxy- methamphetamine (MDMA)	500 or 1000 ng/ml
Barbiturates	200 ng/ml
Benzodiazepines	200 ng/ml
Benzoylecgonine (cocaine metabolite)	300 ng/ml
Cannabinoid	20, 50, or 100 ng/ml
Buprenorphine	5 ng/ml
Heroin metabolites	10 ng/ml
LSD	0.5 ng/ml
Methadone	300 ng/ml
Methadone metabolite	1000 ng/ml
Methaqualone	300 ng/ml
Opiates	300 or 2000 ng/ml
Oxycodone	100 or 300 ng/ml
Phencyclidine	25 ng/ml
Propoxyphene	300 ng/ml

cutoff concentrations for screening of drugs of abuse by commercial immunoassays.

HOMOGENEOUS VERSUS HETEROGENEOUS ASSAY FORMAT

Most of the immunoassay methods require no sample pre-treatment, are easy to use, and require very small amounts of specimen (less than 100 μl). There are two immunoassay formats: competition and sandwich. Competition immunoassays work best for small molecules such as drugs of abuse, while sandwich assays are used for analysis of larger molecules (for example, troponin I or troponin T). Immunoassays for drugs-of-abuse testing are usually based on the competition format. In the competition format, the assay design is sub-classified into homogeneous and heterogeneous assay formats. In general, in the competition assay format analyte molecules (drug or metabolite; antigen) in the specimen compete with the same analyte, which is tagged with a specific label (added in specific amount to the reaction mixture as a part of the immunoassay reagent) for limited antibody-binding sites. Therefore, when more analyte molecules are present, less labeled antigen is bound to antibody and vice versa. If the labeled antigen bound to an antibody behaves differently than the free labeled antigen, then no separation of bound label from free label is necessary for measuring the signal generated, and the assay is called a homogeneous immunoassay. In this format, either the label bound to antibody or the free label generates the signal after incubation. In the heterogeneous immunoassay format, labeled antigen bound to antibody is separated from free label prior to generating the signal. The radioimmunoassay (RIA) assays are heterogeneous because separation of bound from free form is essential before measuring radioactivity.

HOMOGENEOUS IMMUNOASSAYS

There are variations of competitive immunoassay formats in commercially available immunoassays for screening of urine specimens in drugs-of-abuse testing.

Enzyme multiplied immunoassay technique (EMIT): In this competitive homogeneous immunoassay format, the label enzyme is glucose 6-phosphate dehydrogenase (G6PDH). This enzyme oxidizes glucose 6-phosphate, and in this process the cofactor nicotinamide adenine dinucleotide (NAD) is converted into NADH. While NAD has no absorbance at a 340-nm wavelength, NADH absorbs at 340 nm, and conversion of NAD to NADH can be monitored spectrophotometrically at 340 nm. When the concentration of drug is high in a urine specimen, the intensity of the signal is high because less labeled enzyme is bound to antibody (the enzyme bound to antibody is inactive).[2] This assay format was originally designed by the Syva Company (San Jose, CA) and now is marketed by various other diagnostics companies. A format similar to this one is used by drugs-of-abuse immunoassays reagents originally marketed by Bayer Diagnostics (Tarrytown, NY) for use with its ADVIA analyzer. In 2006 Bayer Diagnostics became part of Siemens Medical Solutions. The DRI assays for drugs-of-abuse screening in urine specimens produced by the Microgenics Corporation (Fremont, CA) are based on a similar principle.

Cloned enzyme donor immunoassay (CEDIA): The CEDIA system uses recombinant DNA technology to produce a unique homogeneous enzyme immunoassay system. The assay principle is based on the bacterial enzyme β-galactosidase, which has been genetically engineered into two inactive fragments. The smaller fragment, called enzyme donor (ED), can freely associate in the solution with the larger part, called enzyme acceptor (EA), producing active enzyme and capable of cleaving a substrate generating a color change in the medium that can be measured spectrophotometrically. In this assay, drug molecules in the specimen compete for limited antibody-binding sites with drug molecules conjugated with ED fragment. If drug molecules are present in a specimen, they bind to antibodies, leaving drug molecules conjugated with ED free to form active enzyme by binding with EA, thus generating a signal.[3,4] The Microgenics Corporation (Fremont, CA) sells drugs-of-abuse immunoassays based on CEDIA technology.

Kinetic interaction of microparticles in solution (KIMS): In this system, in the absence of drug molecules, free antibodies bind to drug microparticle conjugate-forming particle aggregates, causing an increase in absorption. When drug molecules are present in a urine specimen, drug molecules bind with free antibody molecules and thus prevent formation of particle aggregates and diminish absorbance in proportion to drug concentration.[5] The OnLine DAT immunoassays marketed by Roche Diagnostics (Indianapolis, IN) are based on the KIMS format.

Fluorescence polarization immunoassay (FPIA): In this homogeneous competitive assay format the fluorescein-labeled drug molecule competes for limited antibody-binding sites with free drug molecules that are present in the urine specimen. When the label is free the molecule rotates freely, but when the label is bound to antibody its movement is restricted and a polarized fluorescence signal is produced. Because the signal is generated by a bound label, the intensity of the signal is lowered by high amounts of drug molecules in a urine specimen. In this scenario few labeled molecules are bound to antibody. Abbott Laboratories (Abbott Park, IL) manufactures this type of immunoassay.[5]

HETEROGENEOUS IMMUNOASSAYS

In heterogeneous immunoassays, the bound label is physically separated from the unbound label prior to generating the signal. The separation is often done magnetically, where the reagent analyte (or its analog) is provided as coupled to paramagnetic particles (PMP), and the antibody is labeled. Conversely, the antibody also may be provided as conjugated to the PMPs, and the reagent analyte may be tagged with the label. After incubation, a washing step is employed to separate the bound from the free form, and then another reagent is added to generate the signal. In chemiluminescent immunoassays (CLIA), the label may be a small molecule that generates a chemiluminescent signal. The label may also be an enzyme (enzyme-linked immunosorbent assay, or ELISA) that generates a chemiluminescent, fluorometric, or colorimetric signal. In older immunoassay formats, the labels were radioactive.[6] In microparticle enzyme immunoassay (MEIA), antibody-coated microparticles and a drug labeled by alkaline phosphatase enzyme are used in an assay format. The enzyme can hydrolyze a fluorogenic substrate after incubation and the wash protocol to generate a fluorescence signal.[7]

LIMITATIONS OF IMMUNOASSAYS

The major problem of immunoassays is false-positive results due to cross-reactivity of a number of structurally similar compounds. Amphetamine immunoassays are mostly affected because a number of structurally similar compounds (see also Chapter 14 and Chapter 15) such as

buflomedil, brompheniramine, chlorpromazine, ephedrine, fenfluramine, isometheptene, mexiletine, N-acetyl procainamide (a metabolite of procainamide), perazine, phenmetrazine, phentermine, phenylpropanolamine, promethazine, pseudoephedrine, quinacrine, ranitidine, tolmetin, and tyramine are known to cross-react with various amphetamine assays causing false-positive results.[8–10] Dietzen et al demonstrated that ranitidine greater than 43 µg/ml in urine specimens interferes with the Beckman Synchron amphetamine immunoassay (Beckman Coulter, Inc., Fullerton, CA). They concluded that due to the extreme sensitivity of ranitidine within this assay, the Beckman assay has little use in the laboratory because the ranitidine concentration in urine specimens routinely exceeds 43 µg/ml in patients taking ranitidine. However, other Beckman assays such as those for opiates, barbiturates, cocaine metabolite, propoxyphene, and methadone have good specificity, while the cannabinoid assay has 100% predictive value, based on GC/MS confirmation.[11]

Tolmetin, a nonsteroidal anti-inflammatory drug, can interfere with EMIT assays for urine drug screening if the drug is present in a significant amount (1800 mg/L). Tolmetin has characteristic high molar absorbance at 340 nm, which is the wavelength for detection of signal in EMIT assays. A specimen collected from an arthritic patient receiving 100 to 400 mg tolmetin showed decreased signal when mixed with abused drugs and analyzed by EMIT assays. Similar interference of tolmetin in FPIA assays for drugs of abuse was not observed because a different wavelength (525 nm) is used for detecting signal. However, potential false-positive test results using FPIA benzodiazepine assay were observed when urine specimens contained high concentrations of fenoprofen, flurbiprofen, indomethacin, ketoprofen, and tolmetin.[10]

Using GC/MS as the gold standard, and based on analysis of 635 urine specimens for the presence of various abused drugs, Ferrara et al reported that EMIT and FPIA assays for opiates, methadone, cocaine, and cannabinoids had positive predictive values of over 90%, while amphetamines, benzodiazepines, and barbiturates assays had between 80% and 90% positive predictive values.[12] Dietzen et al analyzed results from 2450 routine urine drug screens collected from 947 patients and observed 1034 presumptive positive results based on Beckman Synchron drugs-of-abuse immunoassays (excluding benzodiazepines), out of which 175 specimens (17%) can not be confirmed. The amphetamine assay demonstrated the lowest specificity, as none of the 134 presumptive positive specimens could be confirmed by a second analytical technique. Thirty-three such false-positive specimens for amphetamine had ranitidine, five specimens contained ephedrine/pseudoephedrine, and one specimen showed the presence of phenylpropanolamine. Although 100% false-positive test results were observed with the amphetamine immunoassay, the false-positive rates for opiates, propoxyphene, methadone, barbiturate, cocaine (as benzoylecgonine), and cannabinoids were 29%, 11%, 13%, 4%, 2.2%, and 0%.[11] Although amphetamine assays usually show the highest amount of false-positive test results, other immunoassays are also affected. Hull et al reported a false-positive phencyclidine test result with the EMIT assay in a patient who died from an overdose of tramadol, a prescription analgesic.[13]

THIN-LAYER CHROMATOGRAPHY FOR DRUG ANALYSIS

In thin-layer chromatography (TLC) a thin layer of absorbent material is coated on a plate (glass or metal) or impregnated in a sheet of cellulose or fiberglass. For analysis, specimen is applied at the lower edge of the plate, and then the plate is placed in a chamber containing developing solvent. By capillary action solvent moves up in the plate. In this process, analyte molecules interact with both the stationary phase and the developing solvent (mobile phase). Depending on these interactions the molecules move up into the plate at different rates and are separated into spots. Excess solvent is allowed to evaporate from the plate, and spots can then be visualized under ultraviolet or fluorescent light. Alternatively, a color-developing reagent can be sprayed on the plate in order to visualize the analyte spots. The distance an analyte travels on the plate is termed the R_f value. By comparing the R_f value of an analyte with the R_f value of a known standard, a drug can be identified.[7] Drug analysis in a laboratory can be achieved by using homemade TLC plates or commercially available TLC plates and known drug standards. Commercially available TOXI-Lab plates (Varian, Palo Alto, CA) can also be used for drug analysis in a laboratory. Drugs are extracted from urine specimens using Toxi-tubes, which contain solvent and buffer (Toxi-tube A extracts basic and neutral drug at pH 9, and Toxi-tube B extracts acidic drugs at pH 4.5). After extraction, solvents are evaporated and unknown drugs are deposited onto a disk of chromatographic media. The dried disks are then placed into the center holes of respective A and B chromatograms and are developed by placing the plate in a chamber containing developing solvent. After development the plate is dipped into a chromogenic liquid for color development. Identification of a drug is achieved by comparing the spot in the unknown zone with the same spot in an adjacent area where a known drug standard has migrated in the plate.

MASS SPECTROMETRIC TECHNIQUES FOR DRUG CONFIRMATION

Because of the inherent cross-reactivity problems associated with immunoassays, GC/MS is considered the gold standard for confirmation of the presence of a drug in a urine or alternative specimen. Mass spectrometry is capable of analyzing charged particles based on their mass, thus providing a fingerprint of the molecule for unambiguous identification. A typical mass spectrometer consists of an inlet system that supplies the pure compound (separated from a complex biological matrix by GC or high-performance liquid chromatography, HPLC) to the mass spectrometer, an ion source, a mass analyzer, and a detector. The ion source is responsible for the characteristic fragmentation pattern of the analyte that depends on the functional groups and other structural features of the molecule. The detector plots a chromatogram listing all ions generated and separated by their mass-to-charge ratios (m/z) as well as abundance. Usually the charge on the ions is one, and the m/z value represents the mass of the ion. For analysis of urine specimens containing a suspected drug, the mass spectrometer is often used to detect compounds eluting from a gas chromatograph. Gas chromatography/mass spectrometry is widely used for detection and quantification of drugs of abuse in biological matrix such as urine because of its specificity, sensitivity, and the availability of larger number of mass spectra in standard drug libraries.

Electron ionization (EI) at 70eV produces reproducible mass spectrum, which is a common ion source used in GC/MS analysis of drugs, especially drugs of abuse. After producing charged particles from the analyte eluting from the column, a mass spectrum is produced by detecting these charged particles in the detector of the mass spectrum. The major types of mass spectrometric analyzers are the quadrupole analyzer, ion trap analyzer, and time of flight analyzer. Quadrupole detector is common in commercially available GC/MS instruments. In this type of detector four metal rods are used, each opposing pair is connected electrically, and a radio frequency (RF) is applied superimposed with a direct current (DC) applied between two rods. These metal rods are used as a mass filter device, and for a particular radio frequency and electric current only certain ions with a specific m/z value (resonant ions) can pass through this set of metal rods to finally reach the detector. Other ions (nonresonant) collide with the metal rods and fail to reach the detector. By varying RF and voltage applied, an entire set of m/z values can be scanned in a fraction of a second. Usually ranges of m/z 40 to 500 are scanned for analysis of most drugs of abuse, although some commercially available GC/MS may allow scanning up to m/z 600 or 700. Quadrupole detector is useful for both confirmation and quantification of drugs. Although quadrupole mass spectrometer–based GC/MS instruments make up the majority of the instruments used in drug confirmation, the ion trap mass spectrometer, which is also commercially available, can also be used for confirmation of drug tests.[14] **Figure 7-1** shows a GC/MS instrument.

Figure 7-1. *A Gas Chromatograph Combined with a Mass Spectrometer, Commonly Used to Confirm Drug-Testing Results*

Source: Memorial Hermann Hospital at Texas Medical Center.

In addition to gas chromatography, high performance liquid chromatography (HPLC) can also be used for separation of drugs, and then, using a specially designed mass spectrometer, confirmation of drugs can also be achieved. Although most drug molecules are small and relatively volatile, GC can only be used for separation of small, volatile molecules that can easily be transferred into the gas phase for separation. However, HPLC can be applied for separation of both volatile and nonvolatile molecules. Because the mass spectrometer can work only in a vacuum, it is technically easier to apply strong vacuum after the molecules travel though GC and then allow the molecules to enter the mass spectrometer in a relative vacuum. Unfortunately, in HPLC a liquid mobile phase is used, and a sophisticated interface is needed to remove most of the solvent before an eluting compound enters the mass spectrometer. As far as combining HPLC with a mass spectrometer, only moving belt and particle beam interfaces are compatible with electron ionization technique.[15] The electrospray interface is very common in the HPLC/MS analyzers used by clinical laboratories. The electrospray interface produces single or multiple charged ions directly from a solvent system by creating a fine spray of highly charged droplets in the presence of a strong electric field with assistance from heat or from pneumatics. In this process nonvolatile and polar compounds can be ionized. The atmospheric pressure chemical ionization interface produces sample ions by charge transfer from reagent ions. The reagent ions are produced from solvent vapor of the mobile phase.

In general, the HPLC/MS instrument is much more expensive than GC/MS, and therefore GC/MS is more commonly used for analysis of drugs. Nevertheless, HPLC/MS has some advantages over GC/MS in drugs-of-abuse testing, including more sensitivity and more simplified pre-analytic steps prior to analysis. For example, LSD and its glucuronide are found in very small concentrations in urine and can easily be analyzed by HPLC/MS, while GC/MS does not have enough sensitivity to detect the presence of very small amounts of LSD in urine or other biological matrices, such as hair. For analysis of the heroin metabolite 6-acetyl morphine, HPLC/MS is superior to GC/MS. Morphine glucuronide can be analyzed directly by HPLC/MS, while for GC/MS analysis, hydrolysis of morphine glucuronide is needed, followed by extraction into an organic solvent and derivatization.[16]

GC/MS FOR DRUG CONFIRMATION

Although urine specimens can be analyzed directly using immunoassays, significant sample preparation is needed before such specimens can be subjected to GC/MS confirmation. First, the analyte is extracted from urine into an organic solvent. Sometimes, small derivatized silica columns are used for extraction (solid-phase extraction) in which an analyte is finally eluted from the column using a proper organic solvent. One advantage of solid-phase extraction is that some components of urine such as creatinine and urea can be removed from an analyte, thus producing a cleaner extract. For certain drugs that are found mostly as a conjugate in urine (for example, morphine, which is excreted in urine mostly as morphine-3-glucuronide), hydrolysis of the urine specimen to release free morphine is required.

In order to ease the quantitation of a drug or metabolite present in urine, a compound called an internal standard, which is similar in structure to the drug or metabolite, is added in a specified amount to the urine specimen prior to extraction. In many GC/MS protocols, a deuterated analog of the analyte of interest is added because these deuterated derivatives behave chemically similar to the analyte of interest. For example, for analysis of amphetamine and methamphetamine, d_3-amphetamine and d_5-methamphetamine are used as internal standards. For analysis of barbiturates, d_5-pentobarbital is used as an internal standard.

After extraction, another step, the process of derivatization, is needed for certain analytes prior to GC/MS analysis. Derivatization is a chemical modification of the compound by which a polar function group such as an amino group, a carboxylic group, or a hydroxyl group is transformed chemically in order to achieve a derivatized molecule that is less polar and more volatile than the original molecule. During derivatization the internal standard is derivatized at the same time as the analyte of interest. After derivatization the analyte can be analyzed by GC/MS. For GC/MS analysis, derivatized specimen dissolved in a proper solvent in injected in the column of the gas chromatograph (GC). Usually 1 to 2 μl of specimen is injected because capillary columns used in the GC are very sensitive and capable of analyzing a small amount of specimen. Usually the capillary column has a thin film of derivatized silica; for example, methyl silicone. A typical capillary column is 15 to 30 m long with an internal diameter of 0.3 mm, and film thickness is usually 0.25 mm. Helium is used as a carrier gas that is passed through the GC column at a preset flow rate. The GC is programmed so that the initial oven temperature of 120°C can be gradually increased (usually by 10°C per minute) to achieve a final temperature of 280°C to 290°C. Increasing the temperature renders analyte molecules more volatile in the gaseous phase, and helium gas carries them through the column to the mass detector. The final oven temperature is maintained for 5 to 10 minutes to ensure that all compounds are eluted from the capillary column. The run time for analysis may vary from 15 to 30 minutes depending on the program.

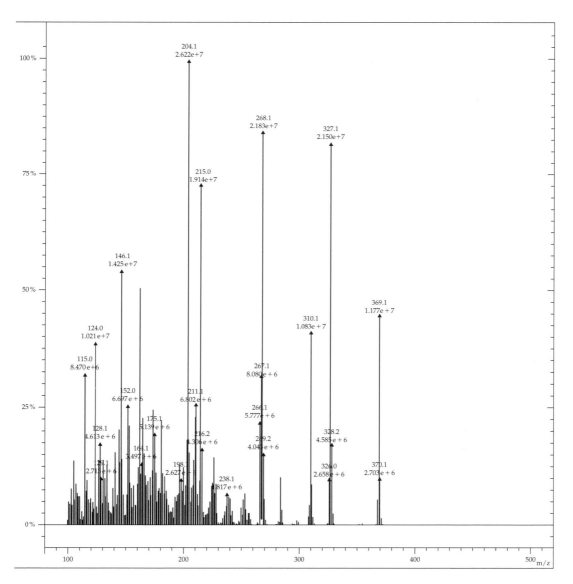

Figure 7-2. *The Full-Scan Mass Spectrum of Morphine After Derivatization with Acetic Anhydride and Pyridine (Acetyl Derivative)*

Gas chromatography/mass spectrometry is the gold standard for drugs-of-abuse testing because each molecule after derivatization produces a unique mass spectrum different from even compounds that which have closely related structures.

Figure 7-2 gives the full-scan mass spectrum of morphine after derivatization with acetic anhydride and pyridine (acetyl derivative). For comparison, **Figure 7-3** gives the full-scan mass spectrum of derivatized codeine, while **Figure 7-4** and

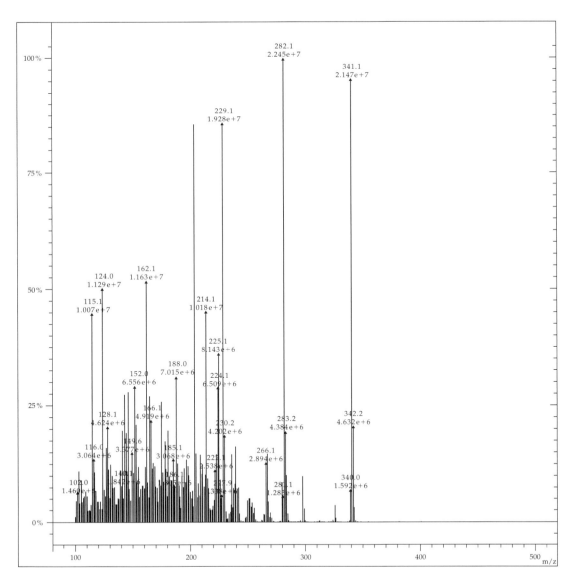

Figure 7-3. *The Full-Scan Mass Spectrum of Derivatized Codeine*

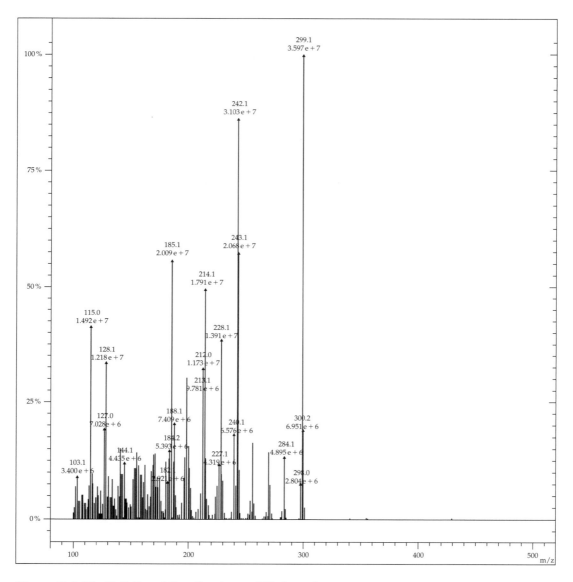

Figure 7-4. *The Full-Scan Mass Spectrum of Hydrocodone*

Figure 7-5 give the mass spectra of hydrocodone and hydromorphone, respectively. These figures show that each drug produces a very characteristic spectrum. Only optical isomers may produce similar mass spectra.

 GC/MS ANALYSIS: SIM VERSUS FULL SCAN

When analytes are eluted from the column, a high vacuum is introduced to remove helium and drug molecules that enter the

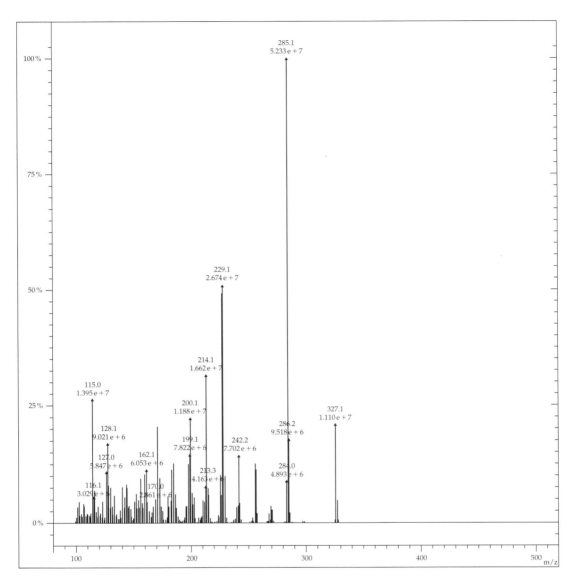

Figure 7-5. *The Full-Scan Mass Spectrum of Hydromorphone*

mass spectrometer in a relative vacuum stage and are bombarded with electrons if the mass spectrometer is operated in electron ionization mode. In order to improve sensitivity of GC/MS identification of an analyte, the mass spectrometer is operated under selected ion monitoring (SIM) rather than scanning for all ions between m/z 40 and 550. Therefore, instead of identifying all ions and using the area under the curve for quantification, a few characteristic ions are selected for unambiguous identification of the analyte and also for quantitation. Because in most drugs-of-abuse testing internal standards are deuterated derivatives of the same drug, both the drug and internal standard are eluted often as a single peak. However, unambiguous identification and quantification are easily achieved by using selected ion monitoring, characteristic ions of the analyte, and the internal standings that differ by 3 to 5 mass units because deuterium has higher mass than hydrogen. Usually 3 ions are selected for the analyte and 2 to 3 ions are chosen for the internal standard for identification, and 1 ion from the analyte and 1 ion from the internal standard are selected for quantification. Because the amount of internal standard added to the urine specimen prior to extraction and derivatization is specified, by comparing the ion ratio of the analyte and the internal standard, quantitation of analyte present in the specimen can be determined.

For example, Broussard et al described a method for simultaneous identification and quantitation of codeine, morphine, hydro-codone, and hydromorphone in urine as trimethylsilyl and oxime derivatives using GC/MS.[17] After adding deuterate codeine, morphine, hydrocodone, and hydromorphone in urine, the authors hydrolyzed conjugated metabolites already present in urine using beta-glucuronidase. For achieving complete hydrolysis, specimen was incubated at 56°C for two hours. After hydrolysis, aqueous hydroxylamine was added in order to derivatize keto opiates. Then derivatized hydrocodone, hydromorphone along with free morphine, codeine, and internal standards were extracted from urine using solid-phase bonded silica extraction columns (Varian, Palo Alto, CA). Further derivatization (trimethylsilyl derivatives) was performed using BSTFA [N,O-bis(trimethylsilyl)

trifluoroacetamide] and trimethylchlorosilane followed by analysis using GC/MS.[17] The mass spectrometer was operated under SIM, and ions selected for codeine were m/z 243, 343, and 371, while ions selected for d_3-codeine were 346 and 374. For quantitation, m/z 371 (for codeine) and 374 (for d_3-codeine) were selected. Similarly, for morphine, the ions selected were m/z 234, 401, and 429, while for d_3-morphine, the ions selected were 417 and 432. Again the m/z 429 and 432 were used for quantitation. For hydrocodone, m/z 297, 371, and 386 were selected, and for d_3-hydrocodone m/z 300 and 389 were selected. For quantitation, m/z 386 and m/z 389 were selected. For analysis of hydromorphone, m/z 355, 429, and 444 were chosen, while for analysis of d_3-hydromorphone, m/z 358 and 447 were selected. For quantification, m/z 355 and m/z 358 were used. **Figure 7-6** gives the total ion chromatogram showing separation of various opiates after derivatization.

ANALYSIS OF AMPHETAMINES

Most amphetamine screening assays use an antibody that specifically recognizes amphetamine or methamphetamine and a variety of structurally related compounds such as amphetamine, 3,4-methylenedioxymethamohetamine (MDMA) and 3,4-methylenedioxyamphetamine (MDA). There are also specific assays that recognize MDMA (ecstasy) primarily. A variety of over-the-counter cold medications and prescription medications interfere with amphetamine/methamphetamine screening assays (see also Chapter 14 and Chapter 15). Because of the cross-reactivity from a wide range of over-the-counter and prescription medications, amphetamine immuno-assays give

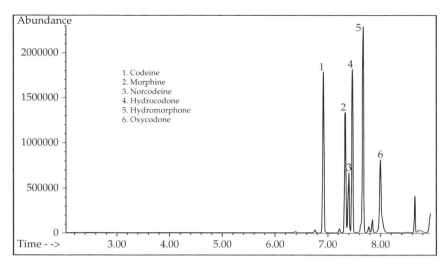

Figure 7-6. *The Total Ion Chromatogram Showing Separation of Various Opiates After Derivatization*

Source: Broussard L, Presley LC, Pittaman T, Clouette R et al. Simultaneous identification and quantitation of codeine, morphine, hydrocodone and hydromorphone in urine as trimethylsilyl and oxime derivatives by gas chromatography-mass spectrometry. *Clin Chem*. 1997;43:1029–1032. Reproduced with kind permission from the American Association of Clinical Chemistry (AACC).

more false-positive results than any other immunoassays used for screening of drugs in urine specimens.

Methamphetamine is metabolized to amphetamine, but after amphetamine use, significant amphetamine is excreted in urine unchanged. Neither methamphetamine nor amphetamine is secreted in urine as a conjugated molecule. Amphetamine, methamphetamine, and related compounds can be extracted from urine using a variety of organic solvents such as 1-butyl chloride. In order to make amphetamine more soluble in organic phase, urine is usually made alkaline using a borate buffer of sodium hydroxide. After extraction and evaporation of organic solvent, amphetamine and related compounds are treated with trifluoroacetic anhydride, pentafluoropropionic anhydride, or haptafluorobutyric anhy-

dride in order to yield corresponding derivatives that can be analyzed directly using GC/MS.

In order to investigate whether amphetamine or methamphetamine is a d- or an l-isomer, a special type of derivatization called chiral derivatization is needed. Chiral derivization is used in cases where the donor claims to use a Vicks inhaler. Gas chromatography/mass spectrometry is used to determine whether a positive methamphetamine result in such a donor is related to d-methamphetamine (which is abused) rather than l-methamphetamine, the main ingredient in the Vicks inhaler. Chiral derivatization can be achieved after extracting amphetamine and methamphetamine from alkaline urine using 1-butyl chloride followed by derivatization using N-trifluoroacetyl-L-propyl chloride.[18]

ANALYSIS OF BENZODIAZEPINES

Benzodiazepines can initially be screened using immunoassays, which are capable of detecting a variety of benzodiazepines. For example, the benzodiazepine immunoassay marketed by Abbott Laboratories (Abbott Park, IL) has sufficient cross-reactivity with alprazolam, bromazepam, chlordiazepoxide, clobazam, clonazepam, demoxepam, diazepam, estazolam, fluni-trazepam, nor-flurazepam, lorazepam, lormetazepam, medazepam, midazolam, nitrazepam, oxazepam, prazepam, temazepam, and triazolam (source: package insert). However, benzodiazepine immunoassays also are subjected to interference. The most common interference is due to the presence of oxaprozin, a non-steroidal anti-inflammatory drug. In one study, 36 urine specimens collected from 12 subjects who received a single oral dose of 1200 mg oxaprozin showed positive test results for benzodiazepine using EMIT-dau and CEDIA benzodiazepine immunoassays. The FPIA benzodiazepine assay provided positive test results for only 25 out of 36 urine specimens.[19]

Benzodiazepines are excreted in urine as their corresponding glucuronide conjugates. Therefore, hydrolysis of conjugate using beta-glucuronidase prior to extraction is recommended. This process usually takes two hours. Then free molecules can be extracted using either solid-phase extraction or organic solvent; for example, chloroform/isopropanol (9:1 by volume). After evaporation of organic-phase trimethylsilyl, derivatives of benzodiazepine/metabolites can be prepared by using N-O-bis (trimethylsilyl) trifluoroacetamide.[20] Instead of trimethylsilyl derivative, tert-butyl-dimethylsilyl derivatives can also be prepared using N-methyl-N-(tertbutyldimethylsilyl)-trifluoroacetamide

(MSBSTFA) prior to GC/MS analysis. West and Ritz analyzed oxazepam, nordiazepam, desalkylflurazepam, temazepam, and α-hydroxyalprazolam by GC/MS using tert-butyl-dimethylsilyl derivatives. The authors used d_5-oxazepam, d_5-nordiazepam, and d_5-α-hydroxyalprazolam as internal standards.[21]

ANALYSIS OF BARBITURATES

Barbiturate immunoassays can recognize a wide variety of commonly abused barbiturates such as amobarbital, butalbital, pentobarbital, secobarbital, and phenobarbital. Secobarbital is used as a calibrator in several commercially available immunoassays.

For GC/MS confirmation of barbiturates, hydrolysis of conjugated metabolites using beta-glucuronidase is carried out prior to extraction using an organic solvent such as ethyl acetate. Liu et al described the solid-phase extraction of barbiturates (after adjusting urine pH to 7) using the Bond-Elute extraction column (Varian, Palo Alto, CA). After extraction, methylation of barbiturates/metabolites was achieved using iodomethane and tetramethylammonium hydroxide by using dimethylsulfoxide as a solvent followed by analysis using GC/MS. The authors used d_5-pentobarbital as an internal standard.[22] Alternatively, barbiturates can also be analyzed by GC/MS as tert-butyl-dimethylsilyl derivates using methyl-N-(tert-butyldimethylsilyl) trifluoroacetamide.[23]

ANALYSIS OF COCAINE METABOLITES

All immunoassays for screening of cocaine in urine specimens recognize benzoylecgonine, the major metabolite of cocaine. Immunoassays for determining the presence of benzoylecgonine in urine usually have good specificity.

No hydrolysis step is needed because benzoylecgonine is not conjugated in urine. Benzoylecgonine can be extracted from urine using liquid extraction or solid-phase extraction using an extraction column. Benzoylecgonine, being a relatively polar molecule, requires derivatization prior to analysis. Silylation, perfluoroalkylation, and alkylation are the most frequently described derivatives in the literature, although benzoylecgonine can also be derivatized with diazomethane. In this process benzoylecgonine is converted back into cocaine, which is relatively less polar and more volatile.[24] Fluconazole interferes with GC/MS confirmation of benzoylecgonine because trimethylsilyl derivative of fluconazole is co-eluted with trimethylsilyl benzoylecgonine. (Fluconazole does not interfere with immunoassay screening for benzoylecgonine.)[25] This problem can be circumvented by using the pentafluoropropionyl derivative of benzoylecgonine because fluconazole derivative elutes after elution of derivatized benzoylecgonine.[26]

ANALYSIS OF CANNABINOIDS

The presence of cannabinoid in urine is determined by the presence of the major metabolite 11-nor-9-carboxy Δ^9-tetrahydrocannabinol (THC-COOH), and immunoassays utilize antibodies that can recognize the presence of THC-COOH and its glucuronide conjugate in urine. Immunoassays usually have good specificity, and few false-positive results are observed.

In urine, THC-COOH is mostly present as conjugated with glucuronic acid. Therefore, hydrolysis of glucuronide derivative is necessary. In one study the authors used Δ^9-THC-COOH as the internal standard. After

adding the internal standard to the urine specimen, hydrolysis of conjugated metabolite of THC was achieved by heating the specimen with 6 M of sodium hydroxide solution for 20 minutes at 56°C. Then, free THC-COOH along with the internal standard was extracted using hexane/ethyl acetate (9:1 by volume), followed by derivatization using N-methyl-N-trimethylsilyl) trifluoroacetamide (MSTFA)/ammonium iodide/ethanethiol (380:1:2 by volume). Next, the trimethylsilyliodide derivative of THC was analyzed by GC/MS.[27] The GC/MS analysis of THC-COOH can be also be achieved by derivatizing THC-COOH with MSTFA alone to produce the trimethylsilyl derivative of THC.[28] Another method for derivatization of THC-COOH is using a reagent mixture of tetramethylammonium hydroxide and iodomethane. In addition, absorptive loss of THC-COOH usually takes place upon storage if the urine pH is acidic. Plastic containers also tend to absorb THC-COOH during prolonged storage.[29]

ANALYSIS OF OPIATES

Most opiate assays recognize morphine and its conjugated metabolite and also have significant cross-reactivity with codeine, heroin, and 6-monoacetyl morphine (a metabolite of heroin). Although some opiate assays also have significant cross-reactivity with hydromorphone and hydrocodone, most opiate assays have low cross-reactivity with oxycodone. Therefore, if a sufficient amount of oxycodone is not present in urine, an opiate screening test using immunoassay may produce a negative result. Specific immunoassays are commercially available for screening urine specimens suspected of containing oxycodone. Morphine is found mostly in a conjugated form in urine. Therefore, hydrolysis of urine is necessary prior to extraction and derivatization,[17] which is discussed earlier in this chapter. Analysis of morphine, codeine, hydromorphone, hydrocodone, and oxycodone by GC/MS can also be achieved after derivatization with acetic anhydride and pyridine.[30]

ANALYSIS OF METHADONE

Although methadone is a synthetic opiate, most commercially available immunoassays for opiate have poor cross-reactivity with methadone. Therefore, such immunoassays can not detect the presence of methadone in urine. Methadone immunoassays usually recognize methadone and have poor cross-reactivity with 2-ethylidene-1,5-dimethyl-3,3-diphenyl pyrrolidine (EDDP), the major metabolite of methadone found in urine. There are also specific immunoassays for methadone metabolites in which the antibodies specifically recognize this metabolite. Several drugs are known to interfere with methadone immunoassays, including disopyramide, quetiapine, cyamemazine, and levomepromazine.[31–33]

Methadone and its metabolites can be extracted from urine using solid-phase extraction and can be analyzed by GC/MS without derivatization. Cheng et al described a method for simultaneous analysis of methadone, EDDP, 2-ethyl-5-methyl 3,3-diphenpyrroline (EMDP), ketamine, norketamine, and tramadol in urine after solid-phase extraction and without derivatization using GC/MS.[34]

ANALYSIS OF PHENCYCLIDINE

Phencyclidine immunoassays use antibodies that can recognize the presence of phencyclidine in urine. Phencyclidine immunoassays may show false-positive results caused by the presence of dextromethorphan, venlafaxine, thioridazine, and tramadol.[35–37] For GC/MS confirmation, phencyclidine can be extracted from urine using the solvent cyclohexane. Although phencyclidine can be analyzed without derivatization, for simultaneous analysis of phencyclidine and its metabolites, derivatization prior to GC/MS analysis is needed. Cone et al extracted phencyclidine and its monohydroxylated metabolite from urine with or without acid hydrolysis and then derivatized them with heptafluorobutyric anhydride prior to GC/MS analysis.[38]

ANALYSIS OF PROPOXYPHENE

Immunoassays for propoxyphene use propoxyphene antibody. These immunoassays are usually specific and have good predictive values for the presence of propoxyphene in urine. In GC/MS confirmation, the presence of propoxyphene along with its major metabolite norpropoxyphene is analyzed. Although propoxyphene can be analyzed by GC/MS without derivatization, for simultaneous analysis of propoxyphene and norpropoxyphene urine can be treated with sodium hydroxide in order to rearrange by base catalysis norpropoxyphene into norpropoxyphene amide, which is then extracted and analyzed by GC/MS.[39]

DRUG CONFIRMATION IN HAIR, SALIVA, AND SWEAT SPECIMENS

The methods that are applicable for confirmation of various drugs in urine by GC/MS are also applicable to testing of hair, saliva, and sweat specimens. The major challenge of analysis of these specimens is related to sensitivity of the technique because a smaller amount of drugs are found in these alternative specimens compared with urine. However, in most instances the parent drug is found in these matrices, and if the metabolite is present it is not conjugated. Therefore, drugs along with internal standards can be extracted from sweat or saliva followed by derivatization if required prior to GC/MS analysis. Because of its increased sensitivity, liquid chromatography combined with tandem mass spectrometry is superior to GC/MS for analysis of drugs in alternative matrices.

Lachenmeier et al washed hair with organic solvent to remove contamination. They added 4 ml of methanol to the washed hair specimen (50 mg specimen) and subjected it to ultrasonication for 5 hours at 50°C. Then, an aliquot of extract was evaporated to dryness, reconstituted with buffer, and analyzed by an immunoassay for the presence of opiates and cocaine. Another aliquot was subjected to GC/MS analysis. For this purpose, drugs were extracted by solid-phase extraction and derivatized with MSTFA in pyridine followed by analysis using GC/MS.[40]

CONCLUSION

Immunoassay screening of specimens is fast but may also produce false-positive results due to cross-reactivity of a prescription or over-the-counter medication. Although amphetamine immunoassays are subjected to much interference from over-the-counter cold medicines and other prescription medicines, interferences in other immunoassays have also been reported. Therefore, GC/MS confirmation of immunoassay-screened positive specimens is essential in workplace drug testing. Although GC/MS technology is widely used for drug confirmation, liquid chromatography combined with mass spectrometry, which allows conjugated drug metabolites to be analyzed directly without need of hydrolysis and derivatization, is gaining acceptance as a superior technique to GC/MS for drug confirmation. However, because of the high cost of acquisition of this instrument compared to that of GC/MS, fewer laboratories use this technique for drug confirmation.

REFERENCES

1. Reisfield GM, Webb FJ, Bertholf RL, Sloan PA, Wilson GR. Family physicians' proficiency in urine drug test interpretation. *J Opioid Manag*. 2007;3:333–337.

2. Hawks RL, Chian CN, eds. *Urine Testing for Drugs of Abuse*. NIDA research monograph 73. Rockville, MD: National Institute of Drug Abuse (NIDA); Department of Health and Human Services; 1986.

3. Henderson DR, Friedman SB, Harris JD, Manning WB, Zoccoli MA. CEDIA: a new homogeneous immunoassay system. *Clin Chem*. 1986;32:1637–1641.

4. Engel WD, Khanna PL. CEDIA in vitro diagnostics with a novel homogeneous immunoassay technique: current status and future prospects. *J Immunol Methods*. 1992;150:99–102.

5. Armbruster DA, Schwarzhoff RH, Hubster EC, Liserio MK. Enzyme immunoassay, kinetic microparticle immunoassay, radioimmunoassay, and fluorescence polarization immunoassay compared for drugs-of-abuse screening. *Clin Chem*. 1993;39:1326–1341.

6. Dai JL, Spkoll LJ, Chan DW. Automated chemiluminescent immunoassay analyzers. *J Clin Ligand Assay*. 1998;21:377–385.

7. Tsai JC, Lin GL. Drug-testing technologies and application. In: Wong RC, Tse HY, eds. *Drugs of Abuse: Body Fluid Testing*. Totowa, NJ: Humana Press; 2005:29–69.

8. Moore KA. Amphetamines/sympathomimetic amines. In: Levine B, ed. *Principles of Forensic Toxicology*. Washington, DC: American Association for Clinical Chemistry; 2003:341–348.

9. Grinstead GF. Ranitidine and high concentration phenylpropanolamine cross react in the EMIT monoclonal amphetamine/methamphetamine assay. *Clin Chem.* 1989;35:1998–1999.

10. Joseph R, Dickerson S, Wills R, Frankenfield D, Cone EJ, Smith DR. Interference by nonsteroidal anti-inflammatory drugs in EMIT and TDx assays for drugs of abuse. *J Anal Toxicol.* 1995;19:13–17.

11. Dietzen DJ, Ecos K, Friedman D, Beason S. Positive predictive values of abused drug immunoassay on the Beckman Synchron in a veteran population. *J Anal Toxicol.* 2001;25:174–178.

12. Ferrara SD, Tedeschi L, Frison G, et al. Drugs-of-abuse testing in urine: statistical approach and experimental comparison of immunoassays and chromatographic techniques. *J Anal Toxicol.* 1994;18:278–291.

13. Hull MJ, Griggs D, Knoepp SM, Smogorzewska A, Nixon A, Flood JG. Postmortem urine immunoassay showing false-positive phencyclidine reactivity in a case of fatal tramadol overdose. *Am J Forensic Med Pathol.* 2006;27:359–362.

14. Vorce SP, Sklerov JH, Kalasinsky KS. Assessment of the ion trap mass spectrometer for routine qualitative and quantitative analysis of drugs of abuse extracted from urine. *J Anal Toxicol.* 2000;24:595–601.

15. Marquet P, Lachatre G. Liquid chromatography-mass spectrometry in forensic and clinical toxicology. *J Chromatogr B.* 1999;7333:93–118.

16. Marquet P. Progress of liquid chromatography-mass spectrometry in clinical and forensic toxicology. *Ther Drug Monit.* 2002;24:255–276.

17. Broussard L, Presley LC, Pittaman T, Clouette R, Wimbish GH. Simultaneous identification and quantitation of codeine, morphine, hydrocodone and hydromorphone in urine as trimethylsilyl and oxime derivatives by gas chromatography-mass spectrometry. *Clin Chem.* 1997;43:1029–1032.

18. Dasgupta A, Saldana S, Kinnaman G, Smith M, Johansen K. Analytical performance evaluation of EMIT II monoclonal amphetamine/methamphetamine assay: more specificity than EMIT d.a.u monoclonal amphetamine/methamphetamine assay. *Clin Chem.* 2003;39:104–108.

19. Frasewr AD, Howell P. Oxaprozin cross-reactivity in three commercial immunoassays for benzodiazepines in urine. *J Anal Toxicol.* 1998;22:50–54.

20. Valentine JL, Middleton R, Sparks C. Identification of urinary benzodiazepines and their metabolites: comparison of automated HPLC, GC-MS after immunoassay screening of clinical specimens. *J Anal Toxicol.* 1996;20:416–424.

21. West RE, Ritz DP. GC/MS analysis of for five common benzodiazepine metabolites in urine as tert-butyldimethylsilyl derivatives. *J Anal Toxicol.* 1993;17:114–116.

22. Liu RH, McKeehan AM, Edwards C, et al. Improved gas chromatography/mass spectrometry analysis of barbiturates in urine using centrifuge-based solid-phase extraction, methylation with d_5-pentobarbital as internal standard. *J Forensic Sci.* 1994;39:1504–1514.

23. Treston AM, Hooper WD. Metabolic studies with phenobarbitone, primidone and their N-alkyl derivatives: quantification of substrate and metabolites using chemical ionization gas chromatography-mass spectrometry. *J Chromatogr.* 1990;526:59–68.

24. Yonamine M, Silva OA. Confirmation of cocaine exposure by gas chromatography-mass spectrometry of urine extracts after methylation of benzoylecgonine. *J Chromatogr B Analyt Technol Biomed Life Sci.* 2002;773:83–87.

25. Wu AH, Ostheimer D, Cremese M, Forte E, Hill D. Characterization of drug interference caused by coelution of substances in gas chromatography/mass spectrometry confirmation of targeted drugs in full scan and selected ion monitoring modes. *Clin Chem.* 1994;40:216–220.

26. Dasgupta A, Mahle C, McLemore J. Elimination of fluconazole interference in gas chromatography/mass spectrometric confirmation of benzoylecgonine, major metabolite of cocaine using perfluoropropionyl derivative. *J Forensic Sci*. 1996;41:511–513.

27. De Cook KJ, Delbeke FT, DeBoer D, Van Eenioo P, Roels K. Quantitation of 11-nor-Δ^9-tetrahydrocannabinol-9-carboxylic acid with GC-MS in urine collected for doping analysis. *J Anal Toxicol*. 2003;27:106-109.

28. Crockett DK, Nelson G, Dimson P, Urry FM. Solid-phase extraction of 11-nor-Δ^9-tetrahydrocannabinol-9-carboxylic acid from urine drug-testing specimens with cerex polycrom-THC column. *J Anal Toxicol*. 2000;24:245-249.

29. Jamerson MH, McCue JJ, Klette KL. Urine pH, container composition and exposure time influence absorptive loss of 11-nor-Δ^9-tetrahydrocannabinol-9-carboxylic acid. *J Anal Toxicol*. 2005;29:627–631.

30. Huang W, Andollo W, Hearn WL. A solid phase extraction technique for the isolation and identification of opiates in urine. *J Anal Toxicol*. 1992;16:307–310.

31. Moorman P, McCoy M, Hague B, Huge D. Disopyramide cross-reactivity in a commercial immunoassay reagent for methadone. *J Anal Toxicol*. 1999;23: 299–300.

32. Widschwendter CG, Zering G, Hofer A. Quetiapine cross reactivity with urine methadone immunoassay. *Am J Psychiatry*. 2007;164:172.

33. Lancelin F, Kraoul L, Flatischler N, Brovedani-Rousset S, Piketty ML. False-positive results in the detection of methadone in urine of patients treated with psychotropic substances. *Clin Chem*. 2005;51:2176–2177.

34. Cheng PS, Lee CH, Liu C, Chien CS. Simultaneous determination of ketamine, tramadol, methadone and their metabolites in urine by gas chromatography-mass spectrometry. *J Anal Toxicol*. 2008;32:253–259.

35. Schier J. Avoid unfavorable consequences: dextromethorphan can bring a false-positive phencyclidine urine drug screen. *J Emerg Med*. 2000;18:379–381.

36. Santos PM, Lopex-Garcia P, Navarro JS, Fernandez AS. False positive phencyclidine results caused by venlafaxine. *Am J Psychiatry*. 2007;164:349.

37. Long C, Crifasi J, Maginn D. Interference of thioridazine (Mellaril) in identification of phencyclidine. *Clin Chem*. 1996;42: 1885–1885.

38. Cone EJ, Buchwald W, Yousefnejad D. Simultaneous determination of phencyclidine and monohydroxylated metabolite in urine of man by gas chromatography-mass fragmentography with methane chemical ionization. *J Chromatogr*. 1981;223:331–339.

39. Amalfitano G, Bessard, Vincent F, Eysseric H, Bessard G. Gas chromatographic quantitation of dextropropoxyphene, norpropoxyphene in urine after solid-phase extraction. *J Anal Toxicol*. 1996;20:547–554.

40. Lachenmeier K, Musshoff F, Madea B. Determination of opiates and cocaine in hair using automated enzyme immunoassay screening methodologies followed by gas chromatography-mass spectrometric (GC-MS) confirmation. *Forensic Sci Int*. 2006;159:189–199.

CHAPTER 8

Point-of-Care Devices for Drug Testing: Advantages and Limitations

ABSTRACT

Point-of-care devices are designed to test specimens at the collection site. The main advantage is that results can be obtained quickly at a doctor's office or other collection site. Point-of-care testing is available for many tests, including urine pregnancy tests, blood glucose monitoring, testing for cardiac markers at the bedside, as well as point-of-care devices for drugs-of-abuse testing. Although point-of-care devices for drugs-of-abuse testing use immunoassay techniques, like laboratory-based immunoassays, these immunoassays are also subject to interferences. In most cases test results are observed visually, although some devices are able to produce a hard copy of the result. For legal purposes these preliminary test results should be confirmed by a more sophisticated technique such as GC/MS in a laboratory with drug confirmation capability and appropriate accreditation. Currently, devices are available for testing urine and oral fluids at the site of collection. Analysis of hair specimen is complex because drugs become incorporated in hair. Therefore, hair specimens must be sent to a laboratory that has the capability of analyzing hair specimens.

Point-of-care devices for testing urine specimens for the presence of drugs are commercially available for testing at the point of collection. These devices are mostly handheld and are capable of producing results using a very small amount of specimen. Some of these devices require the approval of the U.S. Federal Drug Administration. The major advantage of such devices is ease of operation, but these point-of-care testing devices also suffer from many limitations, including production of false-positive results. Moreover, in point-of-care devices in which the collector needs to visually read the result to determine if the test is positive or negative, a false reading by an unskilled collector may cause serious problems. Currently, point-of-care devices are available for analysis of urine, sweat, and oral fluid specimens.

LATERAL-FLOW IMMUNOASSAY

Most commercially available point-of-care devices for drug testing are based on the lateral-flow immunoassay format. This technique is also known as lateral-flow immunochromatographic assay. A typical device contains a membrane strip (usually made of nitrocellulose) onto which drug conjugates are pre-coated at a particular region called the test region. In addition, colored, colloidal gold nanoparticles conjugated with antibodies (colored antibody conjugate) also are coated on a pad on the device, called a conjugate pad. Urine specimen is added to the sample pad. The sample pad may also contain salt or buffer to make the specimen more compatible with the test matrix. After application of the specimen to the sample pad, migration of specimen takes place through the membrane by capillary action. At the other end of the test strip is an absorbent pad that acts as a sink. If drug molecules are present in urine specimens, then these molecules are bound to colored antibody conjugates, thus preventing colored antibody conjugates from flowing up in the test region and binding to immobilized drug molecules. In this process, no color is formed, and the test is considered positive. In the absence of drug molecules in urine specimen, these colored antibody conjugates will flow up to the test region and bind to the immobilized drug molecules, thus forming a color band (considered a negative test).

In ascending multi-immunoassay techniques (such as Triage Drugs of Abuse Panels, Biosite, San Diego, CA) urine specimen is added into a well containing reagent beads. Drug molecules in urine compete for limited antibody-binding sites with drug molecules labeled with colloidal gold. After 10 minutes of incubation, the mixture is transferred to a test strip onto which specific antibodies are immobilized into different test regions. In the absence of drugs in urine specimens, all collodial gold particles are conjugated with antibodies present in the reagent beads, and none of them are available to bind with immobilized antibodies in the test strip. Therefore, no color is formed. In contrast, when drug molecules are present in urine, drug molecules are bound to respective antibodies in the reagent beads, and drugs labeled with collodial gold are free in the reaction mixture. Therefore, when the reaction mixture is added to the test strip, labeled drugs bind with the respective immobilized antibodies on the test strip. In this process a red band is formed and the test is considered positive.[1]

Various formats of lateral flow immunoassays exist in different point-of-care testing devices: dipstick, cassette, dipcard, and test cup.

POINT-OF-CARE TESTING OF URINE SPECIMENS

Currently, several devices, including dipsticks, cartridge tests, meters, and test-cup format assays, are commercially available for testing of urine specimens at collection sites. **Table 8-1** lists the usual cutoff concentrations of various drugs in point-of-care devices.

In one report authors evaluated the performance of the Signify ER Drug Screen Test (manufactured by Applied Biotech in San Diego, CA, for Abbott Laboratories, Abbott Park, IL) and the Triage Drugs of Abuse Panels. These devices are based on immunochemistry and produce a qualitative response to indicate presence or absence of a drug in urine, and the results are observed visually. The Triage Panels can measure the presence of phencyclidine, barbiturates, benzodiazepines, amphet-

Table 8-1	Usual Cutoff Concentrations for Various Drugs in Point-of-Care Testing Devices for Urine Specimens

Drug	Cutoff Concentration
Amphetamine	1000 ng/ml
Benzodiazepines	200 or 300 ng/ml
Barbiturates	200 or 300 ng/ml
Cocaine (as benzoylecgonine)	300 ng/ml
Opiates	300 ng/ml
Cannabinoids	50 ng/ml
Phencyclidine	25 ng/ml

amines, cocaine (as benzoylecgonine), marijuana metabolite (11-nor-9-carboxy Δ^9-tetrahydrocannabinol; THC-COOH), and opiates at cutoff concentrations similar to those used in screening urine specimens by immunoassays using automated analyzers. The Signify ER Drug Screen Test also has the capability of detecting the presence of tricyclic antidepressants at a cutoff concentration of 1000 ng/ml. Using 693 positive urine samples, the authors demonstrated that the Signify ER Drug Screen Test and the Triage Panels have sensitivities of 99.8% and 99.3%, respectively, with accuracies of 99.9% and 99.6%. The Signify ER Drug Screen Test produces results in 8 minutes after application of specimen in 3 sample wells. A positive result is indicated by the absence of a red line, while the red line is present if the specimen is negative. The Triage Panels are multistep. A measured amount of urine is pipetted into a well containing reagent beads and incubated for 10 minutes. The resulting solution is pipetted onto the detection area and allowed to absorb completely in the membrane. Three

drops of wash solution are added to the detection area, and results are read within 5 minutes, with the presence of a red line indicating a positive result and absence of a red line indicating a negative result.[2]

Peace et al evaluated performances of four on-site drug-testing devices for screening urine for the presence of drugs. These devices include QuickScreen Pro-Multi-Drug Screening Tests (Pharmatech, San Diego, CA), Syva Rapid Test d.a.u. 5 and d.a.u. 2 (Dade Behring, Deerfield, IL), Rapid Drug Screen (Integrated Corporate Solutions, Mogadore, OH), and Triage Panels for drugs of abuse plus tricyclics. All devices are capable of simultaneous determination of the presence of amphetamine, benzoylecgonine, opiates, phencyclidine, and marijuana metabolite (THC-COOH). Triage and Rapid Drug Screen also simultaneously test for benzodiazepines and barbiturates, whereas QuickScreen and Syva Rapid Test require separate devices for analysis of benzodiazepines and barbiturates. Sensitivity and specificity calculations demonstrate that Triage performs most reliably for the donor urine specimens as well as for specimens where drugs were added. In addition, Triage required the least amount of specimen and was the only device in which a colored line indicated a positive test result.[3]

Another study evaluated performance of the Roche OnTrak Testcup-er (Tc-er; Roche Diagnostics, Indianapolis, IN), an on-site drug-testing device based on the principle of competitive binding microparticle immunoassay for simultaneous detection of amphetamine (1000 ng/ml cutoff), barbiturates (200 ng/ml cutoff), benzodiazepines (200 ng/ml cutoff), benzoylecgonine (300 ng/ml cutoff), and opiates (300 ng/ml cutoff). The authors tested 149 specimens obtained from emergency departments using Tc-er and EMIT II monoclonal immunoassay simultaneously. They found 98% agreement between the two methods. The authors concluded that Tc-er can be used as a point-of-care device for urine drug screen.[4] Schilling et al evaluated performance of two on-site urine testing devices, EZ Screen (Environmental Diagnostics, Burlington, NC), and OnTrak (Roche Diagnostics, Indianapolis, IN), by comparing results they obtained by using the Abbott Diagnostics ADx machine and reagents (Abbott Laboratories, Abbott Park, IL). The authors concluded that out of the two visual test kits, OnTrak was a more specific assay than EZ Screen, while the ADx fluorescent immunoassays, which are performed in a laboratory using the ADx machine, are the most sensitive as well as the most specific.[5]

Moody et al compared the ability of Instant-View test cards (Alfa Scientific Designs, Poway, CA) and OnTrak TesTcup Pro 5 (Roche Diagnostics, Indianapolis, IN) to detect the presence of amphetamines, benzodiazepines, cannabinoids, cocaine metabolite, and opiates in urine specimens. The authors observed that compared with GC/MS, the respective overall accuracy of Instant-View test cards was 97.1%, and the respective overall accuracy of TesTcups was 96.5%. Although the relative accuracy of both devices was similar, the Instant-View test card was less precise than the TesTcup at or near the cutoff concentration with clinical specimens.[6]

In one study, authors compared cost of on-site urine drug testing versus sending specimens to a laboratory for testing (off-site testing) and found that on-site testing had a significantly lower variable cost, and the total cost was lower than that of off-site testing once a threshold of 27 employees tested was attained.[7] In addition to the devices described here, many other commercially available devices are available for

urine drug screening at the collection site, at home, or in a doctor's office. These types of devices are usually exempt from the federal regulations set by the Clinical Laboratory Improvement Amendments (CLIA). These devices are packaged with instructions for use and have all the components necessary for testing. They are precalibrated and require no additional calibration or validation prior to use.

POINT-OF-CARE TESTING DEVICES FOR ORAL FLUID

Although oral fluid specimens can be transported to a laboratory for analysis, point-of-care devices are also available. Several devices are commercially available for testing of oral fluid specimens at collection sites. In general, drugs are present in much lower amounts in oral fluid compared with urine. Therefore, SAMHSA–mandated cutoff concentrations of oral fluid are much lower than the respective concentrations of drugs in urine specimens. The sensitivity and specificity of point-of-care devices for oral fluid are generally lower than those for urine drug screening. **Table 8-2** gives the SAMHSA-proposed cutoff concentrations of various drugs in oral fluid specimens.

In one study authors evaluated four point-of-care testing devices: OralLab (Ansys Technologies, Lake Forest, CA), Cozart RapiScan (Cozart Bioscience Ltd., Oxfordshire, United Kingdom), Drugwipe (Securetec, Brunnthal, Germany), and SalivaScreen. They concluded that in general most devices performed well for detecting methamphetamine and opiates, but all performed poorly for detecting cannabinoids (THC). None of the devices had the sensitivity in detecting the presence of THC at the proposed SAMHSA cutoff of 4 ng/ml. The ability to accurately and reliably detect

| Table 8-2 | SAMHSA-Proposed Initial Screen Cutoff Concentration of Drugs of Abuse in Oral Fluid Specimens |

Analyte	Screen Test Cutoff Level
Marijuana or metabolite	4 ng/ml
Cocaine metabolite (benzoylecgonine)	20 ng/ml
Opiate metabolite	40 ng/ml
Phencyclidine	10 ng/ml
Amphetamine	50 ng/ml
MDMA	50 ng/ml

cocaine and amphetamine was dependent on the individual device. The OralLab devices showed the highest sensitivity to produce positive results in specimens containing drug levels near the SAMHSA cutoff levels.[8]

Crouch et al evaluated the performances of the Oratect (Branan Medical Corporation, Irvine, CA) and UPlink (OraSure Technologies, Bethlehem, PA) devices in detecting the presence of amphetamine, cocaine, opiates, and cannabinoids, and they evaluated the performance of Drugwipe in detecting the presence of cannabinoids and cocaine in oral fluids. In general, the Oratect and UPlink devices detected amphetamines, opiates, and cannabinoid metabolite (11-nor-9-carboxy Δ^9-tetrahydrocannabinol; THC-COOH) well when these substances were present in oral fluid in concentration ranges approximating the cutoff concentrations proposed by SAMHSA, but all three devices performed poorly in detecting THC at the proposed SAMHSA cutoff. The ability to accurately

and reliably detect cocaine was device dependent, but in general the Oratect and Drugwipe devices performed better than the UPlink device.[9]

Walsh et al evaluated the performances of the Oralstat (American Bio Medica, Kinderhook, NY), SmartClip (EnviteC, Wismar, Germany), Impact (LifePoint, Ontario, Canada), and OraLine IV s.a.t. (Sun Biomedical Laboratories, Blackwood, NJ) devices in detecting the presence of amphetamine, cocaine, opiates, and cannabinoids (Oralstat can also detect benzodiazepines) in oral fluid specimens. Previously the authors had studied perform-ances of six other oral fluid point-of-care devices, including OralLab, Cozart RapiScan, Drugwipe, SalivaScreen, Oratect, and UPlink (OraSure Technologies, Bethlehem, PA). The authors concluded that most of the devices performed well for detecting opiates and amphetamines, but only four devices (Oralstat, Oratect, Smart-Clip, and Uplink) had amphetamine cutoff concentrations at or lower than the SAMHSA–proposed cutoff of 50 ng/ml. Only three devices (Oralstat, Impact, and OraLine IV s.a.t.) can detect cocaine at the SAMHSA–proposed cutoff of 20 ng/ml. They also observed a number of false-negative results. Only four devices (Oralstat, Impact, Oraline IV s.a.t., and Drugwipe) met the proposed cutoff of 4 ng/ml in detecting the presence of THC-COOH in oral fluid. The authors concluded that point-of-care drug-testing devices are still problematic for detecting the presence of cannabinoids (marijuana) in urine.[10]

POINT-OF-CARE TESTING FOR SWEAT SPECIMENS

For testing of drugs in sweat specimens, sweat is usually collected using a sweat patch, and the sweat patch is sent to a laboratory for analysis (also see Chapter 17). Drugs are extracted from the sweat patch to be screened by appropriate immunoassays. Gas chromatography/mass spectrometry is used for drug confirmation. However, using Drugwipe, an on-site immunochemical test for the presence of drugs on body surfaces and oral fluid, the presence of drugs in a swab collected by wiping the armpit can be determined. Different devices are needed for each drug class (opiates, cannabinoids, cocaine, and amphetamines). In one study, the authors recruited two volunteers and gave each of them a single oral dose of 100 mg of 3,4-methylenedioxymethamphetamine (MDMA). Then MDMA and its main metabolite 4-hydroxy-3-methoxymethamphetamine (HMMA) were analyzed in both plasma and urine using GC/MS. The presence of MDMA in sweat was also analyzed using Drugwipe. Armpits of subjects were swabbed for 10 seconds at 0 hours, 2 hours, 6 hours, 8 hours, 12 hours, and 24 hours after MDMA administration. The authors detected the presence of MDMA in sweat 2 hours after administration of MDMA using Drugwipe and found that MDMA can be detected in sweat for up to 12 hours. Plasma MDMA and HMMA concentrations peaked at 2 to 4 hours after MDMA administration, and MDMA can be detected in urine up to 48 hours after administration.[11]

CONCLUSION

Point-of-care testing is gaining popularity for testing urine specimens and oral fluid specimens. Testing for drugs in hair specimens is complex and can not be performed on site. Although in general point-of-care testing devices for testing urine specimens have adequate sensitivity and good predictive values, on-site testing devices for analysis of oral fluid specimens still have certain limitations, especially for detecting the

presence of low amounts of cannabinoids in oral fluid specimens. This is because concentrations of drugs and metabolites are significantly lower in oral fluid compared with urine, thus posing analytical challenges in accurately detecting such low levels of drugs and metabolites in oral fluid specimens. However, it is expected that in the near future commercially available point-of-care devices for testing oral fluid will be able to meet this challenge.

REFERENCES

1. Tsai JC, Lin GL. Drug testing technologies and application. In: Wong RC, Tse HY, eds. *Drugs of Abuse: Body Fluid Testing*. Totowa, NJ: Humana Press; 2005:29–69.

2. Phillips JE, Bogema S, Fu P, et al. Signify ER Drug Screen Test evaluation: comparison to Triage Drugs of Abuse panel plus tricyclic antidepressants. *Clin Chem Acta*. 2003;328:31–38.

3. Peace MR, Tarnai LD, Poklis A. Performance evaluation of four on-site drug-testing devises for detection of drugs of abuse in urine. *J Anal Toxicol*. 2000;24:589–594.

4. Peace MR, Poklis JL, Tarnai LD, Poklis A. An evaluation of the On Trak Testcup-er on site urine drug testing for drugs commonly encountered from emergency departments. *J Anal Toxicol*. 2002;26:500–503.

5. Schilling RF, Bidassie B, El-Bassel N. Detecting cocaine and opiates in urine: comparing three commercial assays. *J Psychoactive Drugs*. 1999;31:305–313.

6. Moody DE, Fang WB, Andrenyak DM, Monti KM, Jones C. A comparative evaluation of the instant-view 5-panel test card with OnTrak TsetTcup Pro 5: comparison with gas chromatography-mass spectrometry. *J Anal Toxicol*. 2006;30:50–56.

7. Ozminkowski RJ, Mark T, Cangianelli I, et al. The cost of on-site versus off-site workplace urinalysis testing for illicit drug use. *Health Care Manag (Frederick)*. 2001;20:59–69.

8. Walsh JM, Flegel R, Crouch DJ, Cangianelli L, Baudys J. An evaluation of rapid point of collection oral fluid drug-testing devices. *J Anal Toxicol* 2003;27:429–439.

9. Crouch DJ, Walsh JM, Flegel R, Cangianelli L, Baudys J, Atkins R. An evaluation of selected oral fluid point of collection drug testing devices. *J Anal Toxicol.* 2005;29: 244–248.

10. Walsh JM, Crouch DJ, Danaceau JP, Cangianelli L, Liddicoat L, Adkins R. Evaluation of ten oral fluid point-of-care drug-testing devices. *J Anal Toxicol.* 2007;31: 44–54.

11. Pacifici R, Farre M, Pichini S, et al. Sweat testing of MDMA with the Drugwipe analytical device: a controlled study with two volunteers. *J Anal Toxicol.* 2001;25:144–146.

CHAPTER 9

"Beating" Drug Tests with Flushing, Detoxifying Agents, and Synthetic and Substituted Urine

ABSTRACT

Searching the Internet with the key words "beat" and "drug test" produces more than 14,000 results, a reflection of the depth of the problem of people trying to invalidate drug tests. Products available to "beat" drug tests can be classified under three general categories: (1) Drinks and flushing agents commercially available for the purpose of detoxifying the body and thus getting rid of abused drugs. (2) Adulterants that are added in vitro to the specimen after collection, provided the collection process is not supervised. These chemicals are usually toxic and should not be ingested. (3). Readily available household chemicals such as table salt, soap, and vinegar, which are added in vitro after collection of the urine specimen. This chapter discusses the effect of the commercially available flushing and detoxifying agents on the drugs-of-abuse testing. Most of these products do not affect drugs-of-abuse testing, except for some products that may dilute urine and thus lower the sensitivity of screening assays, the first step in drugs-of-abuse testing. Substitution of urine specimen or providing synthetic urine is a serious problem because a laboratory has no means to identify substituted specimens. Chapter 10 discusses the effects of common household chemicals used as urinary adulterants on drugs-of-abuse testing. Chapter 11 discusses the effects of commercially available in vitro adulterants, such as Urine Luck, UrinAid, and Stealth.

Commercially available products to beat drug tests can be classified into two broad categories. The first category includes specific fluids or tablets that are taken with substantial water to flush out drugs and metabolites. Many of these products can produce diluted urine, and the concentrations of drugs or metabolites can be significantly reduced. Because each drug of abuse has mandatory federally guided cutoff values, analysis of diluted urine is a problem for drugs-of-abuse testing. For example, the cutoff for amphetamines in the immunoassay screening step is 1000 ng/ml. Therefore, if the concentration of amphetamine is below 1000 ng/ml, the specimen is considered negative. If a person has amphetamine concentration just over the cutoff, and the individual drinks plenty of water and detoxifying agents, which usually contain caffeine, a diuretic, the urine specimen will be diluted, pushing the concentration of amphetamine below the screening cutoff of 1000 ng/ml. Because a specimen tested negative by the immunoassays usually does not undergo further analysis by a more sophisticated and specific confirmation technique such as GC/MS, the individual may pass the drug test.

COMMERCIALLY AVAILABLE FLUSHING AND DETOXIFYING PRODUCTS

The costs of detoxifying products vary widely depending on the type of detoxifying desired and also on the Internet sites from which they are available. For $109.95, one Internet site offers seven-day detoxifying products designed for drug users weighing more than 180 lbs. The manufacturer claims that the kit removes all toxins and comes with four easy-to-use personal drug-test kits of the customer's choice so that the individual can ensure that drugs are being flushed out of the system. The five-day detoxifying formula designed for heavy to moderate users who weigh less than 180 lbs. costs $79.95 and comes with two drug-testing options. Another Internet site sells a premium detoxifying seven-day comprehensive cleansing program for $59.99 and also sells THC/marijuana cannabis dip-strip urine drug tests for $3.99. A fast-working THC/marijuana detoxifying kit for people weighing less than 200 lbs. sells for $51.99, while the two-step THC/marijuana detoxifying kit for people under 200 lbs. sells for $45.99. The fast cocaine detoxifying kit for people

weighing over 200 lbs. sells for $55.99. The same site also sells cheaper products, such as the Absolute De-Tox carbohydrate drink (grape flavor) for $34.99, ZYDOT Natural Blend Cleansing Tea for $19.99, Flax Boost for $19.99, and Detoxifying Quick Flash capsules for $24.99. The Aqua Clean Cleansing system is available from another Internet site for $31.99. Users are instructed to dissolve two tablets in water and drink the water one hour before the scheduled drug test; the effects last for up to five hours. A variety of other products (for example, Absolute De-Tox XXL drink, Absolute Carbo-Drinks, Ready Clean Drug Detox Drink, Fast Flush Capsules, Ready Clean Gel Capsules) are available from various Internet sites. Home urine drug-test kits are also commercially available so that an individual may monitor the progress of the detoxifying process. Some of the Internet sites that sell products for invalidating drugs-of-abuse tests also sell home test kits for detecting the presence of various abused drugs in urine specimens.

SYNTHETIC AND SUBSTITUTED URINE: A BIG CHALLENGE

Synthetic urine, which has the characteristics of natural urine, is commercially available and presents a challenge for workplace drug-testing programs in which the collection of urine is not supervised. Many of the same Internet sites that sell flushing agents, detoxifying products, and in vitro urinary adulterants also sell synthetic urine as well as drug-free urine to substitute for original specimens that may contain abused drugs. One Internet site sells Quick Fix synthetic urine for $31.99. Quick Fix synthetic urine is unisex so that either males or females can use it to pass drug or nicotine testing. The

Quick Fix container is microwaved for 10 seconds with the cap open to achieve a temperature between 94°F and 100°F (34.4°C and 37.7°C), the normal temperature range of urine after collection. Then the cap is closed. A heater pad is provided with Quick Fix synthetic urine, which should be also heated with the urine and then taped to the urine specimen. The manufacturer claims with the heating pad, synthetic urine can maintain the desired temperature for up to six hours in an inside pocket of clothing being worn. The price of synthetic urine ranges from $31.99 to $109 (depending on the manufacturer) and can be ordered through the Internet or by calling toll-free numbers.

Human urine specimens not containing any drugs (frozen or dehydrated urine) are also available for substitution purposes. Fortunately, in many states, including South Carolina, North Carolina, Nebraska, and New Jersey, it is illegal to sell or give away urine for the purpose of defrauding a drug test. One South Carolina man was selling his urine for $69 per sample. He was arrested and found guilty by the Supreme Court of South Carolina. Unfortunately, if substituted urine specimen is not identified by temperature index at the collection site, no other laboratory test can identify it.

SPECIMEN INTEGRITY TESTING

Both the collection site and the laboratory have a number of ways to detect adulterated specimens. The temperature of a urine specimen should be checked within 4 minutes of collection. The temperature should be between 32°C and 38°C (90°F and 100.4°F), but the urine specimen may remain warmer than 33°C for up to 15 minutes. The pH of normal urine varies within the same day but should be between 4.5 and 8.0. The specific gravity should be between 1.005 and 1.030. The creatinine concentration of normal urine varies between 20 and 400 mg/dl. A specimen is considered diluted if the creatinine is less than 20 mg/dl and the specific gravity is less than 1.003. Additional tests are also recommended to detect the presence of other adulterants. Determination of specific gravity is mandatory for any specimen with a creatinine concentration of less than 20 mg/dl.

Although substituted urine should have normal creatinine concentration, specific gravity, and pH, the temperature may not be within the acceptable limit if the person being tested did not carefully heat the synthetic or substituted specimen to achieve the desired temperature or failed to maintain the desired temperature of the urine while coming to the testing facility. This may be apparent in a cold climate where the individual might have walked several blocks from a parking spot.

Another important method of identifying synthetic urine is visual inspection of the specimen. Sometimes the contents of synthetic urine settle down in the form of precipitate if it is not vigorously shaken prior to submitting it as a specimen. Observing objects floating in a urine specimen or sedimentation may also provide a clue that the specimen is not authentic.

DILUTED URINE AND DRUGS-OF-ABUSE TESTING

A negative result for the presence of abused drugs in a urine specimen does not mean that no drug is present. It is possible that the amount of drug is below the cutoff value for the detection of a particular abused drug in the laboratory. Most certified laboratories follow federally mandated guidelines for drugs-of-abuse testing. The criteria for testing of military personnel are extremely stringent. Diluting urine is a simple way to make an otherwise positive drug test negative provided that the original concentration of the abused drug in the specimen collected is moderate and not significantly above the cutoff of the drug assay. Federal guidelines recommend that testing sites place a bluing agent in the toilet tank if possible so that the reservoir of water in the toilet bowl always remains blue. There should be no other source of water in the enclosure where urination takes place. If tap water is available in the rest room where the specimen is collected, there should be no hot water supply. The laboratory can easily tell if an individual has diluted the collected specimen with cold tap water, as it would cause the temperature of the specimen to fall well below the lowest acceptable limit.

Consumption of a large amount of fluid prior to drug testing is a possible way to avoid a positive test.[1] Fraser et al used the criteria of creatinine less than 20 mg/dl and specific gravity below 1.003 as indicators of diluted urine.[2] Creatinine analysis in urine is a very effective method to detect diluted urine. According to Needleman and Porvaznik a creatinine value of less than 10 mg/dl suggests that a urine specimen has been largely diluted by water.[3] Beck et al reported that 11% of all urine specimens submitted to their laboratory for drugs-of-abuse testing was diluted.[4] The SAMHSA program does not currently allow analysis of dilute urine specimens at lower screening and confirmation cutoffs than the recommended guidelines. However, the Correctional Services of Canada (CSC) incorporates lower screening and confirmation cutoffs for drugs and their metabolites (amphetamine: screening cutoff 100 ng/ml, confirmation cutoff 100 ng/ml; benzoylecgonine: screening and confirmation cutoff 15 ng/ml; opiates, screening and confirmation cutoff 120 ng/ml; phencyclidine, screening and confirmation cutoff 5 ng/ml; and cannabinoids, screening cutoff 20 ng/ml, confirmation cutoff 3 ng/ml) for diluted urine specimens. Fraser and Zamecnik reported that 7912 urine specimens collected and analyzed between 2000 and 2002 by the CSC were diluted. Out of that number, 2057 specimens screened positive using SAMSHA cutoff values. When the lower CSC values for cutoff and confirmation were adopted, 1100 specimens tested positive for one or more illicit drugs. The positive rate of diluted specimens was 18.2% in CSC institutes and 22.3% in parolee specimens. The drug most often confirmed positive in a diluted specimen is marijuana. Codeine and morphine are also commonly confirmed in these specimens and rank second after marijuana in prevalence.[5] Soldin reported in 1991 that there was more than a 100% increase in cocaine-positive specimens when the cutoff was lowered to 80 ng/ml from the recommended 300 ng/ml in a pediatric population because neonates are not capable of concentrating urine to the same extent as adults.[6] Luzzi et al investigated the analytic performance criteria of three immunoassay systems (EMIT, Beckman EIA, and Abbott FPIA) for detecting abused drugs below established cutoff values. The authors concluded that drugs can be screened at concentrations much lower than that established by SAMSHA cutoff values. For example, the authors proposed a THC-COOH cutoff value of 35 ng/ml using EMIT, and 14 ng/ml for the Beckman EIA and the FPIA assays, in contrast to the SAMSHA cutoff of 50 ng/ml. The proposed cutoff values were based on the studies of precision of the assays at the proposed lower detection limit in which the coefficient of variation (CV) was less than 20%. This lowering of the cutoff values increased the number of positive specimens in the screening tests to 15.6%. A 7.8% increase was also observed in the confirmation stage of drugs-of-abuse testing.[7]

In February 2000, SAMHSA published the National Laboratory Certification Program (NLPL) State of the Science—Update 1, titled "Urine specimen validity testing: evaluation of the scientific data used to define a urine specimen as 'substituted.'"[8] A substituted specimen was defined as urine creatinine less than or equal to 5 mg/dl and a urine specific gravity less than or equal to 1.001 or greater than or equal to 1.020. Edgell et al performed a controlled hydration study using 56 drug-free volunteers to investigate whether it is possible to produce such diluted urine. Subjects were given 2370 ml of fluid, and urine specimens were collected at the end of each hour for a 6-hour test period. No urine specimen satisfied the paired substitution criteria (specific gravity ≤ 1.001 or above 1.020 and creatinine ≤ 5.0 mg/dl) for diluted urine, although 55% of subjects produce at least one dilute urine specimen during the first 3 hours of hydration with creatinine less than 20 mg/dl and specific gravity less than 1.003. This finding supports the criteria set by SAMSHA for classifying a specimen as substituted if creatinine is below 5 mg/dl and specific gravity less than or equal to 1.001 because such low values are not consistent with normal human physiology.[9] Barbanel et al studied specific gravity and/or creatinine concentrations in 803,130 random urine specimens. Of these, 13,467 specimens had both creatinine and specific gravity measurements performed; none of them met the lower limits of specific gravity (1.001) and creatinine (5 mg/dl). The patients who met one of the two criteria

Table 9-1 Criteria for Diluted Urine

Test	Values
Creatinine and specific gravity	<5 mg/dl ≤1.0010 or >1.020
Creatinine and specific gravity	≥2mg/dl and <20 mg/dl ≥1.0010 or ≥ 1.020
Creatinine[3]	<10 mg/dl
Creatinine and specific gravity[2,11]	<20 mg/dl <1.003

(creatinine < 5.0 mg/dl or specific gravity < 1.001) were neonatal or severely ill, unlike anyone in the workforce undergoing testing for abused drugs. Eleven patients met the criteria of substituted urine (creatinine < 5 mg/dl, specific gravity > 1.020), but all of them were seriously or terminally ill.[10] **Table 9-1** gives criteria for determining diluted urine.

FLUSHING, DETOXIFICATION AGENTS, DIURETICS, AND HERBAL TEA

Flushing and detoxification are frequently advertised as effective means of passing drug tests. Many of these products contain caffeine or other diuretics to increase the output of urine, sugar, and natural or artificial flavoring agents. The objective is to produce dilute urine so that concentrations of abused drugs and or metabolites can be pushed below the recommended cutoff concentrations of the drugs-of-abuse testing program. Cone et al evaluated the effect of excess fluid ingestion on false-negative marijuana and cocaine urine test results. The authors studied the ability of Naturally Clean herbal tea, goldenseal root tea, and hydrochlorothiazide to cause false-negative results. Volunteers drank one gallon of water (divided in 4 doses over a 4-hour period), or herbal tea or hydrochlorothiazide 22 hours after smoking marijuana cigarettes or intranasal administration of cocaine. The creatinine levels dropped below the cutoff 2 hours after intake of excessive fluid. Marijuana and cocaine metabolite levels (as measured by both EMIT and FPIA) decreased significantly and frequently switched from positive to negative in subjects after consuming 2 quarts of fluid. Even excess water was effective in diluting a urine specimen to cause false-negative results. Subjects who consumed herbal tea produced dilute urine faster compared with subjects who drank only water.[11]

Diuretics are used in sports for two purposes: first, to flush out previously taken banned substances by forced diuresis, and second, to achieve quick weight loss to qualify for a lower weight class. The Medical Commission of the International Olympic Committee bans diuretics. There is no commercially available immunoassay for detecting diuretics such as hydrochlorothiazide in urine, and a sophisticated technique such as liquid chromatography combined with tandem mass spectrometry is necessary to confirm the presence of diuretics in doping analysis.[12]

ASPIRIN AND OTHER NONSTEROIDAL ANTI-INFLAMMATORY DRUGS

Wagener et al reported that ingestion of aspirin interfered with the EMIT (enzyme multiplied immunoassay technique) drugs-of-abuse screening assays. The authors observed that urine specimens containing salicylate (15–420 mg/dl) provided a lower rate of change of absorbance compared with drug-free urine. This phenomenon may cause false-negative test results using the EMIT assays. No effect was observed when salicylate was added in vitro to urine specimens containing no salicylate, but when volunteers ingested aspirin tablets and their urine specimens were subsequently analyzed, negative bias was observed. The authors concluded that ingestion of therapeutic doses of aspirin may cause false-negative results for drug screens in urine specimens by this method.[13]

Another study indicated that ingestion of the nonsteroidal anti-inflammatory drugs ibuprofen or fenoprofen cause false-positive results with the FPIA (fluorescence polarization immunoassay; Abbott Laboratories, Abbott Park, IL) benzodiazepine assays. The specimens containing fenoprofen also tested positive by the FPIA assay for barbiturates. In contrast, when tested using a more sophisticated GC/MS method, all but one specimen tested negative. The authors concluded that both ibuprofen and fenoprofen cause false-positive results with the FPIA assays for drugs-of-abuse screening.[14] Rollins et al reported that there is a small likelihood of a false-positive immunoassay screening test for marijuana metabolite (cannabinoids), benzodiazepines, or barbiturates after acute or chronic ingestion of ibuprofen, or after chronic ingestion of fenoprofen or naproxen.[15] In our experience, this small number of false-positive tests results does not cause any problem with drugs-of-abuse testing because all urine specimens that test positive by the immunoassay are automatically confirmed by the more sophisticated GC/MS method. None of the nonsteroidal anti-inflammatory drugs interfere with the GC/MS method of drug confirmation.

BITTER ORANGE AND AMPHETAMINE IMMUNOASSAY SCREENING

Bitter orange is used recently as an ingredient in ephedra-free dietary supplements. Bitter orange contains synephrine, which is structurally similar to amphetamine. Although few earlier reports suggested potential interference of bitter orange with amphetamine screening assays, a more recent article by Nguyen et al clearly established that a single dose of Nature's Way bitter orange did not cause false-positive response in the CEDIA amphetamine assay (Microgenics Corporation, Fremont, CA).[16] Moreover, there are subtle differences between the structure of synephrine and amphetamine, and the GC/MS confirmation seep will be negative if only synephrine and its metabolites are present in the urine specimen.

GOVERNMENT CRITERIA FOR DETERMINING DILUTED OR SUBSTITUTED URINE

SAMHSA has developed criteria to identify diluted or substituted specimens. In general, normal human urine should contain creatinine at concentrations of 20 mg/dl or higher, and normal values of specific gravity of human urine range from approximately 1.0020 to 1.0200. Increased specific gravity may occur from a number of conditions, including dehydration, diarrhea, excessive sweating, water restriction, heart failure, and proteinuria, while decreased specific gravity may be due to excessive fluid intake. A donor may produce dilute urine if he or she has been working in a hot environment and drinking a large amount of fluid, drinking fluid

immediately before providing a urine specimen, or taking a diuretic. The federal guidelines for reporting diluted or substituted urine are as follows[17]:

- *Diluted urine:* A laboratory will report a urine specimen as "diluted" in conjunction with a positive or negative drug test that is greater than or equal to 2 mg/dl and less than 20 mg/dl and has a specific gravity between 1.0010 and 1.0030.

- *Substituted urine:* A laboratory will report a urine specimen as substituted when both the initial and confirmatory tests (ie, tests on separate aliquots) record creatinine concentration less than 2 mg/dl and have specific gravity less than or equal to 1.0010 or greater than or equal to 1.0200.

A Case Study[18]

A laboratory reported that a urine specimen submitted was substituted (creatinine 1.5 mg/dl; specific gravity 1.0005). During the interview the donor claimed to have been performing strenuous activity in a hot climate and drinking a large amount of fluid for several days before submitting the specimen. The MRO requested the agency to have the donor provide another urine specimen under similar conditions using a direct-observation collection process. The laboratory reports that the creatinine concentration in the urine specimen following supervised collection was 5.5 mg/dl and the specific gravity was 1.003. The MRO reported the result as "Refusal to Test (Substituted)."

CONCLUSION

A variety of products are available through the Internet and toll-free telephone numbers to help users pass drug testing by getting rid of unwanted drugs from the body prior to testing. Moreover, all manufacturers recommend drinking plenty of fluid along with these products in order to achieve the desired results. Many of these products contain caffeine or diuretics and result in diluted urine. Specimen integrity testing is very important to identify diluted urine specimens. Abnormally low specific gravity or creatinine or both are indicative of diluted or substituted specimen. It is important for the laboratory to document these levels because diluted or substituted specimen can be considered refusal of the individual to undergo drugs-of-abuse testing. Ingestion of certain nonsteroidal anti-inflammatory drugs may cause a false positive in drugs-of-abuse screening tests, but such drugs do not interfere with the confirmation step of drugs-of-abuse tests using GC/MS. Moreover, taking herbal supplements containing the ingredient bitter orange should not cause false-positive amphetamine results.

REFERENCES

1. George S, Braithwaite RA. An investigation into the extent of possible dilution of specimens received for urinary drugs-of-abuse screening. *Addiction*. 1995;90:967–970.

2. Fraser AD, Zamecnik J, Keravel J, McGrath L, Wells J. Experience with urine drug testing by the correctional service of Canada. *Forensic Sci Int*. 2001;121:16–22.

3. Needleman SD, Porvaznik M. Creatinine analysis in single collection urine specimens. *J Forensic Sci*. 1992;37:1125–1133.

4. Beck O, Bohlin M, Bragd F, Bragd J, Greitz O. Adulteration of urine drug testing: an exaggerated cause of concern [Swedish]. *Lakartidningen*. 2000;97:703–706.

5. Fraser AD, Zamecnik J. Impact of lowering the screening and confirmation cutoff values for urine drug testing based on dilution indicators. *Ther Drug Monit*. 2003;25:723–727.

6. Soldin SJ, Morales AJ, D'Angelo LJ, Bogema SC, Hicks JC. The importance of lowering the cut-off concentrations of urine screening and confirmatory tests for benzoylecgonine/cocaine [Abstract]. *Clin Chem*. 1991;37:993.

7. Luzzi VI, Saunders AN, Koenig JW, et al. Analytical performance of immunoassays for drugs of abuse below established cutoff values. *Clin Chem*. 2004;50:717–722.

8. U.S. Department of Health and Human Services, Substance Abuse and Mental Health Services Administration. NLCP: State of the Science—Urine Specimen Validity Testing: Evaluation of the Scientific Data Used to Define a Urine Specimen as Substituted. February 14, 2000. http://www.workplace.samhsa.gov/DrugTesting/Files_Drug_Testing/Notices_Docs_Resources/Archives/NLCP%20State%20of%20the%20Science%20Update%201.aspx. Accessed October 22, 2008.

9. Edgell K, Caplan YH, Glass LR, Cook JD. The defined HHS/DOT substituted urine criteria validated through controlled hydration study. *J Anal Toxicol*. 2002;26:419–423.

10. Barbanel CS, Winkelman JW, Fischer GA, King AJ. Confirmation of the department of transportation criteria for a substituted urine specimen. *J Occup Environ Med*. 2002;44:407–416.

11. Cone EJ, Lange R, Darwin WD. In vivo adulteration: excess fluid ingestion causes false negative marijuana and cocaine urine test results. *J Anal Toxicol*. 1998;22:460–473.

12. Deventer K, Delbeke FT, Roels K, Van Ecnoo P. Screening for 18 diuretics and probenecid in doping analysis by liquid chromatography-tandem mass spectrometry. *Biomed Chromatogr.* 2002;16:529–535.

13. Wagener RE, Linder MW, Valdes R Jr. Decreased signal in EMIT assays of drugs of abuse in urine after ingestion of aspirin: potential for false-negative results. *Clin Chem.* 1994;40:608–612.

14. Larsen J, Fogerson R. Nonsteroidal anti-inflammatory drugs interfere in TDx assays for abused drugs. *Clin Chem.* 1988;34: 987–988.

15. Rollins DE, Jennison TA, Jones G. Investigation of interference of nonsteroidal anti-inflammatory drugs in urine tests for abused drugs. *Clin Chem.* 1990;36:602–606.

16. Nguyen DT, Bui LT, Ambrose PJ. Response of CEDIA amphetamines assay after a single dose of bitter orange. *Ther Drug Monit.* 2006;28:252–254.

17. U.S. Department of Heath and Human Services, Substance Abuse and Mental Health Services Administration. Medical Review Officer Manual for Federal Agency Workplace Drug-Testing Programs. Effective November 1, 2004. http://www.workplace.samhsa.gov/DrugTesting/Level_1_Pages/HHS%20MRO%20Manual%20(Effective%20November%201,%202004).aspx. Accessed October 22, 2008.

18. U.S. Department of Heath and Human Services, Substance Abuse and Mental Health Services Administration. MRO Case Studies: Case #1. February 2005. http://workplace.samhsa.gov/DrugTesting/Files_Drug_Testing/MROs/MRO%20Case%20Studies%20-%20February%202005.pdf. Accessed October 22, 2008.

CHAPTER 10

Household Chemicals as Urinary Adulterants

ABSTRACT

Persons abusing drugs sometimes attempt to adulterate urine specimens in order to escape detection. Household chemicals such as bleach, table salt, laundry detergent, toilet bowl cleaner, vinegar, lemon juice, and eye drops can be used for adulterating urine specimens. Most of these adulterants, except Visine eye drops, can be detected by routine specimen integrity tests (creatinine, pH, temperature, and specific gravity). Many of these adulterants interfere with the immunoassay screening step of drugs-of-abuse testing. Because the confirmation step is usually not performed by a laboratory if the initial screening test is negative, detecting these adulterants by specimen integrity testing prior to analysis is crucial.

People attempt to beat drug testing by adding various household chemicals to their urine after collection. The simplest approach is to dilute urine with tap water after collecting the specimen. However, hot water in bathrooms is not available in many collection facilities in order to discourage this practice. The temperature of the urine is routinely checked after collection to ensure that the temperature is within the normal physiological range. Although dilution of urine with water reduces the concentration of drugs or metabolites and might help to cheat drug testing, such an adulteration effort can be easily detected because of the lower temperature and lower creatinine concentration of tampered urine.

Another approach to beat drug testing is for the donor to substitute the specimen with synthetic urine. Internet sites sell synthetic urine as a sure method to beat a drug test in settings (e.g., pre-employment drug testing) where collection of a urine specimen is not supervised (see Chapter 9).

Household chemicals that are available at grocery stores are popular adulterants to invalidate drug testing. The first report of the use of household chemicals as urinary adulterants appeared in 1988. Milkkelsen and Ash reported the effects of eight adulterants (sodium chloride, Visine eye drops, hand soap, Drano drain cleaner, bleach, vinegar, goldenseal root tea, and lemon juice) on the immunoassay screening step for drugs-of-abuse testing.[1] Several later papers were published later on the effects of common household chemicals and drinks (goldenseal root tea, herbal tea, and lemon juice) on drugs-of-abuse testing in both the screening step and the confirmation step using GC/MS. In the mid-1990s several companies began to market in vitro urinary adulterants through the Internet. Despite the availability of these commercial adulterants for cheating drug tests, household chemicals are still the most popular. Technicians at the Memorial Hermann–Texas Medical Center in Houston report that they frequently encounter urinary pH outside the normal range (pH 4–8) and the smell of bleach in urine specimens they are analyzing for drug tests.

Because the presence of certain adulterants in sufficient quantities invalidates screening assays for abused drugs, it is essential for drug abuse testing facilities to be able to identify adulterated specimens prior to analysis. Specimen integrity tests can detect the presence of most adulterants in urine specimens.

SPECIMEN INTEGRITY TESTS

Both the collection site and the laboratory at a testing site have a number of mechanisms to detect adulterated specimens. The temperature of a urine specimen should be checked within 4 minutes of collection. The temperature should be between 32°C and 38°C (90°F and 100.4°F), although a urine specimen may remain warmer than 33°C for up to 15 minutes. The pH of normal urine varies within the same day but

should be within 4.5 and 8.0. The specific gravity should be between 1.005 and 1.030. The creatinine concentration of normal urine varies between 20 and 400 mg/dl. A specimen is considered diluted if the creatinine level is less than 20 mg/dl and the specific gravity is less than 1.003. Additional tests are recommended to detect the presence of other adulterants. Determination of specific gravity is mandatory for any specimen with a creatinine concentration of less than 20 mg/dl. Substituted urine specimens have creatinine concentrations less than 5 mg/dl and a specific gravity of less than 1.001 or over 1.020. The urine is adulterated if pH is less than 3 or greater than 11.[2,3] **Table 10-1** summarizes the effects of household chemicals that are often used as urinary adulterants on different parameters of specimen integrity tests.

COMMON HOUSEHOLD CHEMICALS AND DRINKS AS URINARY ADULTERANTS

Several adulterants can affect drug testing performed by immunoassays because antibodies used in immunoassays are sensitive to the pH and the ionic strength of the urine matrix. Common adulterants used for beating drug tests are listed below.

- Table salt (sodium chloride)
- Vinegar
- Hand soap
- Liquid drain cleaner (e.g., Drano)
- Liquid dishwashing detergent (e.g., Joy)
- Liquid bleach (e.g., Clorox)
- Toilet bowl cleaner (e.g., Vanish)
- Lime solvent
- Sodium bicarbonate or sodium hypochlorite

Table 10-1	Common Household Chemicals and Specimen Integrity Tests			
Household Chemicals	**Specimen Integrity Tests***			
	pH	Creatinine	Temperature	Specific Gravity
Diluted urine		X	X	
Sodium chloride				X
Vinegar	X			
Bleach[a]	X			
Liquid soap	X			
Liquid drain cleaner	X			
Sodium bicarbonate	X			
Sodium hypochlorite	X			
Lemon juice	X			
Goldenseal root[b]				
Ascorbic acid (vitamin C)	X			
Visine eye drops				

X An abnormal test indicates presence of the adulterant

a. Cloudy appearance of specimen

b. Dark urine

- Denture-cleaning tablets (sodium perborate)
- Hydrogen peroxide (3% solution available commercially)
- Concentrated lemon juice
- Ascorbic acid (vitamin C)
- Goldenseal root tea
- Eye drops (e.g., Visine)
- Ethyl alcohol and isopropanol
- Liquid antiseptic (e.g., Dettol)

Although in general the fluorescence polarization assay (FPIA; Abbott Laboratories, Abbott Park, IL) is less subject to interference from adulterants compared with the enzyme multiplied immunoassay technique (EMIT) assay, some interference has also been reported with FPIA assays.

The assay for 11-nor-9-carboxy-Δ^9-tetrahydrocannabinol, the major metabolite of tetrahydrocannabinol (THC), is most susceptible to urine adulteration because many adulterants can cause false-negative results if present in sufficient concentrations regardless of the assay technique (EMIT or FPIA). The adulterants that interfere with the testing of marijuana metabolite by the EMIT assay are sodium chloride, vinegar, soap, bleach, liquid drain cleaner, eye drops, and goldenseal root tea. Similarly, ascorbic acid, vinegar, bleach, lime solvent, eye drops, and goldenseal root can cause false-negative results with the FPIA assay for THC metabolite. Several studies have demonstrated that the pH of urine has a significant effect on the results of drug screening tests. Many readily available household chemicals are capable of drastically altering the pH of urine when added to urine in sufficient quantities.[1-5]

The adulterants do not have the same effect on all commercially available immunoassays for drug-of-abuse screening because immunoassays differ in assay design. Nevertheless, some adulterants in sufficient concentrations can also invalidate assays for screening of drugs in urine by producing false-negative results. Because the GC/MS confirmation step is usually not performed for urine specimens that test negative by immunoassay screening tests, the presence of adulterants may invalidate the entire purpose of workplace drug testing. The following factors play important roles in the effectiveness of an adulterant to mask a drug screen successfully:

- *Minimum amount of adulterant needed*: For example, a minimum of 50 gm of sodium chloride per liter of urine (1.5 gm for a typical 30 mL specimen) is needed to mask drug screening by the EMIT assay (**Table 10-2**).

- *Concentration of abused drug or metabolite in the specimen*: If the concentration of a drug is very high, the test may be positive even if a sufficient amount of adulterant is added to the specimen.

- *Immunoassay design:* In general, the FPIA assay is less affected than the EMIT assay.

Sodium chloride: Sodium chloride is effective in masking many tests that rely on the EMIT assay. Sodium chloride (50 gm/L of urine or a higher amount) will cause false-negative test results with many drugs tested by the EMIT assay, while reducing only the sensitivity of the FPIA benzodiazepine assay. The amount of sodium chloride required to mask an EMIT assay also depends on the particular drug assay. For example, 75 gm sodium chloride per liter of

Table 10-2	Amount of Adulterant Needed to Invalidate a Screening Assay for an Abused Drug

Adulterants	Amount Needed for 30 mL of Urine
Sodium chloride	1.5 gm (50 gm/L)
Vinegar	2.6 mL (85 mL/L)
Liquid bleach	0.4 mL (12 mL/L)
Liquid drain cleaner	0.4 mL (12 mL/L)
Lemon juice concentrates	15 mL (500 mL/L)
Ethanol	5% by volume
Isopropanol	5% by volume

urine is needed to cause a false negative by the EMIT assay in a urine specimen containing 1420 ng/ml of amphetamine (the cutoff level of amphetamines in the EMIT assay is 1000 ng/ml). The same amount of sodium chloride will also invalidate a barbiturate test at a barbiturate concentration of 380 ng/ml (the cutoff level of barbiturates is 300 ng/ml).[1] Salt has no effect on the immunoassay screening of amphetamines, barbiturates, benzodiazepines, phencyclidine, benzoylecgonine (cocaine metabolite), opiates, and marijuana metabolites using a different set of immunoassays (cloned enzyme donor immunoassays, known as CEDIA) available from Microgenics Corporation (Concord, CA) (**Table 10-3**). The amount of sodium chloride required for masking a drug test by the EMIT assay increases the specific gravity of the urine to greater than 1.035. Routine specimen integrity tests can easily detect such an adulterated specimen (Table 10-1).

Vinegar: Vinegar at the minimum concentration of 85 mL per liter of urine can invalidate the immunoassay screen for

Table 10-3	Effect of Adulterants on Immunoassay Screening of Drugs of Abuse	
Adulterant	**Drugs Affected**	**Comments**
Sodium chloride	Amphetamines, barbiturates Benzodiazepines, cannabinoids Cocaine (as benzoylecgonine) Opiates, phencyclidine (PCP)	Produces false-negative results using EMIT assay
Sodium chloride	Benzodiazopines	Produces slight decreases in response using FPIA assay
Hydrogen peroxide	Benzodiazepines	Produces decreased level using EMIT assay
Hydrogen peroxide	Benzodiazepines	Produces false positive using FPIA assay
Liquid dishwashing detergent	Cannabinoids, PCP, benzodiazepines	Produces decreased level using EMIT assay
Sodium bicarbonate	Opiates	Produces decreased levels using EMIT assay
Sodium hypochlorite	Cannabinoids, benzodiazepines	Produces false negative using EMIT assay
Sodium hypochlorite	Amphetamines, opiate, PCP	Produces false negative using FPIA assay
Denture-cleaning tablets	Benzoylecgonine, methyl-enedioxyamphetamine (MDMA)	Produce false negative using FPIA assay
Alcohol/isopropanol	Methaqualone	Invalidates EMIT assay

marijuana (Δ^9-tetrahydrocannabinol; THC) as carboxylic acid (11-carboxy-THC), which is mostly conjugated in urine. Vinegar has minimal effect as an adulterant to mask immunoassay screens of various drugs-of-abuse assays. The CEDIA (Microgenics Corporation, Fremont, CA) drugs-of-abuse assays are not affected by vinegar at all (Table 10-3).[4] Furthermore, routine specimen integrity tests easily detect the presence of vinegar: the amount of vinegar required to invalidate the test would also shift the urine pH outside the normal physiological range (Table 10-1).

Hand soap: Hand soap is very effective as an adulterant for marijuana metabolite, barbiturate, methaqualone, and benzodiazepine screening by EMIT assays. Conversely, soap may cause false-positive test results with the FPIA assays for amphetamines and barbiturates. Liquid hand soap can be easily obtained from a dispenser in the bathroom of the collection facility. However, the presence of hand soap in a urine specimen is usually easy to detect: it makes the specimen look cloudy.

Liquid drain cleaner, liquid dishwashing detergent, and liquid bleach: Drain cleaner (e.g., Drano) causes concentration-dependent interference with the EMIT assays for testing for the presence of cocaine metabolite (benzoylecgonine), opiates, THC, and amphetamines in urine. Drain cleaner causes false-negative results with benzodiazepine, THC, and barbiturate assays.[1] Liquid drain cleaner also causes false-negative results in the screening of benzoylecgonine by the FPIA assay. Routine specimen integrity tests easily detect the presence of liquid drain cleaner because it shifts the pH of urine outside the normal physiological range.

Liquid dishwashing detergent (e.g., Joy) affects the benzodiazepine, phencyclidine, and marijuana metabolite assays. Dishwashing liquid causes falsely elevated levels of barbiturates, benzodiazepines, THC, and amphetamines when FPIA assays are used for urine drug screen. High concentrations of bleach and liquid drain cleaner also invalidate most screening assays for abused drugs using CEDIA DAU assays.[4] Although the presence of dishwashing liquid in urine does not cause any change in appearance, pH, or specific gravity, it can be detected by vigorously shaking a small amount of urine.[5]

Liquid bleach invalidates the FPIA assay for THC metabolite by causing a false-negative result and also is capable of destroying THC metabolite in urine as demonstrated by GC/MS analysis (Table 10-3). However, like liquid drain cleaner, bleach shifts the pH of urine outside the normal physiological range, making it easily identified during specimen integrity testing.[1,5]

Toilet bowl cleaner: Toilet bowl cleaner (e.g., Vanish) has minimal effect on drugs-

of-abuse testing by the FPIA assay. Moreover, toilet bowl cleaner can be easily detected in urine by specimen integrity testing because it produces a low urinary pH (Table 10-1).

Lime solvent: Lime solvent is concentrated acidic cleaner for tile surfaces and dark-colored bricks. Lime solvent causes a false negative with the FPIA assay for THC metabolite. The lime in the lime solvent in urine is detected by observing low urinary pH.

Sodium bicarbonate ($NaHCO_3$) and sodium hypochlorite ($NaHClO_4$): The presence of sodium bicarbonate in a sufficient amount in urine invalidates the EMIT assay for opiates and also the FPIA assay for phencyclidine. Sodium hypochlorite affects the EMIT assays for amphetamines, opiates, phencyclidine, benzodiazepine, and marijuana metabolite. Screening of amphetamine, opiates, phencyclidine, and marijuana metabolite using the FPIA assays is also affected.[5] Bicarbonate has no effect on CEDIA assays for drugs of abuse.[4] Baiker et al reported that hypochlorite (a common ingredient of household bleach) adulteration of urine causes a decreased concentration of marijuana metabolites (THC-COOH) as measured by GC/MS. They also observed a false-negative result with the FPIA screen as well as the Abuscreen (Roche Diagnostic Systems, Inc., Branchburg, NJ).[6]

However, the presence of sodium bicarbonate in urine causes a suspiciously high pH, and the presence of sodium hypochlorite lowers the pH significantly below the acceptable physiological limit (Table 10-1).

Denture-cleaning tablets (sodium perborate): Denture-cleaning tablets can be used as a urinary adulterant. One published report indicates that a tablet for cleaning dentures (Steradent) that contains 1.5%

sodium perborate and various salts can invalidate immunoassays for screening drugs. When a powdered denture-cleaning tablet was added to urine at a concentration of 1.0 gm/ML, tests for benzoylecgonine (cocaine metabolite), 3,4-methylenedioxy-methamphetamine (MDMA), and marijuana using the FPIA assays (Abbott Laboratories, Abbott Park, IL) were significantly affected, causing false-negative results. At the lowest concentration of denture tablet tested (0.1 gm/mL), assays for MDMA and marijuana metabolite were affected moderately. The magnitude of the effect of denture tablets in causing false-negative test results with these three drugs depends on the concentration of the adulterant. The possible mechanism is oxidation of the drug or metabolite by sodium perborate. Moreover, the high salt concentration of the tablets also interferes with the immunoassay. Adulteration with sodium perborate is easily detected by a qualitative test using a tumeric reagent.[7]

Hydrogen peroxide: Hydrogen peroxide causes false-positive results with the FPIA assay for benzodiazepines. Some effects (like false positives) may also be observed with the FPIA assay for marijuana metabolite.[5,8]

Concentrated lemon juice: Concentrated lemon juice usually has a minimal effect on drugs-of-abuse testing by immunoassays. The presence of concentrated lemon juice can be easily detected in a urine specimen by the specimen integrity test: the pH is usually on the acidic side (pH of 4 or less) (Table 10-1).

Ascorbic acid (vitamin C): Ascorbic acid can invalidate the assay of marijuana metabolite using the FPIA (producing false-negative results). Ascorbic acid causes false-positive results with creatine analysis using the assay kit available from Abbott Laboratories (Abbott Park, IL). However, in the presence of ascorbic acid the urine may also show low pH (acidic).

Goldenseal root tea: Goldenseal root tea causes a dark appearance of urine and is easily detected by visual inspection. Goldenseal tea interferes with CEDIA assays for the screening of amphetamine and marijuana metabolites in urine.[4]

Visine eye drops: The ability of Visine eye drop to cause false-negative drug tests in the screening phase of the analysis is troublesome. Neither routine specimen integrity testing nor any routine urine analysis is able to detect their presence. Pearson et al studied the effect of Visine eye drops on drugs-of-abuse testing as well as the mechanism by which components of the eye drops produce false-negative drug-testing results.[9] Visine eye drops are effective in causing false-negative results in the analysis of the THC metabolite 11-nor-9-carboxy-Δ^9-tetrahydrocannabinol (Table 10-3). The GC/MS analysis showed that there was no modification in the structure of marijuana metabolite (THC-COOH) by the components of the eye drops. At low concentrations of eye drops, the false-negative cannabinoid result was due to the benzalkonium chloride, an active ingredient of Visine. Visine decreased the THC assay results in both EMIT-d.a.u. assays and the FPIA (Abbott Laboratories, Abbott Park, IL), although Visine had no effect on the glucose 6-phosphate dehydrogenase-drug conjugate used in the EMIT assay. Results of ultrafiltration studies with Visine eye drops suggest that the THC metabolite partitions between the aqueous solvent and the hydrophobic interior of benzalkonium chloride micelles, thus reducing the availability of THC metabolite in antibody-based assays.[8] Visine eye drops and analgesic ointment (e.g., BenGay) can also cause false-negative results with sweat testing.[10] The components of eye drops in urine may be detected by using high-performance liquid chromatography combined with ultraviolet detection at 262 nm, a method originally developed for analysis of ophthalmic formulations.[11]

Ethyl alcohol (alcohol) and isopropanol: Uebel and Wium reported that addition of alcohol or isopropanol to a urine specimen in any concentration (5%, 10%, 20%, or 40%) invalidates the EMIT assay for methaqualone.[8]

Topical antiseptic: The topical antiseptic Dettol is popular in India, some Asian countries, and South Africa. Dettol's active ingredient, chloroxylenol, interferes strongly with the EMIT assays for methaqualone and marijuana metabolite.[8]

Schwarzhoff and Cody conducted a comprehensive study investigating the effect of 16 different adulterating agents: ammonia-based cleaner, L-ascorbic acid, Visine eye drops, Drano drain cleaner, goldenseal root, lemon juice, lime solvent, Clorox bleach, liquid hand soap, methanol, sodium chloride, tribasic potassium phosphate, toilet bowl cleaner (e.g., Vanish), white vinegar, ionic detergent, and whole blood anticoagulated with ethylenediamine tetraacetic acid (EDTA) on FPIA analysis of urine for abused drugs. The authors tested these adulterating agents at a urine concentration of 10% by volume, with the exception of goldenseal, because of its insolubility. For goldenseal root tea, one capsule was suspended in 60 mL urine. Out of six drugs tested (cocaine metabolites, amphetamines, opiates, phencyclidine, cannabinoid, and barbiturates), the cannabinoid test was found to be the most susceptible to adulteration. Approximately half of the agents (ascorbic acid, vinegar, bleach, lime solvent, Visine eye drops, goldenseal) that were tested caused false negatives. Both cannabinoid and opiate assays were susceptible to bleach, and actual degradation of THC was confirmed by GC/MS analysis. The PCP and benzoylecgonine (BE, the metabolite of cocaine) analyses were affected by alkaline agents.[12]

CONCLUSION

Although many readily available household chemicals can be added in vitro after the collection of urine specimens for invalidating drugs-of-abuse testing, most of these adulterants can be readily detected in urine by routine specimen integrity tests (measuring temperature, pH, creatinine, and specific gravity). Because routine tests for specimen integrity are mandated, such readily available household chemicals do not pose a threat to invalidate drug tests. Unfortunately, eye drops are the only over-the-counter product that, if added in sufficient amount to a urine specimen, can invalidate drugs-of-abuse testing by EMIT assays. However, other screening assays, such as the FPIA assay, are less affected by the presence of eye drops in a specimen.

REFERENCES

1. Milkkelsen SL, Ash KO. Adulterants causing false negatives in illicit drug testing. *Clin Chem.* 1988;34:2333–2336.

2. Burrows DL, Nicolaides A, Rice PJ, Duforc M, Johnson DA, Ferslew KE. Papain: a novel urine adulterant. *J Anal Toxicol.* 2005;29:275–295.

3. Moeller KE, Lee KC, Kissack JC. Urine drug screening: practical guide for clinicians. *Mayo Clin Proc.* 2008;83:66–76.

4. Wu AH, Forte E, Casella G, et al. CEDIA for screening drugs of abuse in urine and the effect of adulterants. *J Forensic Sci.* 1995;40:614–618.

5. Warner A. Interference of household chemicals in immunoassay methods for drugs of abuse. *Clin Chem*. 1989;35:648–651.

6. Baiker C, Serrano L, Lindner B. Hypochlorite adulteration of urine causing decreased concentration of delta-9-THC-COOH by GC/MS. *J Anal Toxicol*. 1994;18:101–103.

7. Stolk LM, Scheijen JL. Urine adulteration with denture cleaning tablets [Letter]. *J Anal Toxicol*. 1997;21:403.

8. Uebel RA, Wium CA. Toxicological screening for drugs of abuse in samples adulterated with household chemicals. *S Afr Med J*. 2002;92:547–549.

9. Pearson SD, Ash KO, Urry FM. Mechanism of false negative urine cannabinoid immunoassay screens by Visine eye drops. *Clin Chem*. 1989;35:636–638.

10. Fogerson R, Schoendorfer D, Fay J, Spiehler V. Qualitative detection of opiates in sweat by EIAS and GC-MS. *J Anal Toxicol*. 1997;21:451-458.

11. Rojsitthisak P, Wichitnithad W, Pipitharome O, Sanphanya K, Thanawattanawanich P. Simple HPLC determination of benzalkonium chloride in ophthalmic formulations containing antazoline and tetrahydrozoline. *PDA J Pharm Sci Technol*. 2005;59:323–327.

12. Schwarzhoff, R, Cody, JT. The effects of adulterating agents on FPIA analysis of urine for drugs of abuse. *J Anal Toxicol*. 1993;17:14–17.

CHAPTER 11

Urine Luck, Klear, Urine Aid, Stealth, and Related Urinary Adulterants

ABSTRACT

Several adulterants are commercially available through the Internet or toll-free telephone numbers for the purpose of beating drug tests. Conventional urine specimen integrity testing (pH, temperature, specific gravity, and creatinine) is unable to detect the presence of these products in urine. These adulterants contain strong oxidizing agents and are capable of invalidating drugs-of-abuse tests by destroying drug metabolites present in the urine. However, toxicology laboratories have tests that allow them to identify these adulterants. Several states have banned the possession or sale of adulteration products. Individuals who attempt to defraud drug-testing procedures face misdemeanor charges.

Popular Internet sites sell products they claim are tested and proven to help people pass drug tests. Drug users have a wide choice of products that make use of a variety of chemicals. These products pose a considerable challenge to drug-testing laboratories because they can not be detected in urine by routine specimen integrity testing of temperature, specific gravity, pH, and creatinine. Laboratories must perform special spot tests or urine dipstick tests to identify the presence of such adulterants in urine. Failure to detect such adulterants may invalidate drugs-of-abuse testing.

Table 11-1 lists the most common commercially available products.

Currently, 15 states have laws restricting the sale or use of these adulterating products (**Table 11-2**). As early as 1988 Nebraska passed a law to prevent drug-testing fraud. New Jersey and North Carolina passed similar laws in 2002, as did Arkansas and Maryland in 2003. In 2007 Wyoming made it illegal to possess, manufacture, or sell adulteration products or attempt to defraud a drug test by any means.

Table 11-1 Commercially Available Urinary Adulterants			
Urinary Adulterant	**Composition**	**Price**	**Detection Method**
Urine Luck	Pyridinium chlorochromate	$25–32	Spot test, dipstick
LL-418	Pyridinium chlorochromate	$30	Spot test, dipstick
Randy's Klear II	Pyridinium chlorochromate	$20–35	Spot test, dipstick
Klear	Potassium nitrite	$25–30	Spot test, dipstick
Whizzies	Potassium nitrite	$25–30	Spot test, dipstick
Randy's Klear	Potassium nitrite	$30–40	Spot test, dipstick
UrinAid	Glutaraldehyde	$30	Spot test, dipstick
Instant Clean ADD-IT-ive	Glutaraldehyde	$35–40	Spot test, dipstick
Clear Choice	Glutaraldehyde	$30	Spot test, dipstick
Amber-13	Strong inorganic acid	Low pH (< 3)	
THC-Free	Strong inorganic acid	Low pH (< 3)	

OXIDIZING AGENTS

Wu et al reported on the popular adulteration product Urine Luck (Spectrum Labs, Cincinnati, OH; $35). The active ingredient of Urine Luck is pyridinium chlorochromate (PCC), a strong oxidizing agent. The product is meant to be added directly to a urine specimen (60–90 ml) in order to invalidate a drug test. The manufacturer claims that its new, advanced formula is undetectable by laboratory tests and that it destroys drugs in urine, thus invalidating even GC/MS confirmation of drug tests. Wu et al observed the presence of this adulterant in 2 out of 50 specimens submitted under the chain of custody for workplace drug testing in their laboratory. Pyridinium chlorochromate at a concentration of 100 g/l caused significant decreases in response rate for all EMIT II drug screens, indicating the possibility of false-negative results. In contrast, for the Abuscreen test (Abbott Laboratories, Abbott Park, IL) only morphine and THC metabolite (11-nor-9-carboxy-Δ^9-tetrahydrocannabi-

Table 11-2 States That Have Taken Legal Steps Against Adulteration and Drug Fraud	
Florida	Oklahoma
Illinois	Oregon
Kentucky	Pennsylvania
Louisiana	South Carolina
Maryland	Texas
Nebraska	Virginia
New Jersey	Wyoming
North Carolina	

nol; THC-COOH) assays were affected. The authors observed no effect of PCC on the results of benzoylecgonine (cocaine metabolite) and phencyclidine (PCP) using the Abuscreen assay. However, a false-positive result was observed with the amphetamine assays. The presence of Urine Luck did not alter GC/MS confirmation of methamphetamine, benzoylecgonine, and PCP, but the validity of GC/MS test results for opiates

Table 11-3 Effects of Commercially Available Adulterants on Drugs-of-Abuse Tests	
Urinary Adulterants	**Test Affected**
Urine Luck	THC-COOH; opiate (FPIA, EMIT, CEDIA, KIMS)
Randy's Klear II	EMIT (all assays); THC-COOH; false-negative result by GC/MS
Klear, Whizzies	THC-COOH (FPIA, EMIT, CEDIA, KIMS)
Randy's Klear	THC-COOH; false-negative result by GC/MS
Stealth	THC-COOH; opiate (FPIA, EMIT, CEDIA, KIMS)
UrinAid	EMIT; CEDIA (all tests); some effect on FPIA
Instant Clean ADD-IT-ive	Some false-positive PCP tests by KIMS and FPIA
Iodine	6-monocaetylmorphine and morphine; some effect on THC-COOH

Abbreviations: EMIT, enzyme multiplied immunoassay (Syva, Dade Behring, Deerfield, IL); FPIA, fluorescence polarization immunoassay (Abbott Laboratories, Abbott Park, IL); CEDIA, cloned enzyme donor immunoassay (Microgenics Corporation, Fremont, CA); KIMS, kinetic interaction of microparticles in solution (Roche Diagnostics, Indianapolis, IN)

and THC metabolites was significantly reduced.[1] In summary, Urine Luck had the greatest effects on the opiate and THC-COOH assays (**Table 11-3**).

Paul et al also studied the effect of Urine Luck on tests for drugs of abuse. The authors treated urine specimens containing THC-COOH with 2 mmol/l of PCC, which reduced the THC-COOH concentrations by 58% to 100% of the initial concentrations. The loss increased with decreasing pH, and more loss of THC-COOH was observed with increasing time of incubation (0–3 days). The authors also reported significant reductions in free morphine concentrations if the pH of the urine was below 7.0. The concentrations of amphetamine, methamphetamine, benzoylecgonine, and PCP were unaffected in the presence of pyridinium chlorochromate at urinary pH between 3.0 and 7.0.[2]

Similar adulterants available through the Internet (such as Clear Choice, Lucky Lab LL 418, Randy's Klear II, and Sweet Pea's Spoiler) also contain pyridinium chlorochromate and have similar effects on drugs-of-abuse testing to those of Urine Luck. Table 11-1 summarizes the effects of readily available adulterants on drugs-of-abuse tests.

Pyridinium chlorochromate is a strong oxidizing agent. It is a yellow crystalline solid and when present in urine produces a dark yellow color. However, visual inspection alone is not enough to identify PCC in urine because very concentrated urine may also appear dark yellow. Wu et al described the protocol for detection of pyridinium chlorochromate in urine using a simple spot test using 1,5-diphenylcarbazide in methanol (10 g/l). The 1,5-diphenylcarbazide solution in methanol is colorless, but in the presence of chromium ion, a reddish purple color develops. This spot test is not specific for the presence of chromate because molybdenum, mercury, and vanadium salts may also produce positive results. However, it is unlikely that such high amounts of these compounds would be present in a normal urine sample.[1]

Dasgupta et al also developed a simple spot test for detecting PCC in adulterated urine. Addition of a few drops of hydrogen peroxide (3% solution available commercially in drug stores) to approximately 0.5 mL of urine specimen causes immediate development of a dark brown color and dark brown precipitate if PCC is present in the urine. If no PCC is present, the urine turns colorless. Moreover, being a strong oxidizing agent, PCC can also liberate iodine from potassium iodide solution in acidic medium, and this reaction can be used in a laboratory setting for detecting PCC as an adulterant in the urine.[3]

NITRITE-CONTAINING AGENTS

The chemical nitrite can also invalidate drug testing. It is available in the commercial products Klear and Whizzies. Klear (which usually sells for $35) is supplied in two small tubes containing 500 mg of white crystalline material. Both products readily dissolve in urine without affecting color or temperature and have no effect on the specimen integrity tests.

ElSohly et al first reported that Klear contains potassium nitrite and provided evidence that nitrite leads to decomposition of THC-COOH and its internal standard (Table 11-3). The authors found that using a bisulfite step at the beginning of sample preparation could eliminate this problem.[4]

Tsai et al further investigated the effects of nitrite on immunoassay screenings of five abused drugs: benzoylecgonine (cocaine metabolite), morphine, THC metabolites (THC-COOH), amphetamine, and phency-

clidine. Nitrite at a concentration of 1.0 m had no effect on the Abuscreen assays. At a higher nitrite concentration, the amphetamine assay was more sensitive (causing a false positive), and the THC-COOH assay was less sensitive (causing a false negative). The GC/MS analyses of benzoylecgonine, morphine, amphetamine, and phencyclidine were not affected.[5]

Both duration of nitrite exposure and the urine matrix also have significant effects on the THC-COOH assay. In an in vitro study, 40 urine specimens confirmed positive for THC-COOH were supplemented with 1.15 or 0.30 m nitrite. The results indicated that the pH of the urine and the original drug concentrations are major factors in determining the effectiveness of nitrite in causing false-negative THC-COOH tests. With acidic pH, significant decreases in the immunoassay screening results were observed in all urine specimens within 4 hours of adulteration with nitrite regardless of original concentrations of THC-COOH (range of concentrations 33–488 ng/ml, as determined by GC/MS). All specimens were negative for THC-COOH after 24 hours. In contrast, the immunoassay results of urine specimens with basic or neutral pH were less affected by nitrite exposure. Approximately two-thirds of the samples with pH values greater than 7.0 were immunoassay positive even three days after supplementing with nitrite.[6]

Other commercially available adulterants contain sodium nitrite and other similar products, including the popular Whizzies as well as Randy's Klear, Purafyzit, Krystal Klean, and Urine Clear. These adulterants all sell for about $35 (Table 11-1).

Nitrite in urine may arise in vivo and is found in urine in low concentration. Prescription medications such as nitroglycerin, isosorbide dinitrate, nitroprusside, and ranitidine may cause increased nitrite levels in the blood. However, concentrations of nitrite were below 36 µg/ml in specimens cultured positive for microorganisms, and nitrite concentrations were below 6 µg/ml in patients receiving medications that are metabolized to nitrite. In contrast, nitrite concentrations were 1910 to 12,200 µg/ml in urine specimens adulterated with nitrite.[7] Although adulteration of urine specimens with nitrite may destroy THC-COOH, resulting in false-negative test results in both the immunoassay screening and GC/MS confirmation, the nitrite concentrations in urine that might arise from all possible natural sources—including microorganisms, pathological conditions, or medications—do not affect the analysis of THC-COOH by either immunoassays or GC/MS confirmation.[5]

The presence of nitrite in urine can be easily detected by simple spot tests. Addition of a few drops of a nitrite-adulterated urine specimen to 0.5 ml of 1% potassium permanganate solution, followed by the addition of a few drops of 2N hydrochloric acid, turns the pink permanganate solution colorless with effervescence. Another spot test to detect nitrite uses 1% potassium iodide solution. Addition of a few drops of nitrite-adulterated urine to 0.5 ml of potassium iodide solution, followed by addition of a few drops of 2N hydrochloric acid, results in immediate release of iodine from the colorless potassium iodide solution. If any organic solvent, such as hexane, is added the iodine is readily transferred in the organic layer, giving the layer a distinct color of iodine. If no nitrite is present, the potassium iodide solution remains colorless. There is no interference from high glucose or ketone bodies if present in the urine.[3] Nitrite can also be detected by diazotizing sulfanilamide and coupling the product with N-(1-napthyl) ethylenediamine.

PEROXIDASE

Peroxidase is another chemical that provides an effective way for a drug user to pass a urine drug test. It is available in a product called Stealth (which sells for $42). Stealth consists of two vials, one containing a powder (the peroxidase) and another containing a liquid (hydrogen peroxide). Both products are added to the urine specimen. Stealth is capable of invalidating both Roche OnLine assays (Roche Diagnostics, Indianapolis, IN) and CEDIA assays (Microgenics Corporation, Fremont, CA) for THC-COOH, lysergic acid diethylamide (LSD), and opiates (as morphine) if these drugs or their metabolites are present in modest concentrations (125%–150% of cutoff values) (Table 11-3). Cody and Valtier further found that adding Stealth to an authentic positive sample provided by a marijuana user caused that sample to screen negative.[8]

Stealth is also capable of producing a false-negative screening test if morphine is present in modest concentration (2500 ng/ml). However, specimens containing higher concentrations of morphine (> 6000 ng/ml) tested positive by both immunoassays (Roche OnLine and Microgenics CEDIA). Confirmation by GC/MS can be affected if Stealth is present in the urine. Cody et al reported that GC/MS analysis of Stealth-adulterated urine using standard procedures proved unsuccessful in several cases, and in 4 out of 12 cases neither the drug nor the internal standard was recovered.[9]

Valtier and Cody described a rapid color test to detect the presence of Stealth in urine. Addition of 10 µl of urine to 50 µl of Tetramethylbenzidine (TMB) working solution, followed by addition of 500 µl of 0.1 m phosphate buffer solution, caused a dramatic color change of the specimen to dark brown. Peroxidase activity can also be monitored with a spectrophotometer. Routine specimen integrity testing of pH, creatinine, specific gravity, and temperature did not detect the presence of Stealth in urine.[10] Our investigation shows that if a few drops of a urine specimen adulterated with Stealth are added to potassium dichromate followed by few drops of 2N hydrochloric acid, a deep blue color develops immediately, which usually fades with time.

GLUTARALDEHYDE

Glutaraldehyde, first marketed in the 1990s under the brand name UrinAid, is also used to invalidate drugs-of-abuse testing. Several commercially available adulterants contain glutaraldehyde. UrinAid contains 4 to 5 ml of glutaraldehyde solution, which should be added to 50 to 60 ml of urine after collection. Instant Clean ADD-IT-ive, another urinary adulterant available through the Internet, also contains glutaraldehyde, while Clear Choice contains glutaraldehyde and squalene. Glutaraldehyde solutions are also available in hospitals and clinics as cleaning or sterilizing agents. A 10% solution of glutaraldehyde is available from pharmacies as over-the-counter medication for treatment of warts.

Glutaraldehyde inhibits the enzymes used in the EMIT II drugs-of-abuse assays, thus invalidating all drugs-of-abuse testing by this method. Urine specimens adulterated with glutaraldehyde demonstrate strong negative absorbance readings (final absorbance reading after incubation lower than the initial absorbance), which should alert the technologist performing the screening assays that something is wrong with the specimen. Urine specimens adulterated with glutaraldehyde also smell like ripe fruits or vegetables, like a very ripe apple or pumpkin.

Glutaraldehyde at a concentration of 0.75% volume can lead to false-negative screening results for a cannabinoid test using the EMIT II drugs-of-abuse screen. Amphetamine, methadone, benzodiazepine, opiate, and cocaine metabolite tests can be affected at glutaraldehyde concentration between 1% and 2% using EMIT II immunoassays. At a concentration of 2% by volume, the assay of benzoylecgonine (cocaine metabolite) is significantly affected (apparent loss of 90% sensitivity). Similarly, a loss of 80% sensitivity was also observed with the benzodiazepine assay.[11]

Wu et al reported that glutaraldehyde interfered strongly with most drugs-of-abuse assays using the CEDIA immunoassay method.[12] Goldberger and Caplan evaluated the effect of glutaraldehyde on testing of five abused drugs (amphetamines, THC-COOH, benzoylecgonine, opiate. and phencyclidine) using 15 drug-positive and 15 drug-negative urine specimens for each drug. The authors reported that glutaraldehyde caused false-negative results with EMIT assays in approximately 58% of the specimens, while 15% of the results were invalid using the fluorescence polarization immunoassay (FPIA, Abbott Laboratories, Abbott Park, IL) because of an increase in background fluorescence and failure to pipette grossly abnormal specimens. In contrast, 76% of specimens negative for phencyclidine produced positive test results with the FPIA, and 96% of specimens negative for phencyclidine produced false-positive results with a kinetic interaction of microparticles in solution immunoassay (KIMS; Roche Diagnostics, Indianapolis, IN). Amphetamine produced variable results in the presence of glutaraldehyde using the KIMS assay.[13]

Wu et al described a simple fluorometric method for the detection of glutaraldehyde in urine. When 0.5 ml of urine was heated with 1.0 mL of 7.7 mmol/l potassium dihydrogen phosphate (pH 3.0) saturated with diethylthiobarbituric acid for 1 hour at 96° to 98°C in a heating block, a yellow green fluorophore developed if glutaraldehyde was present. Shaking the specimen with n-butanol resulted in the transfer of this adduct to the organic layer, which can be viewed under long-wavelength ultraviolet light. Glutaraldehyde in urine can also be estimated using a fluorometer.[14]

OTHER URINARY ADULTERANTS

Mary Jane Super Clean 13 is a detergent and surfactant used for invalidating drug testing. Surfactant can invalidate the testing of THC-COOH because it can shield the marijuana metabolite from reacting with antibody utilized in the assay. The lipophilic nature of marijuana metabolite may cause this drug metabolite to migrate inside the micelles formed because of the presence of surfactant/detergent in the urine specimen. However, the presence of such an adulterant may cause a soapy specimen, a red flag that the integrity of the specimen has been compromised.

Before 1998, Urine Luck was composed of a solution of strong hydrochloric acid. Two other products available for invalidating drug tests, Amber-13 and THC-Free, are also made up of a strong solution of hydrochloric acid. These products can interfere with the immunoassay screening step of drugs-of-abuse testing because immunoassays are very sensitive to the pH of the matrix and usually perform well within the normal physiological pH of urine (pH 4–9). However, routine integrity tests easily detect the presence of such adulterants in urine specimens because the pH levels of the adulterated specimens are abnormally low (< 3).

Iodine, a strong oxidizing agent, can be used as a urinary adulterant because it destroys morphine and 6-monoacetylmorphine (heroin metabolite) almost immediately. The effect of iodine is less significant on THC-COOH. Iodine is a particularly effective way to beat a morphine drug test because it can mask the drug and still remain undetected. Iodine can not be detected in the urine specimen because it is converted to iodide. Iodine is poorly soluble in water, but it dissolves in a solution of potassium iodide. Paul and Jacobs described a spectrophotometric method for detection of iodide in adulterated urine after oxidation to iodine. They showed that iodide in urine is oxidized by sodium nitrite to iodine. Excess sodium nitrite is destroyed by sulfamic acid, and iodine can be detected by chromogenic substrate ABTS [2,2'-azino-bis(3-ethylbenzthiazoline-6-sulfonic acid)].[15]

MECHANISM OF ACTION OF ADULTERANTS

Strong oxidizing agents, like Klear (potassium nitrite), Urine Luck (pyridinium chloro-chromate), and Stealth (peroxidase and hydrogen peroxide), cause false-negative results in the immunoassays used for screening drugs by directly destroying THC metabolites (THC-COOH). These adulterants interfere with both the confirmation phase and the extraction phase of THC-COOH because they destroy THC-COOH and the internal standard. Use of reducing agents such as sodium hydrosulfite or sulfamic acid prior to extraction will overcome this problem.[16] Unfortunately, although this step can allow detection of remaining THC-COOH, it can not recover the lost concentration of the marijuana metabolite from the point of specimen collection to analysis.

Most oxidizing agents used as adulterants are more effective if the pH of urine is acidic. To prevent destruction of drugs by oxidizing agents, addition of carbonate as a buffering agent prior to or after urine void has been recommended.[17] Other oxidizing agents such as potassium permanganate, hydrogen peroxide/ferrous ammonium sulfate, periodic acid, potassium persulfate, and sodium oxychloride can also destroy THC-COOH within 48 hours. The effect of oxidizing agents on THC-COOH primarily depends on the reduction potential (E°), pH, temperature, time of reaction, and urine constituents. Horseradish peroxidase along with hydrogen peroxide (Stealth), as well as a combination of hydrogen peroxide and Japanese radish, black mustard seed, and red radish, can destroy THC-COOH in urine specimens.[18]

Adulterants can also interfere with the extraction process. Stealth is known to interfere with the extraction of codeine and morphine for GC/MS confirmation. Our experience indicates that PCC is effective in decreasing the semi-quantitative response rate for THC and opiates using FPIA. The incubation time played an important role in decreasing the response rate. Nitrite is very effective in reducing the response rate of THC, but the PCP assay is also affected.

IDENTIFYING ADULTERATED SPECIMENS

Laboratory professionals have various means at their disposal to identify adulterated specimens. Moreover, both state and federal governments are stepping up protocols to prevent drug test fraud. In our experience fewer than 2% of urine specimens submitted for pre-employment drug testing are adulterated. After Texas made it illegal to sell or possess adulteration products to invalidate drug tests, we have not observed any nitrite- or chromated adulterated urine. The most common adulterant we have observed in our laboratory is the smell of bleach in urine specimens.

Federal guidelines require additional tests for urine specimens with abnormal physical characteristics. A laboratory is allowed to report a urine specimen as adulterated when both the initial and confirmatory test results (i.e., tests on separate aliquots) meet the following criteria:[19]

- The pH of a urine specimen is less than 3 or greater than 11.

- The concentration of nitrite in urine is equal to or greater than 500 μg/ml.

- Chromium (VI) is present and verified by a specific confirmation step.

- Glutaraldehyde is present and verified by GC/MS.

- Pyridine (pyridinium chlorochromate) is present and confirmed by GC/MS.

- A surfactant is present and the dodecylbenzene sulfonate equivalent concentration is greater than or equal to 100 μg/ml.

- The specimen contains a substance that is not a normal constituent of urine. The presence of the substance should be verified by a specific confirmatory test.

- The specimen contains an endogenous substance at much higher concentration than expected from normal physiological process. The presence of the endogenous substance must be confirmed by an appropriate confirmatory test.

URINE DIPSTICKS TO DETECT URINARY ADULTERANTS

Although federal guidelines require specific tests for identifying adulterated specimens for SAMHSA-certified laboratories, standard urinalysis test strips such as Multistix from Bayer Diagnostics and Combur-Test from Roche Diagnostics, which are routinely used in clinical laboratories as a part of urinalysis protocol, also can be used to detect the presence of various adulterants. Cody and Valtier reported that urine specimens adulterated with Stealth showed strong positive response for glucose, blood, and nitrite. The glucose reaction in the dipstick is a peroxidase-based couple reaction, and Stealth has peroxidase and hydrogen peroxide, which react with this agent. Blood tests are also based on peroxidase activity. Moreover, Stealth is capable of converting any urinary nitrate to nitrite, which then reacts with the nitrite reaction pad in the dipstick.[8] In our experience, nitrite-adulterated urine not only produces a strong response to nitrite in the dipstick but also shows strong response to the glucose pad. Specimen adulterated with pyridinium chlorochromate also shows strong response with glucose.

On-site adulterant detection devices are now commercially available. These dipstick devices offer an advantage over spot tests because an adulteration check can be performed at the collection site. Peace and Tarani evaluated the performance of three on-site devices, Intect 7 (Branan Medical Corporation, Irvine, CA), MASK Ultrascreen (Kacey, Asheville, NC) and AdultaCheck 4 (Sciteck Diagnostics, Arden, NC). Intect 7 can simultaneously test for creatinine, nitrite, glutaraldehyde, pH, specific gravity, PCC, and bleach. Ultrascreen tests for creatinine, nitrite, pH, specific gravity, and oxidants. AdultaCheck 4 tests creatinine, nitrite, glutaraldehyde, and pH. The authors adulterated urine specimens with Stealth, Urine Luck, Instant Clean ADD-IT-ive, and Klear at their optimum usage concentrations and concluded that Intect 7 was the most sensitive of the group and identified adulterants correctly. AdultaCheck 4 did not detect Stealth, Urine Luck, or Instant Clean ADD-IT-ive. Ultrascreen detected a broader range of adulterants than AdultaCheck 4. However, in practice, it detected these adulterants only at levels well above their normal usage, making it less effective than Intect 7 for identifying adulterated urine specimens.[20] In our experience, AdultaCheck 6 and Intect 7 are equally effective in identifying adulterated specimens.[21]

Urine specimen validity (adulteration) test dipsticks are also available from Craig Medical Distribution (Vista, CA). This test strip detects creatinine, nitrite, glutaraldehyde, pH, specific gravity, and oxidants. Another dipstick product, AdultaCheck 10 (Sciteck Diagnostics, Arden, NC), has 10 test pads providing tests for specific gravity, pH (abnormal range 2–12), pH (normal range 5–9), oxidants (including but not limited to Urine Luck, Stealth, Stealth 51, nitrite, and chromate), creatinine, nitrite, aldehyde (including glutaraldehyde), chromate, peroxidase (peroxidase and similar compounds), and halogens (including chlorine and bromine).

LEGAL IMPLICATIONS OF ADULTERATED SPECIMENS

According to federal guidelines, the medical review officer (MRO) is required to contact an individual who produces an adulterated specimen to give him or her an opportunity to explain why the specimen was adulterated. The individual needs to

A Case Study[22]

A laboratory reported that a urine specimen was adulterated with nitrite and the concentration of nitrite was 850μg/mL. Federal guidelines identify an adulterated specimen as having nitrite concentration equal to above 500μg/mL. During the interview with the MRO, the person who submitted the urine specimen claimed to have been eating cured meats for dinner. However, eating nitrite-containing food could not cause such a high amount of nitrite in urine. Because the person did not have a legitimate explanation for such a high amount of nitrite in the urine, the MRO reported the case as "Refusal to Test (Adulterated— Nitrite 850 μg/ml)."

provide convincing evidence that adulteration (for example, high nitrite content of the urine) actually originated from a normal physiological process, such as taking a nitrite-containing medication. In reality the criteria for adulterated specimens prove adulteration, and there can be no other valid medical explanation.[19] From a legal point of view, submitting an adulterated specimen is equivalent to "refusal to test," which will be the written report on the drug test results.

CONCLUSION

Products are available through the Internet and toll-free telephone numbers for the purpose of invalidating drugs-of-abuse testing. These products are composed of glutaraldehyde, nitrite, or chromate. The presence of the product Urine Luck (pyridinium chlorochromate) renders the urine specimen dark yellow, while other products do not change the color of urine.

Although the presence of such adulterants can not be detected by routine specimen integrity tests (temperature, pH, creatinine, and specific gravity), inexpensive spot tests and specially designed urine dipsticks are available for identifying such adulterants. If an adulterant is detected in a specimen, the laboratory will record the result as "refusal to test."

REFERENCES

1. Wu A, Bristol B, Sexton K, Cassella-McLane G, Holtman V, Hill DW. Adulteration of urine by Urine Luck. *Clin Chem.* 1999; 45,1051–1057.

2. Paul BD, Martin KK, Maguilo J, Smith ML. Effects of pyridinium chlorochromate adulterant (Urine Luck) on testing of drugs of abuse and a method for quantitative detection of chromium (VI) in urine. *J Anal Toxicol.* 2000;24:233–237.

3. Dasgupta A, Wahed A, Wells A. Rapid spot tests for detecting the presence of adulterants in urine specimens submitted for drug testing. *Am J Clin Pathol.* 2002; 117:325–329.

4. ElSohly MA, Feng S, Kopycki WJ, et al. A procedure to overcome interferences caused by adulterant "Klear" in the GC-MS analysis of 11-nor-Δ^9-THC-9-COOH. *J Anal Toxicol.* 1997;20:240–242.

5. Tsai SC, ElSohly MA, Dubrovsky T, Twarowska B, Towt J, Salamone SJ. Determination of five abused drugs in nitrite-adulterated urine by immunoassay and gas chromatography-mass spectrometry. *J Anal Toxicol.* 1998;22:474–480.

6. Tsai LS, ElSohly MA, Tsai SF, Murphy TO, Twarowska B, Salamone SJ. Investigation of nitrite adulteration on the immunoassay and GC-MS analysis of cannabinoids in urine specimens. *J Anal Toxicol.* 2000;24: 708–714.

7. Urry F, Komaromy-Hiller G, Staley B, et al. Nitrite adulteration of workplace drug testing specimens: sources and associated

concentrations of nitrite and distinction between natural sources and adulteration. *J Anal Toxicol.* 1998;22:89–95.

8. Cody JT, Valtier S. Effects of Stealth adulteration on immunoassay testing for drugs of abuse. *J Anal Toxicol.* 2001;25:466–470.

9. Cody JT, Valtier S, Kuhlman J. Analysis of morphine and codeine in samples adulterated with Stealth. *J Anal Toxicol.* 2001;25: 572–575.

10. Valtier S, Cody JT. A procedure for the detection of Stealth adulterant in urine samples. *Clin Lab Sci.* 2002;15:111–115.

11. George S, Braithwaite RA. The effect of glutaraldehyde adulteration of urine specimens on Syva EMIT II drugs of abuse assay. *J Anal Toxicol.* 1996;20:195–196.

12. Wu AH, Forte E, Casella G, et al. CEDIA for screening drugs of abuse in urine and the effect of adulterants. *J Forensic Sci.* 1995;40:614–618.

13. Goldberger BA, Caplan YH. Effect of glutaraldehyde (UrinAid) on detection of abused drugs in urine by immunoassay [Letter]. *Clin Chem.* 1994;40:1605–1606.

14. Wu A, Schmalz J, Bennett W. Identification of Urin-Aid adulterated urine specimens by fluorometric analysis [letter]. *Clin Chem.* 1994;40:845–846.

15. Paul B, Jacobs A. Spectrophotometric detection of iodide and chromic (III) in urine after oxidation to iodine and chromate (VI). *J Anal Toxicol.* 2005;29:658–663.

16. Cody JT, Schwarzhoff RH. Impact of adulterants on RIA analysis of urine for drugs of abuse. *J Anal Toxicol.* 1989;13:277–284.

17. Lewis SA, Lewis LA, Tuinman A. Potassium nitrite reaction to 11-nor-Δ^9-tetrahydrocannabinol-9-carboxylic acid in urine in relation to the drug screening analysis. *J Forensic Sci.* 1999;44:951–955.

18. Paul BD, Jacobs A. Effects of oxidizing adulterants on detection of 11-nor-Δ^9-THC-9-carboxylic acid in urine. *J Anal Toxicol.* 2002;26:460–463.

19. U.S. Department of Heath and Human Services, Substance Abuse and Mental Health Services Administration. Medical review officer manual for federal agency workplace drug-testing programs. Effective November 1, 2004. http://www.workplace.samhsa.gov/DrugTesting/Level_1_Pages/HHS%20MRO%20Manual%20(Effective%20November%201,%202004).aspx. Accessed October 22, 2008.

20. Peace MR, Tarnai LD. Performance evaluation of three on-site adulteration detection devices for urine specimens. *J Anal Toxicol.* 2002;26:464–470.

21. Dasgupta A, Chughtai O, Hannah C, Davis B, Wells A. Comparison of spot tests with AdultaCheck 6 and Intect 7 urine test strips for detecting the presence of adulterants in urine specimens. *Clin Chem Acta.* 2004; 34:19–25.

22. U.S. Department of Heath and Human Services, Substance Abuse and Mental Health Services Administration. MRO Case Studies: Case #1. February 2005. http://workplace.samhsa.gov/DrugTesting/Files_Drug_Testing/MROs/MRO%20Case%20Studies%20-%20February%202005.pdf. Accessed October 22, 2008.

CHAPTER 12

Alternative Explanations for True Positives in Drug Testing

Poppy-Seed Products, Health Tea, Passive Marijuana Inhalation, and Hemp Oil

ABSTRACT

There are a few legitimate explanations for testing positive on a drug test. For example, eating food containing poppy seeds may cause analytical true-positive results in both screening and confirmatory drug tests because poppy seeds contain various amounts of morphine. Coca tea containing cocaine is readily available in South American countries. Drinking such tea will cause an individual to test positive for benzoylecgonine, the metabolite of cocaine in urine. Hemp oil, available in certain drinks, contains a small amount of cannabinoids, which may cause a positive test for marijuana metabolite (11-nor-9-carboxy-Δ^9-tetrahydrocannabinol; THC-COOH) in urine. Passive inhalation of marijuana smoke, however, does not cause a positive test.

Eating certain types of food may cause false-positive drug test results. Therefore, both individuals going through pre-employment drug testing or workplace drug testing and human resources personnel should be aware of the possibility of such false-positive test results. Medical review officers are well trained to identify such instances where a positive test for morphine is due to ingestion of food containing poppy seeds. However, an individual undergoing drug testing should be sure to document consumption of such food along with any prescription or non-prescription drugs he or she may be taking. Many prescription pain medications cause true-positive test results for morphine, codeine, and related drugs. Several tranquilizers contain drugs in the benzodiazepine class and may cause true-positive results in drugs-of-abuse testing. Numerous over-the-counter cold medications contain ephedrine, pseudoephedrine, or related compounds, which interfere with the immunoassay screening for amphetamine.

POPPY PLANTS AND POPPY SEEDS

The history of cultivation of poppy plants can be traced to ancient Mesopotamia, eventually spreading to India and China. In nineteenth-century China, opium addiction led to the banning of opium and to the Opium War between China and Britain. Opium addiction was also widespread among early immigrants in the United States, where new laws were introduced to deal with the growing addiction problem. Today, growing opium poppies (*Papaver somniferum*) is illegal in the United States. The sale of poppy seed from *Papaver somniferum* is banned in Singapore and Saudi Arabia. Possession of food containing poppy seeds is banned by law in the United Arab Emirates.

The raw opium used in pharmaceuticals in the United States comes from other parts of the world, mainly India and Turkey. The import of poppy seeds is not banned in the United States. Poppy seeds are widespread in American food, added to muffins, bagels, and cakes. Some ethnic cooking uses a concentrated paste of poppy seeds.

The amount of opium in poppy seeds is very low compared with the other parts of the plant. Opium is found in the latex (a milky fluid) collected from immature seed capsules of the plants one to three weeks after flowering by incision of green seed pods. More than 20 alkaloids have been isolated from *Papaver somniferum*, out of which three alkaloids (morphine, codeine, and noscapine [antitussive]) are used in therapy. Thebaine is a biosynthetic intermediate of the morphine pathway that is used by the pharmaceutical industry for synthesis of oxycodone and the opiate antagonist naloxone. Many other alkaloids found in poppy plants have no narcotic properties.[1]

MORPHINE AND CODEINE CONCENTRATIONS FOLLOWING CONSUMPTION OF POPPY SEEDS

The amount of opiates in poppy seeds is not enough to produce a narcotic effect after consumption. However, the concentrations of morphine and codeine vary widely among different brands of poppy seeds; for example, the morphine content of Australian poppy seed can be 40 times higher than that of Dutch and Turkish poppy seed.[1] Positive opiate screening and eventually confirmed presence of codeine and morphine have been widely documented after consumption of food containing poppy seeds. The reported concentrations of both codeine and morphine vary widely among individuals in the same study and also among studies, with values ranging from "none detected" to several thousand nanograms of codeine and/or morphine per milliliter of the specimen.

Meadway et al analyzed the morphine and codeine content of poppy seeds by having four subjects ingest two poppy-seed-containing foods. The maximum morphine and codeine content of the poppy seed the authors analyzed was 33.2 μg of morphine per gram of the seed and 13.7 μg of codeine per gram of the seed. Following consumption of bread rolls (containing mean 0.76 g of seed), all urine specimens tested negative for opiate by the EMIT screening assay (using a 300 ng/ml cutoff for opiates), with the exception of one subject (with 63 kg body weight). This subject demonstrated opiate-positive urine specimens up to 6 hours post ingestion, as well as a maximum morphine concentration of 832.0 ng/ml and a maximum codeine concentration of 47.9 ng/ml in urine that was observed 2 to 4 hours post ingestion.[2] In another study, the concentrations of morphine and codeine were 2797 ng/ml and 214 ng/ml, respectively, in one healthy volunteer who ingested three poppy-seed bagels. Opiate was present in the urine 25 hours post ingestion.[3] No opiate was present 45 hours post ingestion. In response to these findings, in 1998 the Department of Health and Human Services (DHHS) increased the screening cutoff of opiate immunoassays from 300 ng/ml to 2000 ng/ml.

In another study, four volunteers ate three poppy-seed bagels each. Neither morphine nor codeine was detected in oral fluids. However, the levels of morphine ranged from 312 to 602 ng/ml in urine. When three volunteers ate one poppy-seed bagel and then an unlimited amount of poppy seeds in one hour (volunteer 1: 14.82 g, volunteer 2: 9.82 g, and volunteer 3: 20.82 g), the oral fluid tested positive up to one hour after ingestion at a 40 ng/ml cutoff (highest morphine content: 205 ng/ml). Urine specimens were positive for 8 hours.[4]

In Germany, the blood level of free morphine should be less than 10 ng/ml in drivers. Moeller et al studied blood and urine morphine levels after consumption of poppy-seed products. All five volunteers in their study showed positive opiate urine drug tests (up to 2079 ng/ml by a semi-quantitative Abbott assay; urine morphine 147–1300 ng/ml by GC/MS). No blood specimen tested positive for free morphine, but the specimens did yield morphine levels up to 24 ng/ml following hydrolysis.[5]

Hill et al investigated the effect of ingesting high amounts of poppy seed by measuring the urinary concentrations of morphine in volunteers. The study used Australian poppy seed because it contains the highest amount of morphine of any poppy seed available in the United States. The morphine content of the Australian

poppy seeds ranges from 90 to 200 μg of morphine per gram of poppy seed, while Dutch and Turkish poppy seed contains only 4 to 5 μg of morphine per gram of poppy seed. Ten subjects (6 male, 4 female) ingested two servings of poppy-seed pastry per week (generally on Monday and Tuesday; 8.1 mg average morphine per serving) for three weeks (total morphine consumed: 49 mg). Hair specimens were collected before and after the study. Urine specimens were collected for a 24-hour period following poppy seed ingestion and then 3 to 5 hours after subsequent ingestion of poppy-seed pastry. The maximum values of urinary morphine ranged from 2929 to 13,857 ng/ml (as determined by GC/MS). Moreover, urinary morphine levels remained above the 2000 ng/ml cutoff for as long as 10 hours. Seven out of 10 subjects reported drowsiness for 1 hour after taking poppy-seed pastry. The effect lasted 2 to 4 hours. Despite high urinary morphine levels, all subjects reported hair level morphine below the standard cutoff (0.04–0.48 ng of morphine/10 mg of hair; cutoff 2 ng/morphine/10 mg of hair).[6] **Table 12-1** gives typical morphine and codeine concentrations in volunteers after they consumed poppy-seed-containing products.

HEROIN ABUSE VERSUS POPPY SEED CONSUMPTION

Heroin is first metabolized to 6-monoacetylmorphine, which is further metabolized to morphine. It has been suggested that 6-monoacetylmorphine is a marker of heroin abuse because this metabolite is not found in urine after eating food containing poppy seeds. Moreover, DHHS guidelines require that the laboratory test for 6-monoacetylmorphine when the morphine concentration is greater than or equal to 2000 ng/ml. Thebaine is a natural con-

Table 12-1	Typical Concentrations of Morphine and Codeine in Volunteers After Consumption of Poppy-Seed Products		
Time Post-Consumption	**Morphine, ng/ml**	**Codine, ng/ml**	**Reference**
2–4 hours (one subject)[2]	832	47.9	2
Other subjects (all specimens)[2]	None detected[a]	None detected[a]	2
2–4 hours (same subject)[2]		83.8	2
0–2 hours (same subject)[2]	302.1		2
3 hours	2797	214	3
22 hours	676	16	3
3–5 hours	2929	208	6
3–5 hours	5651	552	6
3–5 hours	13,857	1174	6

a. Following cutoff of 300 ng/ml concentration using EMIT assays.

stituent of poppy seed, and it has been suggested that thebaine can be used as a marker for poppy seed consumption. One study detected thebaine in concentrations ranging from 2 to 91 ng/ml in volunteers who consumed 11 g of poppy seed.[7] The elimination of thebaine varies widely among individuals, however, and absence of thebaine in a specimen does not necessarily mean that the detection of morphine and codeine in urine was not from consumption of poppy-seed products.

HEALTH INCA TEA AND MATE DE COCA TEA

The drinking of coca tea is common in South America. Coca tea is prepared from coca leaves, which contain various amounts of cocaine. The tea is usually packed in tea bags containing approximately 1 g of plant material. Drinking such tea is equivalent to consumption of cocaine and other alkaloids present in the coca leaves. Jenkins et al reported an average of 5.11 mg cocaine per tea bag of coca tea in tea from Peru and an average of 4.86 mg of cocaine per tea bag in coca tea from Bolivia. When the tea was prepared, one cup of Peruvian coca tea had an average of 4.14 mg of cocaine, while one cup of Bolivian tea had an average of 4.29 mg of cocaine. When one volunteer drank one cup of Peruvian tea, a maximum benzoylecgonine concentration (metabolite of cocaine) of 3940 ng/ml was observed 10 hours post consumption. Similarly, after consumption of one cup of Bolivian tea, a volunteer showed a peak benzoylecgonine concentration of 4979 ng/ml 3.5 hours after consumption of tea. These results clearly indicate that significant amounts of cocaine can be found in coca tea from Bolivian and Peru, and drinking such tea may cause a failed drug test for cocaine.[8]

Although U.S. custom regulations require that no cocaine should be present in any herbal tea, tea made of coca leaves nevertheless can be found on the U.S. market. These products are sold under the names of Health Inca tea and Mate de Coca tea. Rohrig et al reported a urinary concentration of benzoylecgonine after ingestion of a cup of Health Inca tea by volunteers. Benzoylecgonine was detected in the urine specimens up to 26 hours post ingestion. The maximum urinary benzoylecgonine concentration of 1.4 to 2.8 mg/L (1400–2800 ng/ml) was observed 4 to 11 hours post ingestion of Health Inca tea.[9] Turner et al prepared tea by immersing one Mate de Coca tea bag in 250 ml of boiling water for 25 minutes. They took a 5 ml sample for analysis, and volunteers drank the rest. Urinary samples were collected at 2, 5, 8, 15, 21, 24, 43, and 68 hours after drinking the tea. All urine samples tested positive for benzoylecgonine by immunoassay. The amount of cocaine in the tea was estimated to be 2.5 mg.[10] **Table 12-2** gives the typical cocaine content of various coca teas.

PASSIVE INHALATION OF MARIJUANA

Exceeding the cutoff limit for marijuana tests is difficult to achieve through passive inhalation. The Department of Transportation states that medical review officers should not recognize passive drug exposure as a legitimate medical explanation for a positive test.[11,12] Tetrahydrocannabinol (THC, marijuana) released in air is most likely to exist as an aerosol particle whose concentration following mixing becomes highly dilute. Passive inhalation of marijuana may lead to positive screening and confirmation tests in oral fluid up to 30 minutes after exposure.[13] Niedbala et al later studied the effect of passive inhalation of marijuana on urine and oral fluid testing using high marijuana–containing cigarettes. In the first study, four smokers smoked THC mixed with tobacco (39.5 mg THC) in an unventilated eight-passenger van; four volunteers were passive smokers. In the second study, four volunteers smoked

Table 12-2 Typical Cocaine Content of Coca Tea[8,10]	
Tea	**Average Cocaine Content**
Peruvian coca tea	5.11 mg/tea bag
Bolivian coca tea	4.86 mg/tea bag
Peruvian tea (1 cup)	4.14 mg
Bolivian tea (1 cup)	4.29 mg
Mate de Coca (1 cup)	2.5 mg

marijuana only (83.2 mg THC). Oral fluid was collected using the Intercept Oral Specimen Collection Device (OraSure Technology, Bethlehem, PA). Participants were allowed to go outside the van 60 minutes after exposure. Oral fluid was collected at baseline (30 minutes before exposure) and 0, 15, and 45 minutes inside the van and 1, 1.25, 1.5, 1.75, 2, 2.5, 3.5, 4, 6, and 8 hours outside the van. Oral fluid collection continued up to 72 hours after exposure. Urine specimens were also collected. Oral fluid was tested for THC metabolites (11-nor-9-carboxy-Δ^9-tetrahydrocannabinol) using a Cannabinoids Intercept Micro-Plate Enzyme Immunoassay with a cutoff of 3 ng/ml (for the confirmation assay: 2.0 ng/ml). A 50 ng/ml cutoff was used for the urine specimens. All urine specimens tested negative (50 ng/ml cutoff) for the passive smokers (GC/MS showed THC metabolite concentrations in the range of 5.8–14.7 ng/ml 6–8 hours after exposure). In study 1, where oral fluid was collected inside the van, some subjects showed a positive response due to contamination of the oral fluid collection device with THC smoke, but in study 2, when all oral fluid specimens were collected outside the van, no positive specimens were observed. In contrast, all smokers showed significant THC content in both oral fluid and urine as expected. The mean urinary concentration was 75 ng/ml 4 hours after smoking.[14] The later study by the same authors clearly demonstrates that passive inhalation of marijuana should not lead to positive oral fluid testing.

▰▰▰ HEMP OIL

Industrial hemp comprises a number of varieties of *Cannabis sativa L.*, which are cultivated for industrial and agricultural purposes, mainly for seeds and fiber. *Cannabis* is the only plant genus that contains cannabinoids. However, the industrial hemp plant is different from the plant cultivated for marijuana (medical or illegal) production. The two cannabinoids, THC (marijuana; Δ^9-tetrahydrocannabinol) and cannabidiol, are important constituents of industrial hemp plants. THC is psychoactive, while cannabidiol is antipsychoactive and counteracts the effect of THC. Industrial hemp is characterized by low THC and high cannabidiol content, while the plants cultivated for production of marijuana are high in THC content and very low in cannabidiol content. The THC level is so low in hemp products that it is impossible to get high from taking these products. Cultivation of hemp in the United States is illegal unless special permission is obtained from the Federal Drug Administration, but the import of hemp seed, from which hemp oil is produced, is not illegal in the United States. Moreover, washed industrial-quality hemp seeds contain no or very little THC in the resin sticking to the seed. Hemp oil contains high amounts of essential fatty acids (linoleic acid and alpha-linoleic acid) and thus may have health benefits.[15]

The seeds and hemp oil may contain measurable amounts of THC. Ross et al compared THC content of cannabis seed obtained from fiber-type plants (hemp) and drug-type plants. The authors obtained seeds of *Cannabis sativa* (Mexican, Jamaican, Colombian, and hybrid mix) from the 1995 harvest of plants in the research facility at the University of Mississippi, and fiber-type seeds (hemp seeds) from the International Hemp Association (Amsterdam). As expected, the THC contents of hemp seed were significantly lower than the THC contents of cannabis seeds obtained from drug-type plants. For example, hemp seed originated in Yugoslavia contained 9 μg of THC per gram of seed. In contrast, Jamaican cannabis seed showed the presence of 124 μg of THC per gram of seed.[16] **Table 12-3** gives concentrations of THC in cannabis seeds (fiber-type plants such as hemp versus drug-type plants). A 1997 survey found that the THC content of hemp oil was 11 to 117 μg/g (ppm).[17] In 2000, oil containing 10 to 20 μg/g of THC and hull seeds containing 2 to 3 μg/g were reported in the United States (K. Cole, personal communication, 2000).

Studies conducted in 1998 or earlier reported significant amounts of THC metabolites after consumption of hemp oil because the THC content in most hemp oil exceeded 50 μg/g. Now the THC content in most commercial hemp oil is as low as 5 μg/g. Therefore, studies conducted in 1998 or later concluded that ingestion of a reasonable amount of hemp oil should not cause positive THC results in drug testing. In 1997 Struempler et al also reported positive cannabinoid workplace drug testing following ingestion of commercially available hemp oil preparation. The first specimen that tested negative was obtained 53 hours after ingestion.[18] In 1998 Alt and Reinhardt reported the presence of THC metabolites 80 hours post ingestion of 40 to 90 ml of hemp seed oil by volunteers.[19] The authors also reported the presence of THC

Table 12-3	Concentration of Δ^9-Tetrahydrocannabinol (Δ^9-THC) in Cannabis Seeds	
Seed Type	**Δ^9-THC Concentration (μg/g)**
Fiber Type	
Hemp seeds (dioecious), Hungary 1995	8
Hemp seeds, Yugoslavia, 1995	9
Hemp seeds, Unisex, uniko-B, Hungary, 1995	12
Hemp seeds, Fururs, France, 1994 (with fungicide)	0
Drug Type	
Mexican seeds	66
Jamaican seeds	124
Colombian seeds	41
Hybrid seeds, mix (no plant particles)	79

Source: Ross SA, Mehmedic Z, Murphy TP, ElSohly MA. GC-MS analysis of the total Δ^9-THC content of both drug-and fiber-type cannabis seeds. *J Anal Toxicol.* Reproduced with permission from Preston Publications, a division of Preston Industries, Inc.

in hemp food products like hemp bar, hemp flour, and hemp liquor. A report from Switzerland indicated the presence of very high amounts of THC after ingestion of 11 or 22 g of cannabis seed oil due to very high THC content (1500 μg/g) of the oil. Urine samples were positive up to 6 days after ingestion of the oil. The THC metabolite concentrations (THC-COOH) ranged from 5 to 431 ng/ml, as determined by GC/MS.[20] Another report from Switzerland confirmed THC poisoning in four patients who ate a salad preparation containing hemp oil because the concentrations of THC in the hemp oil far exceeded

the recommended tolerance dose.[21] Following that report, the Swiss Federal Office of Public Health issued a warning concerning consumption of hemp oil. However, there is no case report about marijuana poisoning after consumption of hemp-containing food products in the United States.

Hempen Ale, an alcoholic beverage formulated, brewed, and bottled by the Frederick Brewing Company (Frederick, MD), does not contain any THC because the hemp seeds used are subjected to two wash cycles before brewing so that any vegetative material that potentially may contain THC is removed. Gibson et al reported the absence of THC in Hempen Ale and concluded that ingestion of a moderate amount of this drink is not sufficient to produce a cannabis-positive drug screen.[22] This drink is no longer available on the consumer market.

More recent reports from the United States indicate that drinking moderate amounts of hemp oil should not cause a THC-positive result in workplace drug testing. Leson et al reported that consumption of 125 ml of hemp oil (equivalent to ingestion of 0.6 mg of THC; a very high consumption) produced a highest THC metabolite concentration of 5.2 ng/ml, as determined by GC/MS. This value was below the 15 ng/ml cutoff for GC/MS confirmation. However, several urinary specimens collected from volunteers after consumption of hemp oil tested positive by the immunoassay screen at a 20 ng/ml cutoff, and one specimen tested positive at a 50 ng/ml cutoff. Therefore, programs that rely on immunoassay screening tests only and use a lower screening cutoff can still encounter occasional positives in subjects ingesting hemp food because a significant amount of THC present in hemp-food samples may exist as THC acids A or B. These species are metabolized analogous to free THC but are not quantitated in GC/MS confirmation of THC-COOH, which is derived from free THC.[23] A 2006 study concluded that consumption of hemp oil produced by U.S. manufacturers according to the guidelines of the manufacturers should not lead to positive tests for THC in plasma or whole blood.[24]

CONCLUSION

Ingestion of poppy-seed-containing products may cause a positive opiate screening assay as well as confirmed morphine and codeine levels in urine. In 1998 the federal government increased the cutoff of the opiate assay from 300 ng/ml to 2000 ng/ml. Although one published report has indicated that the concentration of morphine from eating poppy-seed food may reach even 13,857 ng/ml, such a high value is unlikely in routine situations. In our experience and in accordance with published data, morphine and codeine levels after consumption of poppy-seed products should be between 300 ng/ml and 1000 ng/ml, and such levels may persist for 12 to 24 hours. The new opiate testing cutoff of 2000 ng/ml is very reasonable. The presence of 6-monocaetylmorphine in an opiate-positive specimen is indicative of heroin abuse and not from consumption of poppy-seed-containing products.

Despite U.S. customs regulations, coca tea is occasionally found on the legal U.S. market. However, documentation of cocaine in tea leaves can provide evidence of whether a person is abusing cocaine or accidentally ingested coca tea.

Although hemp oil and hemp seeds are legally available in the United States from health food stores, the THC content of hemp oil and hemp seeds is relatively low, and it is unlikely for an individual to test positive for marijuana following consumption of a reasonable amount of hemp oil or hemp-containing foods.

A Case Study[25]

A laboratory report confirmed a marijuana metabolite concentration of 30 ng/ml. The donor claimed that he was at a party on Saturday night where several individuals were smoking marijuana, but he did not smoke a joint. The specimen was collected two days after the party, and the medical review officer determined that a non-smoking individual could not reach a high enough drug concentration from passive inhalation to reach the cutoff of marijuana metabolite used in the federal agency program. The MRO reported the case as "Positive for Marijuana."

REFERENCES

1. Schmidt J, Boettcher C, Kuhnt C, Zenk MH. Poppy alkaloid profiling by electrospray tandem mass spectrometry and electrospray FT-ICR mass spectrometry after [ring-13C]-tyramine feeding. *Phytochemistry.* 2007;68:189–202.

2. Meadway C, George S, Braithwaite R. Opiate concentrations following the ingestion of poppy seed products: evidence for the "poppy seed defense." *Forensic Sci Int.* 1998;96:29–38.

3. Struempler RE. Excretion of codeine and morphine following ingestion of poppy seeds. *J Anal Toxicol.* 1987:11:97–99.

4. Jackson GF, Saddy JJ, Poklis A. The determination of morphine in urine and oral fluid following ingestion of poppy seeds. *J Anal Toxicol.* 2003;27:449–452.

5. Moeller MR, Hammer K, Engel O. Poppy seed consumption and toxicological analysis of blood and urine samples. *Forensic Sci Int.* 2004;143:183–186.

6. Hill V, Cairns T, Cheng CC, Schaffer. Multiple aspects of hair analysis for opiates: methodology, clinical and workplace populations, codeine, and poppy seed ingestion. *J Anal Toxicol*. 2005; 29: 696–703.

7. Cassella G, Wu AH, Shaw BR, Hill DW. The analysis of thebaine in urine for the detection of poppy seed consumption. *J Anal Toxicol*. 1997;21:376–383.

8. Jenkins AJ, Llosa T, Montoya I, Cone EJ. Identification and quantitation of alkaloids in coca tea. *Forensic Sci Int*. 1996;77: 179–189.

9. Rohrig TP, Moore C. Urinary excretion of benzoylecgonine following ingestion of health Inca tea. *Forensic Sci Int*. 1991;49: 57–64.

10. Turner M, McCrory P, Johnston A. Time for tea, anyone? *Br J Sports Med*. 2005; 39–37.

11. Mule SJ, Lomax P, Gross SJ. Active and realistic passive marijuana exposure tested by three immunoassays and GC/MS. *J Anal Toxicol*. 1988;12:113–116.

12. Office of Drug and Alcohol Policy and Compliance. The Ombinus Transportation Employee Testing Act of 1991. 49 CFR Part 40. http://www.dot.gov/ost/dapc. Accessed November 19, 2008.

13. Niedbala S, Kardos S, Salamone D, Fritch D, Bronsgeest M, Cone EJ. Passive cannabis smoke exposure and oral fluid testing. *J Anal Toxicol*. 2004;28:546–552.

14. Niedbala RS, Kardos KW, Fritch D, et al. Passive cannabis smoke exposure and oral fluid testing II. Two studies of extreme cannabis smoke exposure in a motor vehicle. *J Anal Toxicol*. 2005;29:607–615.

15. Schwab U.S., Callaway JC, Erkkilä AT, Gynther J, Uusitupa MI, Järvinen T. Effects of hemp seed and flaxseed oils on the profile of serum lipids, serum total and lipoprotein lipid concentrations and haemostatic factors. *Eur J Nutr*. 2006;45: 470–477.

16. Ross SA, Mehmedic Z, Murphy TP, ElSohly MA. GC-MS analysis of the total Δ^9-THC content of both drug-and fiber-type cannabis seeds. *J Anal Toxicol*. 2000;24:715–717.

17. Bosy TZ, Cole KA. Consumption and quantitation of Δ^9-tetrahydrocannabinol in commercially available hemp seed oils and products. *J Anal Toxicol*. 2000;24:562–566.

18. Struempler RE, Nelson G, Urry TM. A positive cannabinoid workplace drug test following the ingestion of hemp seed oil. *J Anal Toxicol*. 1997;21:283–285.

19. Alt A, Reinhardt G. Positive cannabis results in urine and blood samples after consumption of hemp food products. *J Anal Toxicol*. 1998;22:80–81.

20. Lehman T, Sager F, Brenneisen R. Excretion of cannabinoids in urine after ingestion of cannabis seed oil. *J Anal Toxicol*. 1997;5: 373–375.

21. Meier H, Vonesch HJ. Cannabis poisoning after eating salad. *Schweiz Med Wochenschr*. 1997;127:214–218.

22. Gibson CR, Williams RD, Browder RO. Analysis of Hempen Ale for cannabinoids. *J Anal Toxicol*. 1998;22:179.

23. Leson G, Pless P, Grotenhermen F, Kalant H, ElSohly MA. Evaluating the impact of hemp food consumption on workplace drug tests. *J Anal Toxicol*. 2001;25:691–698.

24. Goodwin RS, Gustafson RA, Barnes A, Nebro W, Moolchan ET, Huestis MA. Δ^9-tetrahydrocannabinol, 11-hydroxy-Δ^9-tetrahydrocannabinol and 11-nor-9-carboxy-Δ^9-tetrahydrocannabinol in human plasma after controlled oral administration of cannabinoids. *Ther Drug Monit*. 2006;28:545–51.

25. U.S. Department of Heath and Human Services, Substance Abuse and Mental Health Services Administration. MRO Case Studies: Case #1. February 2005. http://workplace.samhsa.gov/ DrugTesting/Files_Drug_Testing/ MROs/MRO%20Case%20Studies%20-%20February%202005.pdf. Accessed October 22, 2008.

CHAPTER 13

Miscellaneous Drugs-of-Abuse Testing Issues

Contaminated Currency, Mushrooms, Hallucinogens, and Glue and Solvent Sniffing

ABSTRACT

There are miscellaneous factors that should be taken into consideration in drugs-of-abuse testing. Although cocaine and other abused drugs have been detected in paper currencies, handling paper currencies contaminated with drugs should not cause positive drug-test results. Various hallucinogens such as lysergic acid diethylamide (LSD), psilocybin, psilocin (magic mushrooms), mescaline (peyote cactus), and ketamine are also abused, but these drugs are not usually tested in pre-employment or workplace drug-testing programs. Solvent and glue sniffing are forms of drug abuse that are usually overlooked. Abuse of solvent and glue is a serious problem among young individuals. Even death can occur from such abuse.

Miscellaneous other factors also should be considered in drugs-of-abuse testing. Several reports show that paper currencies are often contaminated with abused drugs. Various other hallucinogens such as lysergic acid diethylamide (LSD), phencyclidine and related drugs, ketamine, magic mushrooms (psilocybin and psilocin), and peyote cactus (mescaline) are also abused. LSD is the most potent hallucinogen. Under the influence of hallucinogens, people see images and feel sensations that are unreal. They may also experience mood swings and a feeling of spiritual energy. Hallucinogenic agents produce their effects by disrupting the interaction of nerve cells and

the neurotransmitter serotonin. Despite abuse, hallucinogens are not routinely tested for in pre-employment or workplace drug testing. Solvent and glue sniffing is a serious problem among young people, possibly even leading to death.

 COCAINE AND OTHER DRUGS OF ABUSE IN PAPER CURRENCY

U.S. currency has been found to contain significant amounts of cocaine.[1,2] Oyler examined $1 bills from several big cities in the United States and found cocaine in amounts above 0.1 μg in 74% of bills. Moreover, 54% of that currency showed cocaine concentrations above 1.0 μg. The highest amount of cocaine found was 1327 μg in a $1 bill.[1] Negrusz et al analyzed ten $20 bills collected from Rockford, Illinois, and four $1 bills collected from Chicago. The concentration of cocaine varied from 10.02 μg to 0.14 μg in $20 bills, and 2.99 μg to none detected in $1 bills. Overall, 92.8% of all bills analyzed were contaminated with cocaine.[2] Jenkins reported the analysis of 10 randomly collected $1 bills from five U.S. cities for cocaine, 6-acetylmorphine (metabolite of heroin), morphine, codeine, methamphetamine, amphetamine, and phencyclidine. The author observed cocaine in 92% of these bills (the amount of cocaine varied from 0.01 to 922.7 μg per bill). 6-acetylmorphine and morphine were detected in three bills, while amphetamine was detected in one bill. The author further reported that methamphetamine was present in three bills and phencyclidine (PCP) in two bills. This report demonstrates that although cocaine is the major contaminant in U.S. paper currency, other abused drugs may also be present.[3]

Lavins et al analyzed 165 randomly collected paper currency notes from 12 U.S. cities and four foreign countries and analyzed for the presence of Δ^9-tetrahydrocannabinol (THC), cannabinol and cannabidiol, 11-nor-9-carboxy-Δ^9-tetrahydrocannabinol, and 11-hydroxy-Δ^9-tetrahydrocannabinol. The authors reported that for U.S. $1 bills ($N = 125$), THC was present in only two bills (1.6%). The authors detected the presence of cannabinol in 13 dollar bills (10.31%) with a range of values between 0.014 and 0.774 μg. For foreign currencies ($n = 40$) THC and cannabinol were detected in 9 notes (22.5%). These currency notes were from Colombia, India, Qatar, and New Zealand. The concentrations of THC ranged from 0.026 to 0.065 μg/bill, and cannabinol concentrations ranged from 0.061 to 0.197 μg/bill.[4] **Table 13-1** gives various amounts of abused drugs detected in U.S. currencies.

Table 13-1 Drugs Found in U.S. Currencies[1–4]		
Drug	**Currency**	**Highest Amount Found**
Cocaine	$1 bill	1327 μg
Cocaine	$1 bill	2.99 μg
Cocaine	$20 bill	10.02 μg
Cocaine	$1 bill	922.7 μg
Heroin	$1 bill	168.5 μg
Morphine	$1 bill	5.51 μg
6-acetylmorphine	$1 bill	9.22 μg
Phencyclidine (PCP)	$1 bill	1.87 μg
Amphetamine	$1 bill	0.85 μg
Methamphetamine	$1 bill	0.60 μg
Tetrahydro-cannabinol (THC)	$1 bill	0.17 μg
Cannabinol	$1 bill	0.77 μg
Cannabidiol	$1 bill	0.09 μg

 ## HANDLING MONEY CONTAMINATED WITH DRUGS

ElSohly investigated whether individuals who handled cocaine-contaminated paper money would test positive by urinalysis. Two $1 bills were immersed in dry, powdered cocaine and then shaken free of loose cocaine. One individual then handled the money several times during the course of the day. Analysis of urine samples collected over a period of approximately 24 hours after handling the contaminated money revealed that the maximum concentration of benzoylecgonine (cocaine metabolite)

observed was 72 ng/ml. This value was significantly below the cutoff level of the benzoylecgonine screening assay (300 ng/ml). The value was even lower than the US military recommended cutoff of 100 ng/ml.[5]

![bullet] ## MAGIC MUSHROOM ABUSE

Magic mushrooms (psychoactive fungi) that grow in the United States, Mexico, South America, and many other parts of the world contain the hallucinogenic compounds psilocybin and psilocin. Psilocybin and psilocin along with other compounds in the tryptamine class of drugs are classified as Class I controlled substances with no known medical use but have a high abuse potential. Unlawful possession of a Class I controlled substance is a felony in the United States. Although individual states do not specifically list "psychoactive mushrooms" as such under controlled substances, many state courts have ruled that it is reasonable to consider such mushrooms as living containers of Class I controlled substances. Therefore, possession of such compounds or growing such plants may be illegal. In 2005 the UK government changed the law and included dried or cooked psychoactive mushrooms under Class A drugs. It is a criminal offense to possess or sell such products in the United Kingdom. Many species of magic mushrooms contain hallucinogenic compounds, but almost all of them are brown or dark tan in color. Magic mushrooms are eaten raw, cooked with food, or dried. These mushrooms can be mistaken for other nonhallucinogenic mushrooms or even poisonous mushrooms such as Amanita mushrooms. Therefore, it is dangerous to try to identify such mushrooms for human consumption. A 2007 article reported death from ingestion of Amanita mushroom due to mistaken identity.[6]

Psilocybin and psilocin are found in over 150 species of mushrooms. The group of psychoactive mushrooms includes species of the genera *Conocybe*, *Gymnopilus*, *Panaeolus*, *Pluteus*, *Psilocybe*, and *Stropharia*.[7] *Panaeolus cyanescens* usually contains the highest amounts of psilocybin and psilocin, while the most common type of magic mushroom in Germany is *Psilocybe semilanceata*, which contains 0.003% to 1.15% psilocybin and 0.01% to 0.90% psilocin.[8] The psilocybin contents in *Psilocybe cubensis* was 0.44% to 1.35% in the cap of the mushroom and 0.05% to 1.27% in the stem, while the corresponding psilocin concentrations were 0.17% to 0.78% and 0.09% to 0.30%, respectively. In general, more hallucinogenic alkaloids are found in the cap of the mushroom than in the stem.[9]

After ingestion, psilocybin, often the major component of the mushroom, is rapidly converted by dephosphorylation into psilocin, which has psychoactive effects similar to those of LSD, but usually the duration of the peak effect is short (0.5–2 hours after ingestion) and declines in 3 to 4 hours. The average half-life is 3 hours.[10] These hallucinogens affect the central nervous system, producing hallucination, hyperkinesis, and ataxia.[7] Eventually, psilocin is conjugated in the liver and excreted as glucuronide. The Federal Drug Administration (FDA) has not approved any commercially available immunoassay for analysis of psilocin in human plasma or urine. Therefore, high-performance liquid chromatography or GC/MS is used for analysis of psilocin in serum or urine. In one report, the total psilocin concentration in serum was 52 ng/ml and the total psilocin concentration in urine was 1760 ng/ml in a person who consumed magic mushroom.[11]

Intoxication from use of magic mushroom is common. Some magic mushroom species contain phenylethylamine, which may cause cardiac toxicity. Beck et al reported that the amount of phenylethylamine may vary much more than that of psilocybin in magic mushrooms. Three young men were hospitalized due to adverse reactions to magic mushroom. The highest amount of phenylethylamine found in the mushroom (*Psilocybe semilanceata*) was 146 μg/g wet weights.[12] Raff et al reported renal failure in a 20-year-old woman who consumed magic mushrooms.[13] There is also a report of a fatal case of magic mushroom poisoning.[14]

PSILOCIN AND AMPHETAMINE SCREENING

Tiscione and Miller identified psilocin in a urine specimen during a routine investigation of an individual driving under the influence of drugs. The urine specimen initially showed a positive result with the fluorescence polarization immunoassay (FPIA) screening for amphetamine/methamphetamine in urine. The authors determined that at a concentration of 50 μg/ml, the cross-reactivity of psilocin with the amphetamine immunoassay is 1.3%. The urine concentration of psilocin decreased rapidly despite the fact that the specimen was stored at 4°C.[15]

PEYOTE CACTUS

Peyote cactus (*Lophophora williamsii*) is a small, spineless cactus that grows in the southwestern part of the United States and Mexico. Peyote cactus is small and round without sharp spines. The top of the cactus that grows aboveground is called the "crown." The crown consists of disc-shaped buttons that contain the psychoactive compound mescaline. Mescaline can be extracted from the peyote cactus, or buttons can be chewed or soaked in water to produce psychoactive liquid. Native North American Indian recognized the psychotropic properties of peyote as many as 5,700 years ago. Using carbon dating, El-Seedi et al analyzed two archaeological specimens of peyote buttons from the collection of the Hangar 9/Edward H. White Museum in San Antonio and observed that the buttons dated back to 3780 to 3660 B.C. The authors also extracted alkaloids from the buttons and demonstrated the presence of mescaline, the active ingredient of peyote.[16] Mescaline is classified as a Class I controlled substance, but approximately 300,000 members of the Native American Church can ingest peyote cactus legally as a religious sacrament during ritual all-night prayer. The members may attend the prayer ceremonies as often as three times a week or infrequently as once a year.[17]

Although mescaline has the lowest potency among naturally occurring hallucinogens, a full dose (200–400 mg) has a long duration of action. The highest psychedelic effect may be achieved within 2 hours of ingestion and may last as long as 8 hours.[18] The psychoactive effects of mescaline are similar to those of LSD, including deeply mystical feelings. Mescaline is metabolized to several different metabolites, but a large amount of mescaline can be recovered unchanged in urine. Even though one study found no evidence of psychological or cognitive deficits among Native Americans who used peyote regularly in a religious setting,[17] toxicity and even death from mescaline overdose have been reported. One person who died under the influence of mescaline showed 9.7 μg/ml of drug in serum and 1163 μg/ml of drug in urine. The corresponding drug concentration in the liver was 70.8 μg/mg/g.[19]

Botulism can occur if peyote buttons are stored in water.[20] Nolte and Zumwalt reported a case in which a 32-year-old Native American man with history of alcohol abuse ingested peyote tea. He later developed respiratory distress and suddenly collapsed. His antemortem blood specimen showed the presence of mescaline (0.48 mg/L), and the concentration of mescaline in urine was 61 mg/L. Other than a trace amount of chlordiazepoxide, no other drug or ethanol was found.[21]

Currently, there is no commercially available immunoassay for analysis of mescaline in body fluids, but GC/MS can be used for determination of concentrations of mescaline in the biological matrix.

![] LYSERGIC ACID

Lysergic acid is a naturally occurring alkaloid found in the ergot fungus (*Claviceps purpurea*). This type of fungus grows on grains such as barley, rye, or wheat. Lysergic acid diethylamide (LSD) is a potent hallucinogen that was synthesized in 1938 by the chemist Albert Hoffman, who later discovered its hallucinogenic effect. The d-isomer of LSD is one of the most potent hallucinogens known to mankind, while the other optical isomer (l-LSD) is relatively inactive. A closely related compound, lysergic acid amide, is found in seeds of morning glory (*Ipomoea violacea*) and Hawaiian baby woodrose (*Argyreia nervosa*). However, lysergic acid amide is much less potent compared with LSD.[22] Use of LSD was very popular in the United States in the 1960s. Between 1999 and 2001, more than two million Americans tried LSD for the first time.[23]

LSD is usually administered orally in small doses (20–140 µg), and the duration as well as the intensity of the hallucinogenic effect are dose dependent.[24] The average elimination half-life of LSD is 3.6 hours, and it has a short detection window (12–22 hours) after a typical use. Only 1% to 3% of the parent LSD is found in urine because LSD is extensively metabolized to several metabolites.[25] Out of five metabolites of LSD characterized from human urine (nor-LSD, 2-oxo-LSD, 2-oxo-3-hydroxy-LSD [OH-LSD], 13-hydroxy-LSD, and 14-hydroxy-LSD), the concentration of OH-LSD is approximately 24 times greater than the LSD concentration. Burnley and George reported the results of a GC/MS measurement of OH-LSD in human urine. The authors reported that the concentrations of OH-LSD varied from 4.3 ng/ml to 55.8 ng/ml in five female patients and from 1.7 ng/ml to 7.4 ng/ml in six male patients.[26]

Although the concentrations of LSD and its metabolites can be accurately determined using GC/MS, the FDA-approved immunoassays are also available for rapid screening of LSD in suspected abusers. Wiegand et al compared EMIT II (Dade-Behring, Deerfield, IL), CEDIA (Microgenics Corporation, Fremont, CA), and RIA (Diagnostic Products Corporation, Los Angeles, CA) assays for detection of LSD in urine. The authors conclude that the CEDIA assay demonstrated superior precision, accuracy, and decreased cross-reactivity to compounds other than LSD compared with the EMIT II assay. The cutoff concentration of LSD is considered to be 200 pg/ml. The authors further analyzed 24 urine specimens containing between 227 pg/ml and 1400 pg/ml LSD (measured by GC/MS) using these three immunoassays, and all three assays correctly identified LSD in 23 out of 24 specimens.[27]

A recent article indicated that bupropion, a medication used to aid cessation of smoking, interferes with the LSD screening assay by CEDIA technique. A 50-year-old patient who arrived at the hospital and was taking bupropion showed positive urine screening of LSD and amphetamine using the CEDIA assays. However, the positive screening results were not confirmed by the more sophisticated GC/MS method. The authors concluded that bupropion interferes with both the amphetamine and the LSD assays using the CEDIA method.[28]

LSD overdose can have serious medical consequences. In one report eight patients who used LSD tartrate powder intranasally collapsed within 15 minutes of abuse. The patients presented with symptoms of hyperthermia, coma, and respiratory arrest. Mild general bleeding was also observed, indicative of platelet dysfunction. The serum concentrations of LSD varied from 2.1 to 26 ng/ml, while the gastric concentrations varied from 1000 to 7000 µg/dl. With supportive care the patients recovered. The authors concluded that massive LSD overdose in humans is life threatening.[29]

▨ KETAMINE

Ketamine is a dissociative anesthetic (the person taking it feels detached from the environment) that is structurally and pharmacologically related to phencyclidine. Ketamine can produce a similar hallucinogenic effect to that of phencyclidine. Ketamine is a Schedule II drug with limited use in medicine but is used more often in veterinary medicine. Ketamine abusers use this drug intravenously, and the effect can be felt immediately. Ketamine is used as a club drug and at "rave" parties. Ketamine comes in a clear liquid or whitish powder. The liquid can be injected, while the powder can be dissolved and injected or can be taken orally or intranasally. Ketamine is very hallucinogenic. Abusers can experience unpleasant flashbacks even weeks after discontinuation of use. The half-life of ketamine is relatively short in humans (2.5

hours). Although few cases of ketamine intoxication with fatal outcome have been reported, a serious overdose with ketamine may produce acidosis, rhabdomyolysis, seizure, respiratory depression, and cardiac arrest.[30]

Ketamine is metabolized to norketamine, which then undergoes further metabolism. Currently, there is no commercially available immunoassay for screening of ketamine and its metabolite in urine. Ketamine is analyzed by gas chromatography with nitrogen-phosphorus or flame ionization detection, GC/MS, or liquid chromatography combined with mass spectrometry. Kim et al analyzed ketamine and norketamine in human urine using gas chromatography combined with positive ion chemical ionization mass spectrometry. The authors demonstrated that the concentrations of ketamine varied from 0.03 µg/ml to 56.16 µg/ml, while the concentration of norketamine ranged from none detected to 29.31 µg/ml in six subjects abusing ketamine.[31] The ketamine concentration was 21 µg/ml in gastric content, 3.8 µg/ml in blood, and 1.2 µg/ml in urine in a 34-year-old woman who died of ketamine poisoning.[32]

Table 13-2 gives street names of various hallucinogens, while **Figure 13-1** gives structures of LSD, ketamine, mescaline, psilocybin, and psilocin. **Table 13-3** lists typical concentrations of hallucinogens in serum and urine after abuse.

▨ SOLVENT AND GLUE SNIFFING

Although solvent (inhalant) abuse is common among adolescents not only in the United States but also worldwide, this problem is often overlooked. One study estimated that in the United States approximately 20% of adolescents have tried

Table 13-2	Street Names of Common Hallucinogens

Hallucinogen	Street Name
LSD	Acid, blotters, trips, sugar cube, blue haven, blue cheer, red dragon
Magic mushroom	Magic mushroom, mushies, shroom, liberty caps, fly agaric
Peyote cactus	Cactus, buttons, peyote, mesc
Ketamine	Special K, vitamin K, K, super K, super caid, jet, cat, aliums

inhalants at least once by the time they reach eighth grade.[33] In the United States, the mean age of solvent abusers is 13, and the rate of abuse is higher in Caucasians and Hispanics compared with Blacks.[34]

Abused inhalants include solvents, glues, adhesives and paint thinners, fuels, and propellants (petroleum products). Inhalant abuse includes breathing directly from a container, soaking a rag with solvent and placing it over the nose and mouth, or pouring the solvent in a plastic bag and then breathing fumes. Abuse of inhalants produces euphoria like that caused by other abused drugs. When an abuser becomes hypoxic by rebreathing

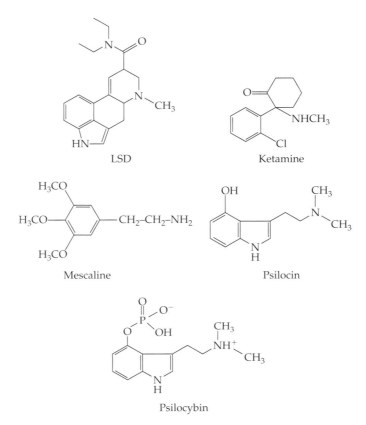

Figure 13-1. *Chemical Structures of LSD, Ketamine, Mescaline, Psilocin, and Psilocybin*

Table 13-3	Typical Concentrations of Hallucinogens After Abuse	
Hallucinogen	**Source**	**Typical Concentration**
Psilocybin	Magic mushroom	Rapidly metabolized to psilocin
Psilocin	Magic mushroom	52 ng/ml in serum, 1760 ng/ml in urine
Mescaline	Peyote cactus	9.7 µg/ml in serum, 1163 µg/ml in urine[a]
LSD	Synthetic	2.1–26 ng/ml in 8 patients
		227–1400 pg/ml (0.23–1.4 ng/ml) in 24 subjects
OH-LSD (metabolite)		4.3–55.8 ng/ml in 5 female subjects
Ketamine	Synthetic	0.03–51.16 µg/ml in 6 subjects
Norketamine (metabolite)		0–29.31 µg/ml in 6 subjects

a. The individual died from the overdose.

from a bag, the euphoric effect may even intensify.[34]

Common household products that are abused include glue, adhesives, nail polish, nail polish remover, cigarette lighter fluid, butane gas, gas (petrol), air fresheners, deodorant, hairspray, pain relieving spray, typewriter correction fluid, paint thinners, paint removers, and a variety of other agents. These household and office products contain toxic solvents such as toluene (paint, spray paint, adhesives, paint thinner, and shoe polish), acetone (nail polish remover, typewriter correction fluid, and markers), hexane (glue and rubber cement), chlorinated hydrocarbon (spot and grease removers), xylene (permanent markers), propane gas (gas to light the grill and spray paints), butane gas (lighter fluid and spray paint), and fluorocarbons (hair spray, analgesic spray, and refrigerator coolant such as Freon). In one study the authors investigated 318,393 exposures and concluded that exposure to hydrocarbons, which are systematically absorbed and have low viscosity (such as benzene, toluene, xylene, halogenated hydrocarbon, kerosene,

and lamp oil), caused the highest hazard values. Moreover, the risk associated with hydrocarbon exposure is greater among older children and adolescents.[35] Chronic abuse of toluene-containing products and chlorinated solvents can produce severe liver, kidney, and brain damage. Drunken behavior, mood changes, and anorexia may also be observed among these abusers.[36]

Solvent abusers often present with nonspecific symptoms, but long-term abusers may present with a wide range of neuropsychiatric symptoms. **Table 13-4** lists the common toxicities encountered in solvent abusers.

The most serious consequence of solvent abuse is death, usually caused by aspiration or asphyxia. Nearly 50% of deaths from solvent abuse are due to sudden sniffing death syndrome. When an acutely intoxicated abuser is startled, a burst of catecholamines may trigger ventricular fibrillation.[34] Steffee et al reported two cases of fatal volatile solvent inhalation abuse: gasoline sniffing in a 20-year-old man and aerosol air freshener inhalation in a 16-year-old girl.[37] Exposure to toluene, one of

Table 13-4	Adverse Effects of Solvent Abuse

Death (sudden sniffing death syndrome)
Cardiac arrhythmia
Anoxia
Respiratory depression
Pulmonary failure
Renal failure
Neurologic effects
Dermatological effects
Hematological effects
Nausea and vomiting
Hepatotoxicity

the major components of glue, can cause cardiac arrhythmia and sudden sniffing death syndrome. Increased QT interval may also be observed in both symptotic and symptomatic toluene abusers.[38] Also, abuse of butane gas (lighter fluid) may cause arrhythmia.

 CONCLUSION

Although paper currencies may be contaminated with cocaine and other drugs of abuse, handling such contaminated money should not cause positive results in drug-of-abuse testing. A variety of hallucinogens such as magic mushroom, peyote cactus, LSD, and ketamine are abused. LSD is the most potent hallucinogen. Although solvent abuse is a less-publicized problem in drugs of abuse, abuse of solvent can cause significant organ damage or lead to death.

 REFERENCES

1. Oyler J, Darwin WD, Cone EJ. Cocaine contamination of United States paper currency. *J Anal Toxicol.* 1996;20:213–216.

2. Negrusz A, Perry JL, Moore C. Detection of cocaine on various denominations of United States currency. *J Forensic Sci.* 1998:43;626–629.

3. Jenkins AJ. Drug contamination in U.S. paper currency. *Forensic Sci Int.* 2001;121: 189–193.

4. Lavins ES, Lavins BD, Jenkins AJ. Cannabis (marijuana) contamination of United States and foreign paper currency. *J Anal Toxicol.* 2004;28:439–442.

5. ElSohly MA. Urinalysis and casual handling of marijuana and cocaine. *J Anal Toxicol.* 1991;14:46.

6. Madhok M. Amanita bisporgera: ingestion and death from mistaken identity. *Minn Med.* 2007;90:48–50.

7. Reingardiene D, Vilcinskaite J, Lazauskas R. [Hallucinogenic mushrooms.] *Medicina (Kaunas).* 2005;41:1067–1070.

8. Musshoff F, Madea B, Beike J. Hallucinogenic mushrooms on the German market: simple instructions for examination and identification. *Forensic Sci Int.* 2000;113: 389–395.

9. Tsujikawa K, Kannamori Y, Iwata Y, et al. Morphological and chemical analysis of magic mushrooms in Japan. *Forensic Sci Int.* 2003;138:85–90.

10. Anastos N, Barnett NW, Lewis SW, et al. Determination of psilocin and psilocybin using flow injection and tris (2,2'-bipyridyl)ruthenium (II) chemiluminescence detection respectively. *Talanta.* 2005;67:354–359.

11. Sticht G, Kaferstein H. Detection of psilocin in body fluids. *Forensic Sci Int.* 2000;113: 403–407.

12. Beck O, Helander A, Karlson-Stiber C, Stephansson N. Presence of phenylethylamine in hallucinogenic Psilocybe mushroom: possible role in adverse reactions. *J Anal Toxicol.* 1998;22:45–49.

13. Raff E, Halloran PF, Kjellstrand CM. Renal failure after eating "magic" mushrooms. *CMAJ.* 1992;147:1339–1441.

14. Gonomori K, Yoshioka N. The examination of mushroom poisonings at Akita University. *Leg Med (Tokyo)*. 2003;5(Suppl 1):S83–S86.

15. Tiscione NB, Miller MI. Psilocin identified in a DUID investigation. *J Anal Toxicol.* 2006;30:342–345.

16. El-Seedi HR, DeSmet PA, Beck O, Possnert G, Bruhn JG. Prehistoric peyote use: alkaloids and radiocarbon dating of archaeological specimens of Lophophora from Texas. *J Ethnopharmacol.* 2005;101:238–242.

17. Halpern JH, Sherwood AR, Hudson JI, Yugerlum-Todd D, Pope HG Jr. Psychological and cognitive effects of long term peyote use among Native Americans. *Biol Psychiatry.* 2005;58:624–631.

18. Nichols DE. Hallucinogens. *Pharmacol Ther.* 2004;101:131–181.

19. Reynolds PC, Jindrich EJ. A mescaline associated fatality. *J Anal Toxicol.* 1985;9:183–184.

20. Hashimoto H, Clyde VJ, Parko KL. Botulism from peyote [Letter]. *N Eng J Med.* 1998;339:203–204.

21. Nolte KB, Zumwalt RE. Fetal peyote ingestion associated with Mallory-Weiss lacerations. *West J Med.* 1999;170:328.

22. Baselt RC, Cravey RH. Lysergic acid diethylamide. In *Disposition of Toxic Drugs and Chemicals in Man.* 4th ed. Foster City, CA: Chemical Toxicology Institute; 1995:43–438.

23. Johnston LD, O'Malley PM, Bachman JG. Monitoring the future: national results on adolescent drug use: overview of key findings, 2002. Bethesda, MD: National Institute on Drug Abuse, Monitoring the Future; 2003. http://www.monitoringthefuture.org/pubs/monographs/overview2002.pdf. Accessed October 22, 2008.

24. Klette KL, Anderson C, Poch G, Nimrod AC, El-Sohly MA. Metabolism of lysergic acid diethylaminde (LSD) to 2-oxo-3-hydroxy LSD (OH-LSD) in human microsomes and cyopreserved human hepatocytes. *J Anal Toxicol.* 2000;24:550–556.

25. Poch GK, Klette KL, Anderson C. The quantitation of 2-oxo-3-hydroxy lysergic acid diethylamide (OH-LSD) in human urine specimens, a metabolite of LSD: comparative analysis using liquid chromatography-selected ion monitoring mass spectrometry. *J Anal Toxicol.* 2000;24:170–179.

26. Burnley BT, George S. The development and application of a gas chromatography-mass spectrometric (GC-MS) assay to determine the presence of 2-oxo-3-hydroxy-LSD in urine. *J Anal Toxicol.* 2003;27:249–252.

27. Wiegand RF, Klette KL, Stout P, Gehlhausen JM. Comparison of EMIT II, CEDIA, and DPC RIA assays for the detection of lysergic acid diethylamide in forensic urine samples. *J Anal Toxicol.* 2002;26:519–523.

28. Vidal C, Skipuletz T. Bupropion interference with immunoassays for amphetamines and LSD. *Ther Drug Monit.* 2007;29:373–375.

29. Kloch JC, Boerner U, Becker CE. Coma, hyperthermia, and bleeding associated with massive LSD overdose: a report of eight cases. *Clin Toxicol.* 1975;8:191–203.

30. Vroegop MP, van Dongen RT, Vantroyen B, Kramers C. [Ketamine as a party drug.] [Article in Dutch.] *Ned Tijdschr Geneeskd.* 2007;151:2039–2042.

31. Kim EM, Lee JS, Choi SK, Lim MA, Chung HS. Analysis of ketamine and norketamine in urine by automatic solid-phase extraction (SPE) and positive ion chemical ionization-gas chromatography-mass spectrometry (PCI-MS). *Forensic Sci Int.* 2008;174:197–202.

32. Tao Y, Chen XP, Qin ZH. A fetal chronic ketamine poisoning. *J Forensic Sci.* 2005;50:173–176.

33. U.S. Department of Health and Human Services. Monitoring the future survey Released: smoking among teenagers decreases sharply and increase on ecstasy use slows. HHS News, December 19, 2001. http://www.nida.nih.gov/MedAdv/01/NR12-19.html. Accessed October 22, 2008.

34. Anderson CE, Loomis GA. Recognition and prevention of inhalant abuse. *Am Fam Physicians*. 2003;68:869–874.

35. Cobaugh DJ, Seger DL, Krenzelok EP. Hydrocarbon toxicity: an analysis of AAPCC TESS data. *Przegl Lek*. 2007;64:194–196.

36. Flanagan RJ, Ives RJ. Volatile substance abuse. *Bull Narc*. 1994;46:49–78.

37. Steffee CH, Davis GJ, Nicol KK. A whiff of death: fatal volatile solvent inhalation abuse. *South Med J*. 1996;89:879–884.

38. Alper AT, Akyol A, Hasdemir H, et al. Glue (toluene) abuse: increased QT dispersion and relation with unexplained syncope. *Inhal Toxicol*. 2008;20:37–41.

CHAPTER 14

Over-the-Counter Drugs That Interfere with Drug Testing

ABSTRACT

Various over-the-counter (OTC) cold medications interfere with amphetamine/methamphetamine screening assays because the components of many cold medications, such as ephedrine and pseudoephedrine, are structurally similar to amphetamine/methamphetamine. The OTC cough medication dextromethorphan causes false-positive test results with phencyclidine (PCP) immunoassays. Common analgesics such as ibuprofen and other nonsteroidal anti-inflammatory drugs also cross-react with various screening assays employed in drugs-of-abuse testing. Ibuprofen also interferes in the immunoassay screen for marijuana metabolite. Fenoprofen may cause false-positive tests with tests for amphetamine, barbiturates, and marijuana metabolites. In addition, ingestion of poppy-seed-containing food products produces a positive test for opiate, while ingestion of excessive amounts of hemp products produces a positive test for marijuana metabolites (see also Chapter 12).

Many over-the-counter (OTC) drugs and some food products interfere with immunoassay screening for drugs. In particular, OTC medications affect immunoassay screening for the presence of amphetamine/methamphetamine. All immunoassays commercially available for screening of abused drugs in urine specimens are subject to interfering substances causing false-positive results. Therefore, any positive result from an immunoassay screening should be validated by a second, more sophisticated analytical technique like GC/MS. Interference in GC/MS is minimal

or nonexistent, making this technique the gold standard for drugs-of-abuse testing.

OTC MEDICATIONS

Many OTC cold and cough medications interfere with immunoassay screening for amphetamine/methamphetamines in urine specimens. Both amphetamine and methamphetamine exist as enantiomers (optical isomers) designed as d- (dextrorotatory) and l- (levorotatory) isomers. The d-amphetamine is the form that is abused, while in pharmaceutical preparations both d- and l-isomers can be present (see also Chapter 15). Most of the antibodies used in amphetamine assays target the amino groups of both amphetamine and methamphetamine. The cross-reactivities of these screening assays with OTC cold medications that contain various hydroxy amines vary widely from one assay to another. In addition, the active ingredients of certain dietary supplements available without prescription can produce false-positive results with urine tests for amphetamine/methamphetamine.[1-3] **Table 14-1** lists OTC products that interfere with amphetamine/methamphetamine screening assays.

Stout et al reported that cross-reactivities of ephedrine, pseudoephedrine, and phenylpropanolamine with amphetamine/methamphetamine immunoassays are generally higher than those reported by the respective manufacturers. In addition, large amounts of ephedrine and pseudoephedrine are found in urine specimens from individuals taking OTC medications containing these compounds. The authors further reported that 833 out of 1044 specimens that failed to confirm positive for the presence of amphetamine, methamphetamine, 3,4-methylenedioxyamphetamine (MDA), or 3,4-methylenedioxymethamphetamine (MDMA) by GC/MS contained ephedrine, pseudoephedrine, or phenylpropanolamine.[4]

Caplan et al reported that the fluorescence polarization immunoassay (FPIA; Abbott Laboratories, Abbott Park, IL) for screening of amphetamine/methamphetamine has a much lower cross-reactivity with pseudoephedrine and phenylpropanolamine than the enzyme multiplied immunoassay (EMIT; Dade Behring, Deerfield, IL).[5] Woodworth et al reported that by using serial dilution of urine specimens, the presence of cross-reactants can be differentiated from the presence of amphetamine/methamphetamine using the EMIT II assay.[3]

Table 14-1	Active Ingredients of OTC Products That Interfere with Amphetamine/Methamphetamine Screening Assays	
Active Ingredient		**Class of Drug**
Brompheniramine		Antihistamine
Ephedra (ephedrine)		Diet pill
Phentermine		Diet pill
Phenylpropanolamine		Decongestant
Pseudoephedrine		Decongestant
Phenylephrine		Decongestant
Ranitidine		H2 receptor blocker (reduces acid production by stomach)
Tyramine		Diet pill

In November 2000 the Food and Drug Administration (FDA) issued warnings about phenylpropanolamine and requested all drug companies to discontinue use of phenylpropanolamine in OTC medications due to the risk of hemorrhagic stroke. In response to this request many pharmaceutical companies voluntarily removed phenylpropanolamine from their products. In December 2005 the FDA issued a notice regarding use of phenylpropanolamine in OTC nasal decongestant and weight-control products. The FDA reclassified phenylpropanolamine as a nonmonograph product (Category II) that is not considered safe or effective.[6]

 ## EPHEDRA-CONTAINING WEIGHT-LOSS PRODUCTS

Dietary supplements are not recommended for weight loss because of concern about their safety. Ma huang (ephedra) is commonly found in herbal weight-loss products that are often referred to as "herbal fen-phen." Some weight-loss clinics and herbal outlets promote ma huang as an alternative to fenfluramine, the prescription drug that has been withdrawn from the market due to toxicity. Herbal fen-phen products sometimes contain St. John's wort and are marketed as "herbal Prozac." Ephedra-containing products are also marketed as decongestants, bronchodilators, and stimulants. Other promoted purposes include bodybuilding and enhancement of athletic performance. "Herbal ecstasy" is also an ephedrine-containing product, used to induce euphoria.[7]

Use of ephedra-containing products is harmful to patients with high blood pressure, glaucoma, and thyrotoxicosis. Prolonged use of ephedra-containing products or overdose with ephedra-containing supplements may result in heart attack, stroke, seizure, or death.

(–) Ephedrine is the predominant alkaloid of ephedra plants. Other phenylalanine-derived alkaloids found are (+) pseudoephedrine, (–) norephedrine, (+) norpseudoephedrine, (+) N-methyl ephedrine, and phenylpropanolamine. Ephedrine is a potent central nervous system stimulant. Phenylpropanolamine is associated with cardiac toxicity. Haller et al analyzed 35 dietary supplements and found that total ephedra alkaloid content varied from 5.97 mg to 29.3 mg per serving.[8] In another report, Haller and Benowitz evaluated 140 reports of ephedra-related toxicity that were submitted to the FDA between June 1997 and March 31, 1999. The authors concluded that 31% of cases were definitely related to ephedra toxicity and another 31% were possibly related. Reports of ephedra toxicity showed that 47% of cases involved cardiovascular problems and 18% involved problems with the central nervous system. Hypertension was the single most frequent

adverse reaction, followed by palpitation, tachycardia, stroke, and seizure. Ten events resulted in death, and 13 events caused permanent disability. The authors concluded that use of a dietary supplement that contains ephedra may pose a health risk.[9]

The FDA banned ephedra alkaloids in April 2004. The banned products were ma huang, *Sida cordifolia L.*, and *Pinellia ternata*, but Chinese herbal products, herbal teas, and drugs containing synthetic ephedrine were not banned. There is a push for companies marketing herbal weight-loss products to produce ephedra-free diet pills. Ephedra-free diet pills may also contain phenylpropanolamine, tyramine, or phentermine, which like ephedrine interferes with the immunoassay screening of amphetamine/methamphetamine in urine specimens. However, GC/MS analysis can distinguish these compounds from amphetamine or methamphetamine. Other diet products that contain hydroxy citric acid, pyruvate, chromium, or bitter orange do not interfere with drugs-of-abuse testing.

EFFECT OF INHALER USE ON AMPHETAMINE/METHAMPHETAMINE SCREENING

OTC nasal decongestant Vicks inhaler contains l-amphetamine. Because immunoassay screening for amphetamine is specifically designed for identification of d-methamphetamine, use of the Vicks Inhaler usually does not cause false-positive results in urine drug testing for amphetamine/methamphetamine. Poklis et al had two subjects use the Vicks Inhaler every hour. They found that the highest concentrations of l-methamphetamine observed in the subjects following the inhaler use were 1390 ng/ml and 740 ng/ml, respectively.

The subjects' urine specimens tested negative with the EMIT II amphetamine/methamphetamine assay (Dade Behring, Deerfield, IL).[10] Another study reported that nasal use of the Vicks Inhaler following the recommended dosage should not cause false-positive amphetamine/methamphetamine urine screening results using FPIA for amphetamine/methamphetamine on the TDxADs/FLx analyzer (Abbott Laboratories, Abbott Park, IL) because the antibody used in this immunoassay is stereoselective. This assay recognized d-methamphetamine or d-amphetamine if present in the urine specimens. However, when two subjects inhaled twice the recommended dosage, a positive test result was obtained by the FPIA screening assay. The concentrations of l-methamphetamine in the urine specimens of these two subjects were 1560 ng/ml and 1530 ng/ml, respectively.[11] However, l-methamphetamine can be distinguished from d-methamphetamine using GC/MS and the chiral derivatization technique.[2] If more than than 80% l-methamphetamine is found in the specimen, the result is considered consistent with use of the Vicks Inhaler.

GC/MS is used to differentiate ephedrine, pseudoephedrine, and related products from amphetamine and methamphetamine. However, Hornbeck et al demonstrated that at a high injector port temperature (where the specimen in introduced into the GC/MS machine) of 300°C and higher, if ephedrine or pseudoephedrine is present in high amounts in urine, it can be thermally dehydrated to methamphetamine, causing false-positive confirmation of methamphetamine.[12] This artifact can be avoided by maintaining the injector port temperature at 180°C. Based on these reports the federal drug-testing guidelines now state that amphetamine, a metabolite of methamphetamine, should be present in the specimen at a concentration of 200 ng/ml or higher in order to report any urine drug test as positive for methamphetamine. **Table 14-2** lists common OTC medications that interfere with amphetamine/methamphetamine immunoassays.

 SOME OTC COLD MEDICATIONS MOVED BEHIND THE COUNTER

In 2006 the U.S. Patriot Act mandated that all medications containing the decongestant pseudoephedrine be stocked behind the pharmacy counter and sold in limited quantities because pseudoephedrine is used in the illegal manufacturing of methamphetamine for abuse. The new law affected several hundred OTC products for children and adults, including Sudafed Nasal Decongestant tablets, Advil Allergy Sinus caplets, Thera-Flu Daytime Severe Cold softgels, Tylenol Flu NightTime Gel Caps, and Vicks Children's NyQuil Cold and Cough. These products are still available without a prescription, but they must be purchased from a pharmacist by presenting a valid identification issued by a government agency (such as a driver's license).

The federal law also limits an individual to buying products containing no more than 3.6 g of pseudoephedrine in a single day and no more than 9 g a month at a retail store. Therefore, many pharmaceutical companies have replaced pseudoephedrine in their formulations with phenylephrine, which has a similar action to pseudoephedrine but can not be used to make methamphetamine. The law also restricts sale of two other common ingredients in OTC drugs, ephedrine and phenylpropanolamine, because both compounds

Table 14-2	Some Common OTC Medications That Interfere with Amphetamine/Methamphetamine Immunoassays	
Interfering Compound	**Product Name(s)**	
Brompheniramine	Allent, Andehist syrup, Bromadrine PD, Bromfed-DM, Bromfenex, Dallergy, Dexaphen SA, Dimetapp, Drixoral Allergy Sinus, Lodrane, Rondec syrup	
Phentermine	Adipex-P	
Phenylephrine	Actifed Cold and Allergy, Ami-Tex LA, Neo-Synephrine, Sudafed PE	
Phenylephrine (nasal)	Afrin, Alconefrin nasal drops, Neo-Synephrine, Rhinall, Vicks Sinex	
Pseudoephedrine	Actifed, Alka-Selzer Plus, Allegra-D, Claritin-D, Comtrex Daytime Maximum Strength Cold and Cough, Comtrex Maximum Strength Non-Drowsy capsules, Contac Cold and Flu day caplets, Despec-SR caplets, Duratuss, Entex LA, Guaifed, Mapap Cold Formula, Ornex Severe Cold No Drowsiness caplets, Tuss-LA, Sudafed, Novafed, Robitussin Cold and Congestion tablets, Robitussin Cold Multi-Symptom Cold and Flu softgels, Theraflu, Tylenol Allergy and Sinus, Tylenol Cold, Tylenol Sinus, Vicks Children's NyQuil Cold and Cough, Vicks 44 Cough and Cold Relief Non-Drowsy LiquiCaps, Vicks DayQuil Multi-Symptom Cold and Flu LiquiCaps, Vicks NyQuil Multi-Symptoms Cold and Flu Relief, Zephrex-LA	
Ranitidine	Zantac	

have the potential to be used illegally to make methamphetamine.[13]

 OTC COLD MEDICATIONS MAY BE FATAL IN INFANTS

Over-the-counter cold and cough medicines may cause severe toxicity and even fatality in infants younger than 2 years. Caregivers sometimes unknowingly give infants more than one OTC cold medication with similar composition, causing life-threatening overdoses. In 2004 and 2005, an estimated 1519 children under 2 years of age were treated for toxicity associated with use of cold and cough medications. The proper dosage of cold and cough medications in children below 2 years old is not known. Therefore, OTC cold and cough medications should not be given to any children under 2 years of age without approval of a physician, and the dosage recommended by the physician should be strictly followed to avoid an adverse drug effect.[14]

Boland et al reported fatal cold medication intoxication in an infant involving pseudoephedrine, brompheniramine, and dextromethorphan. The concentrations of brompheniramine and dextromethorphan in the postmortem blood were 0.40 mg/L and 0.50 mg/L, respectively, and the concentration of pseudoephedrine was 14.4 mg/L.[15] The Philadelphia medical examiner's office reported the deaths of 15 infants below the age of 16 months between

February 1999 and June 2005 in which ingredients of OTC cold medicines were present in the postmortem blood. The most commonly found drug was pseudoephedrine, which was detected in all cases in blood concentrations ranging from 0.10 to 0.17 mg/L, and it was the only drug detected in three cases. Other drugs detected were acetaminophen, dextromethorphan, carbinoxamine, chlorpheniramine, brompheniramine, doxylamine, and ethanol.[16] The Montgomery County coroner's office in Ohio also reported a series of 10 infant deaths over eight months in which toxicological analyses detected the presence of active ingredients of OTC cold and cough medicines.[17]

Pseudoephedrine can even be toxic in adults. Sizemore et al reported that a 31-year-old woman with pheochromocytoma developed hypertensive crisis and congestive heart failure due to use of an OTC cold medicine containing pseudoephedrine. She died from subsequent cardiac arrhythmia and shock.[18]

RANITIDINE AND AMPHETAMINE/ METHAMPHETAMINE SCREENING

Ranitidine is a H_2-receptor blocking agent that reduces stomach acid production. This drug is used for treating ulcers and now is available without a prescription. Dietzen et al reported that ranitidine, if present in urine at a concentration over 43 µg/ml, produces false-positive test results with an amphetamine screen using Beckman Synchron immunoassay reagents (Beckman Diagnostics, Fullerton, CA). This concentration of ranitidine is routinely exceeded in patients taking ranitidine.[19] Poklis also reported that ranitidine interferes with the EMIT d.a.u. amphetamine/methamphetamine assay if the ranitidine concentration in urine exceeds 91 µg/ml. The concentrations of ranitidine in urine specimens collected from 23 patients receiving 150 to 300 mg ranitidine per day varied from 7 µg/ml to 271 µg/ml.[20]

MISCELLANEOUS OTHER INTERFERENCES

Dextromethorphan is an antitussive agent found in over 125 OTC cough and cold medications. **Table 14-3** lists just some of the available products that contain dextromethorphan.

Dextromethorphan is also abused in high dosages, mostly by young adults. High doses of dextromethorphan (over 30 mg) produce false-positive opiate and phencyclidine (PCP) test results with immunoassays.[22,23] In another report, the authors observed three false-positive PCP tests in pediatric urine specimens using an on-site testing device (Instant-View multitest drugs-of-abuse panel; Alfa Scientific Designs, Poway, CA). The authors concluded that the false-positive PCP tests were due to the cross-reactivities of ibuprofen, metamizol, and dextromethorphan and their metabolites with the PCP assay. These drugs were detected in high amounts in the urine specimens collected from these pediatric patients.[23] Pheniramine and methylphenidate also produce false-positive results with the PCP screen.[23]

Anecdotal reports also indicate that nonsteroidal anti-inflammatory drugs may produce false-positive results in immunoassay screening tests for the presence of drugs of abuse in urine specimens. Rollins et al studied the effect of such drugs on drugs-of-abuse screening by using 60 volunteers

Case Studies

Case 1: A medical review officer (MRO) received a laboratory result confirming the presence of methamphetamine (1250 ng/ml) and amphetamine (225 ng/ml). During the interview the donor informed the MRO she had used the Vicks Vapor Inhaler and diazepam. The laboratory performed a chiral analysis of methamphetamine and confirmed that over 95% of methamphetamine was present as l-methamphetamine, the active ingredient of Vicks Vapor Inhaler. Although benzodiazepine was not tested as a part of the workplace drug-testing protocol, the MRO verified the information that the donor had a prescription for diazepam (Valium). The MRO reported the drug testing as negative to the agency and did not provide the information regarding use of diazepam because the donor had used the medication legally.

Case 2: A laboratory test confirmed the presence of methamphetamine (950 ng/ml) and amphetamine (245 ng/ml) in a urine specimen. The donor denied use of any prescription medication but informed the MRO that he had used a Vicks Vapor Inhaler. Chiral analysis revealed that approximately 90% of the amphetamine and methamphetamine in the specimen were d-isomers. Because the Vicks Vapor Inhaler contains only l-methamphetamine, the d-methamphetamine and d-amphetamine in the specimen could not have come from the use of the Vicks Inhaler but instead indicated illicit use of methamphetamine. The MRO reported the result as positive for methamphetamine.

Table 14-3 Some Products That Contain Dextromethorphan	
Alka-Seltzer Plus	Pertussin DM Extra Strength
Benylin Adult Formula cough suppressant	Robitussin cough gels
Benylin Pediatric cough suppressant	Robitussin Maximum Strength cough
Bromfed	suppressant
Cheracol D cough formula	Robitussin Pediatric cough suppressant
Codal DM syrup	Sinuatus DM
Codimal DM syrup	Sucrets 8-Hour cough suppressant
Comtrex Cold and Cough Multi-Symptom	Sudafed Cold and Cough liquid caps
Relief	Su-Tuss DM
Coricidin HBP Cough and Cold	Theraflu
Coricidin HBP Flu Maximum Strength	Triaminic Cold and Cough soft chews
Cydec DM syrup	Triaminic Cough soft chews
Delsym	Vicks 44 Cough Relief
Diabetic Tussin DM	

and 42 patients taking ibuprofen, naproxen, or fenoprofen. Out of 510 urine specimens collected from 102 individuals, only 2 specimens tested positive for cannabinoids using an EMIT assay, one in an individual who ingested 1200 mg ibuprofen in three divided dosages, and one in a patient taking naproxen regularly. Two urine specimens were false positive for barbiturates using the FPIA, one in a patient taking ibuprofen and one in a patient taking naproxen. The authors concluded that there is a small likelihood of false-positive results in drugs-of-abuse screening assays in individuals taking nonsteroidal anti-inflammatory drugs.[24]

Although most reports in the literature describe false-positive results in drugs-of-abuse testing due to the presence of OTC medications in urine specimens, Brunk reported a false-negative GC/MS confirmation of THC metabolite (THC-COOH) as methyl derivative due to the interference of ibuprofen with the methylation step. The urine specimen tested positive for THC metabolite using the EMIT d.a.u. assay, but it tested negative by GC/MS. Thin-layer chromatography confirmed the presence of THC-COOH.[25]

OTC DRUGS CONTAINING CODEINE AND OPIATE

Codeine-containing products are strictly controlled in the United States, although they are more freely available in Canada. Codeine itself is classified as a Schedule II drug, but a small amount of codeine in combination with other active ingredients is found in some cough formulas classified as Schedule IV drugs, and a few of these medications are available without prescription in some states. However, Canadian law states that OTC products containing codeine must contain two other active ingredients (for example, acetaminophen). A nonprescription codeine-containing product is Kaodene with Codeine, while morphine-containing products include Amogel, Donnagel-PG, Infantol Pink, Paregoric, and Quiagel PG. Most of these products are used as antidiarrheal agents. Use of these products may cause positive opiate test results.[26]

CONCLUSION

Various OTC cold medications containing pseudoephedrine, phenylephrine, and related compounds interfere with various amphetamine/methamphetamine screening assays, but GC/MS confirmatory tests can differentiate these compounds from amphetamine and methamphetamine. Due to a few reports of misidentification of pseudoephedrine as methamphetamine in the GC/MS confirmation step, federal guidelines now require that amphetamine, a metabolite of methamphetamine, be present at a concentration equal to or greater than 200 ng/ml in order to report a positive confirmatory test for methamphetamine. OTC cold medicines containing pseudoephedrine and related compounds are unsafe for young children younger than 2 years and should not be administered without consulting a physician. Infant deaths have been reported from OTC cold and cough medicines containing pseudoephedrine and related compounds. Pseudoephedrine can even be toxic in adults. Dextromethorphan, a common constituent of many OTC cough medications, interferes with screening of phencyclidine. Several OTC nonsteroidal anti-inflammatory drugs also interfere with various screening assays, but such false-positive results can be easily identified by GC/MS.

REFERENCES

1. Moore KA. Amphetamine/sympathomimetic amines. In: Levine B, ed. *Principles of Forensic Toxicology*. Washington, DC: American Association for Clinical Chemistry; 2003:341–348.

2. Dasgupta A, Saldana S, Kinnaman G, Smith M, Johansen K. Analytical performance evaluation of EMIT II monoclonal amphetamine/methamphetamine assay: more specificity than EMIT d.a.u. monoclonal amphetamine/methamphetamine assay. *Clin Chem*. 1993;39:104–108.

3. Woodworth A, Saunders AN, Koenig JW, Moyer TP, Turk J, Dietzen DJ. Differentiation of amphetamine/methamphetamine and other cross-immunoreactive sympathomimetic amines in urine samples by serial dilution. *Clin Chem*. 2006;52:743–746.

4. Stout PR, Klette KL, Horn CK. Evaluation of ephedrine, pseudoephedrine, and phenylpropanolamine concentrations in human urine samples and comparison of the specificity of DRI amphetamines and Abuscreen online (KIMS) amphetamine screening immunoassay. *J Forensic Sci*. 2004;49:160–164.

5. Caplan YH, Levine B, Goldburger B. Fluorescence polarization immunoassay for screening for amphetamine and methamphetamine in urine. *Clin Chem*. 1987;33:1200–1202.

6. U.S. Food and Drug Administration. Phenylpropanolamine (PPA) Information. http://www.fda.gov/cder/drug/infopage/ppa/default.htm. Accessed October 20, 2008.

7. Street drug alternative with ephedra. *FDA Consumer*. 1996;30(5):4.

8. Haller CA, Duan M, Benowitz NL, Jacob P 3rd. Concentrations of ephedra alkaloids and caffeine in commercial dietary supplements. *J Anal Toxicol*. 2004;28:145–151.

9. Haller CA, Benowitz NL. Adverse and central nervous system events associated with dietary supplements containing ephedra alkaloids. *N Eng J Med*. 2000;343:1833–1838.

10. Poklis A, Jortani WSA, Brown CS, Crooks CR. Response of the EMIT II amphetamine/methamphetamine assay to specimens collected following use of Vicks inhalers. *J Anal Toxicol*. 1993;17:284–286.

11. Poklis A, Moore KA. Stereoselectivity of the TDX/ADX/FLx amphetamine/methamphetamine II amphetamine/methamphetamine immunoassay response of urine specimens following nasal inhaler use. *J Toxicol Clin Toxicol*. 1995;33:35–41.

12. Hornbeck CL, Carrig JE, Czarny RJ. Detection of GC/MS artifact peak as methamphetamine. *J Anal Toxicol*. 1993;17:257–263.

13. Bren L. Some cold medications move behind the counter. *FDA Consumer*. 2006;40(4):18–19.

14. Centers for Disease Control and Prevention. Infant deaths associated with cough and cold medications—two states, 2005. *Morb Mortal Wkly Rep*. 2007;56:1–4.

15. Boland DM, Rein J, Lwe EO, Hearn WL. Fatal cold medication intoxication in an infant. *J Anal Toxicol*. 2003;27:523–526.

16. Wingert WE, Mundy LA, Colloins GL, Chmara ES. Possible role of pseudoephedrine and over-the-counter cold medications in the deaths of very young children. *J Forensic Sci*. 2007;52:487–490.

17. Marinetti L, Lehman L, Castro B, Harshbarger K, Kubiczek P, Davis J. Over-the-counter cold medications-postmortem findings in infants and relationship to cause of death. *J Anal Toxicol*. 2005;29:738–743.

18. Sizemore GW, Scrogin KE, Weisenberg ES, Weldon-Linne CM, Madoo OB. Hypertensive crisis, catecholamine cardiomyopathy and death associated with pseudoephedrine use in a patient with pheochromocytoma. *Endocr Pract*. 2008;14:93–96.

19. Dietzen DJ, Ecos K, Friedman D, Beason S. Positive predictive values of abused drug immunoassays on the Beckman Synchron in a veteran population. *J Anal Toxicol*. 2001;25:174–178.

20. Poklis A, Hall KV, Still J, Binder SR. raniti-dine interference with the monoclonal EMIT d.a.u. amphetamine/methampheta-mine assay. *J Anal Toxicol.* 1991;15:101–103.

21. U.S. Department of Heath and Human Services, Substance Abuse and Mental Health Services Administration. MRO Case Studies: Case #1. February 2005. http://workplace.samhsa.gov/DrugTesting/Files_Drug_Testing/MROs/MRO%20Case%20Studies%20-%20February%202005.pdf. Accessed October 22, 2008.

22. Schwartz RH. Adolescent abuse of dextro-methorphan. *Clin Pediatr (Phila).* 2005;44:565–568.

23. Marchei E, Pellegrini M, Pichini S, Martin I, García-Algar O, Vall O. Are false-positive phencyclidine immunoassay instant-view multi test results caused by overdose con-centrations of ibuprofen, metamizol, and dextromethorphan? *Ther Drug Monit.* 2007;29:671–673.

24. Rollins DE, Jennison TA, Jones G. Investi-gation of interference by nonsteroidal anti-inflammatory drugs in urine tests for abused drugs. *Clin Chem.* 1990;36:602–606.

25. Brunk SD. False positive GC/MS assay for carboxy THC due to ibuprofen interference. *J Anal Toxicol.* 1988;12:290–291.

26. Kwong TC. Clinical false positive drug test results. In: Dasgupta A, ed. *Handbook of Drug Monitoring Methods.* Totowa, NJ: Humana Press; 2008:395–406.

CHAPTER 15

Prescription Medications That Interfere with Drug Testing

ABSTRACT

Many prescription medications interfere with the immunoassay screening of drugs. In addition, several prescription medications contain Class II, III, IV, or V drugs, which are also abused. Several prescription medications contain amphetamine, methamphetamine, or drugs that are metabolized to amphetamine or methamphetamine and thus cause analytical true-positive results in the GC/MS confirmation step. Use of opioid-containing pain medications may cause positive opiate test results. Use of benzodiazepines under medical advice also produces a positive benzodiazepine result in drugs-of-abuse testing. The prescription drug Marinol, although used infrequently, is metabolized to THC-COOH. A patient taking Marinol will test positive for cannabinoid in drugs-of-abuse testing. It is extremely important for donors to disclose use of any prescription drugs during pre-employment drug testing or workplace drug testing.

Many OTC cold and cough medicines interfere with urine screening tests but rarely interfere with GC/MS confirmation tests. In contrast, several prescription medicines contain opioid, amphetamine, or methamphetamine, which produce a true-positive drug-testing result. Use of the prescription drug Marinol to control severe pain produces a true-positive confirmatory test for marijuana metabolite (11-nor-9-carboxy-Δ^9-tetrahydrocannabinol; THC-COOH) in urine. Although the presence of benzodi-azepines in urine is not always tested in workplace drug testing, many prescription tranquilizers and anti-anxiolytic drugs contain benzodiazepines. Therefore, taking such medications produces a positive benzodiazepine test result. In addition, several prescription drugs interfere with screening assays for drugs-of-abuse testing, but the GC/MS confirmatory step can distinguish such drugs from illicit drugs if present in urine specimens.

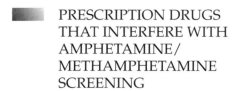
PRESCRIPTION DRUGS THAT INTERFERE WITH AMPHETAMINE/ METHAMPHETAMINE SCREENING

Many OTC cold medicines interfere with the screening for amphetamine/methamphetamine in urine specimens due to structural similarities of these drugs with methamphetamine. In addition, several prescription drugs also interfere with the screening of amphetamine/methamphetamine in urine specimens but do not interfere with the GC/MS confirmation step. **Table 15-1** provides a list of these drugs along with their common brand names and indications for use.

These drugs include buflomedil, chloroquine, fenfluramine, isometheptene, isoxsuprine, perazine, phenmetrazine, promethazine, propylhexedrine, quinacrine, tolmetin, and trimethobenzamide. In addition, the metabolite of procainamide, N-acetyl procainamide, also interferes with the screening of amphetamine/methamphetamine in urine.[1] Papa et al described interference of buflomedil in the monoclonal enzyme multiplied immunoassay technique (EMIT d.a.u.; Dade Behring, Deerfield, IL), but no false-positive result was obtained with the polyclonal EMIT assay.[2] In another study, authors observed that 36% of patients taking promethazine had false-positive test results of urine amphetamine using the EMIT II Plus monoclonal amphetamine/methamphetamine assay (Dade Behring). A separate study did not show any false-positive test results due to the presence of promethazine using EMIT II Plus, Triage (Biosite, San Diego, CA), and TesTcard 9 (Roche Diagnostics, Indianapolis, IN) amphetamine assays.[3] Fenfluramine, a component of fen-phen,

also interferes with immunoassay screening for amphetamine/methamphetamine, but in 1997 this drug was withdrawn from the U.S. market because of its cardiotoxicity.

Methylphenidate is used to treat attention deficit hyperactivity disorder (ADHD). Manzi et al reported a case in which a false-positive amphetamine screening result was reported in a child taking methylphenidate.[4] An old phenothiazine derivative, perazine, which is used as an antipsychotic drug, caused false-positive amphetamine and opiate screening results using the fluorescence polarization immunoassay (FPIA; Abbott Laboratories, Abbott Park, IL) in a patient intoxicated with perazine. In contrast, a more specific technique, high-performance liquid chromatography, did not show any presence of amphetamine or opiate.[5]

Mebeverine is an antispasmodic drug that is a substituted ethyl amphetamine derivative. This drug is metabolized to paramethoxyamphetamine and other derivatives, and it produces positive amphetamine screening results using the FPIA amphetamine/methamphetamine screening assay. However, by detecting specific metabolites of mebeverine using GC/MS, the false-positive screening assay can be shown to be due to prescription use of mebeverine.[6]

PRESCRIPTION DRUGS THAT CONTAIN AMPHETAMINE OR METHAMPHETAMINE

Amphetamine and methamphetamine are listed as Schedule II drugs in the United States and are used to treat ADHD. These drugs contain d-amphetamine, d-methamphetamine, or a racemic mixture of d- and l-isomers. **Table 15-2** gives brand names of these drugs. For example, Adderall contains a mixed amphetamine salt that is widely prescribed as a psychostimulant medication

Table 15-1   Active Ingredients of Prescription Drugs That Interfere with Amphetamine/Methamphetamine Screening Assays

Active Ingredient	Use	Brand Name
Buflomedil	Treating peripheral arterial disease	Buflomedil Merck
Chloroquine	Antimalarial	Aralen
Chlorpromazine	Antipsychotic	Thorazine
Fenfluramine	Weight-loss product	Withdrawn from U.S. market
Isometheptene	Treating migraine and tension headache	Isocom, Isopap, Midchlor, Midrin, Migratine, Mitride
Isoxsuprine	Treating symptoms of central and peripheral vascular disease	Vasodilan, Voxuprine
Methylphenidate	For treating attention deficit hyperactivity disorder	Concerta, Metadate, Methylin, Ritalin
Mexiletine	Antiarrhythmic	Mexitil
Mebeverine	Antispasmodic	Daspatal
Perazine	Old phenothiazine derivative; antipsychotic	Taxilan
Phenmetrazine	Withdrawn from U.S. market	Preludin
Promethazine	Treating severe allergy	Phenergan, Promethergan, Promacot
Propylhexedrine	Treating nasal congestion	Benzedrex
Quinacrine	Antiprotozoal	Atabrine
Tolmetin	Nonsteroidal anti-inflammatory drug	Tolectin
Trimethobenzamide	Treating nausea and vomiting	Tigan
N-acetyl procainamide	Metabolite of procainamide	Procanbid

for ADHD. Use of these drugs produces positive results (both screening and confirmation) in urine drugs-of-abuse testing. Individuals who take these medications should present a valid prescription to the medical review officer (MRO), who may verify the use of such drugs by contacting the physician who prescribed the medication. The use of Adderall is an acceptable explanation for a positive amphetamine test in workplace drug testing. Without valid proof that the drug was taken under medical advice, such results would be reported to the agency as positive, indicating illicit use of amphetamine or methamphetamine.

In January 2002 the FDA approved Paremyd eye drops, which contain the substances hydroxyamphetamine and tropicamide. Hydroxyamphetamine is used outside the United States as a topical nasal decongestant as well as for oral use. Although amphetamine is metabolized to hydroxyamphetamine, hydroxyamphetamine is not metabolized to amphetamine.

Table 15-2   Drugs That Contain Amphetamine or Methamphetamine or are Metabolized to Amphetamine or Methamphetamine

Active Ingredient	Brand Names
Amphetamine	Adderall, Biphetamine, Dexedrine, DextroStat
Methamphetamine	Desoxyn
Amphetaminil	Aponeuron (used in treatment of obesity, but mostly withdrawn from clinical use due potential for abuse)
Clobenzorex	Aselin, Asenlix, Dinintel, Finedal, Rexigen
Ethyl amphetamine	Apetinil (mostly replaced by other anoretic agents)
Fenoproporex	Falagan, Lipolin (mostly replaced by other drugs or withdrawn due to toxicity)
Mefenorex	Rondimen, Pondinil, Anexate
Prenylamine	Segontin, Segentine
Benzphetamine	Didrex
Famprofazone	Gewodin (multi-ingredient medicine containing the analgesic famprofazone)
Furfenorex	Withdrawn due to abuse potential
Selegiline	Carbex, Deprenyl, Eldepryl

Therefore, use of such products should not cause positive amphetamine test results in urine drug testing.[7]

PRESCRIPTION DRUGS THAT ARE METABOLIZED TO AMPHETAMINE OR METHAMPHETAMINE

Several drugs that are metabolized to amphetamine or methamphetamine (and then also to amphetamine) produce positive test results for amphetamine/methamphetamine in drugs-of-abuse testing. Drugs such as amphetaminil, benzphetamine, clobenzorex, dimethylamphetamine, ethyl-amphetamine, famprofazone, fencamine, fenethylline, fenproporex, fenfenorex, mefenorex, mesocarb, selegiline, and prenylamine are metabolized to amphetamine or methamphetamine.[8]

In the past, ethylamphetamine was used for appetite suppression and control of obesity, but it has mostly been replaced by newer drugs. Similarly, amphetaminil, which is also metabolized to amphetamine, was used in the past for treating obesity, but the drug is rarely used clinically because of its abuse potential. Benzphetamine, clobenzorex, fencamine, fenproporex, mefenorex, and furfenorex are also anoretic agents and are used to treat obesity. Prenylamine, which is metabolized to amphetamine, is a calcium channel blocker that causes coronary vasodilation and is used to treat angina pectoris. Selegiline is used to treat Parkinson disease, and this drug is metabolized to methamphetamine.[8]

The amphetamine-containing drug Adderall is widely prescribed for patients suffering from ADHD. Cody et al studied the effect of Adderall on urinary concentrations of amphetamine using five volunteers who each ingested 20-mg Adderall tablets. The peak amphetamine concentrations ranged from 2645 to 5948 ng/ml and had positive amphetamine concentrations above the GC/MS confirmation level of 500 ng/ml as many as 47.5 hours post ingestion. As expected, both d- and l-isomers of amphetamine were observed in urine, which distinguished the profile from illicit use of amphetamine, which contains mostly d-isomer, and also from use of another amphetamine-containing drug, Dexedrine (which contains d-isomer).[9] In another study, volunteers ingested 120-mg oral doses of prenylamine, which is also known to metabolize to amphetamine. The FPIA amphetamine/methamphetamine assay showed wide variations in amphetamine levels. A urine specimen collected from one volunteer showed an amphetamine concentration of 3200 ng/ml, while a urine specimen collected from another volunteer provided a negative screen for amphetamine/methamphetamine. The GC/MS analysis confirmed the presence of both d- and l-isomers of amphetamine because prenylamine is manufactured as a racemic mixture (a mixture of both d- and l-isomers).[10]

Famprofazone is metabolized to methamphetamine, and then methamphetamine is subsequently metabolized to amphetamine. Grenhill et al studied the urine amphetamine and methamphetamine concentrations of subjects who ingested 2 Gewodin tablets containing a total of 50 mg of famprofazone. GC/MS showed peak amphetamine concentrations (148–2271 ng/ml) and methamphetamine concentrations (615–7361 ng/ml) 3 to 7 hours post ingestion. Both d- and l-isomers of amphetamine and methamphetamine were identified in urine specimens.[11]

Selegiline, a drug used in treating Parkinson disease, is metabolized to l-methamphetamine, which is further metabolized to l-amphetamine. Given the stereospecificity of antibody used in designing of immunoassays for screening of amphetamine/methamphetamine in urine, a low dosage of selegiline should not produce a positive screening result. Nevertheless, positive immunoassay screening results using the FPIA amphetamine/methamphetamine assay were observed up to 2 days following ingestion of a 10-mg selegiline tablet. However, mostly l-isomers of both methamphetamine and amphetamine were detected in urine, which indicates that the test is detecting selegiline rather than illegal methamphetamine because if it were methamphetamine, d-isomer would be present.[12] Therefore, stereoselective analysis of both amphetamine and methamphetamine is important to distinguish illicit use of methamphetamine or amphetamine from medical use of certain drugs or use of the Vicks Vapor Inhaler, which contains l-methamphetamine and is available without prescription (see Chapter 14).

OPIOID-CONTAINING PRESCRIPTION DRUGS

Several prescription medications for treating moderate to severe pain contain morphine, codeine, hydrocodone, oxycodone, or related opioids. Oxymorphone is the newest oral opioid used in treating moderate to severe persistent pain. Oxymorphone is structurally similar to hydromorphone.[13] Ingestion of fentanyl-containing drugs (which are also opioid) or use of a fentanyl patch like the Duragesic patch should not cause a positive opiate test result because fentanyl has very poor cross-reactivity with the antibodies used in opiate screening assays, which recognize morphine and related substances. Oxycodone has variable cross-reactivity with different opiate screening assays, and there is also a specific immunoassay that recognizes the presence of oxycodone in urine. However, taking codeine- or morphine-containing analgesic medication produces a positive opiate test result in drugs-of-abuse testing. **Table 15-3** provides a list of these drugs along with their common product names. It is important for donors to disclose the use of such medication during workplace drug testing in order to avoid the negative consequences of a positive opiate test result.

Ethylmorphine, which is used in many countries as an antitussive agent, is metabolized to morphine. Ingestion of ethylmorphine produces 100% positive test results with opiate screening in urine specimens using the EMIT assay during the first 24 hours of administration of the drug. Both ethylmorphine and morphine were detected in urine specimens, while morphine was formed from ethylmorphine at a highly variable rate.[14] After oral ingestion, codeine is metabolized to morphine, and in subjects taking a single dose of codeine-containing medication, the total amount of morphine present in a urine specimen can be more than the concentration of codeine.[15] Therefore, the morphine-to-codeine ratio is not reliable to determine the type of opiate ingestion. Although codeine is metabolized to morphine, morphine is not metabolized to codeine. Therefore, codeine should not be observed in the urine of an individual who has taken a drug containing only morphine.

Opiate testing also tests for the presence of hydrocodone, oxycodone, hydromorphone, and oxymorphone. Moreover, hydromorphone and hydrocodone may produce a positive result in the opiate-screening assay depending on the type on antibody used in the assay, although oxy-

codone and oxymorphone usually have low cross-reactivity with most opiate immunoassays. For example, the Roche On-Line opiate immunoassay (Roche Diagnostics, Indianapolis, IN) has less than 4% cross-reactivity with oxycodone, but the corresponding cross-reactivities with hydromorphone and hydrocodone are 21% and 28%, respectively (according to the package insert). The EMIT d.a.u. and the EMIT II Plus opiate assay have 6.7% and 5.6% cross-reactivity with oxycodone, respectively. Smith et al reported that when a single dose of hydrocodone, hydromorphone, oxycodone, or oxymorphone was administered to volunteers, both parent drugs and their O-demethylated metabolites were excreted, with peak concentrations reached within 8 hours and then declining to below 300 ng/ml within 24 to 48 hours, as measured by GC/MS. Immunoassay screening for opiates using both the EMIT and the FPIA detected hydromorphone, hydrocodone, and oxycodone 6 to 24 hours after ingestion of the respective drug using a cutoff opiate concentration of 300 ng/ml. However, neither assay detected the presence of oxymorphone. The authors concluded that urine specimens containing low to moderate concentrations of hydromorphone, hydrocodone, oxycodone, and oxymorphone will likely test negative using conventional immunoassay screening of opiates. The GC/MS method is more sensitive for detecting these parent drugs and the corresponding metabolites compared with immunoassays.[16]

USE OF MARINOL AND THE MARIJUANA TEST

Although marijuana is a Schedule I drug, a synthetic tetrahydrocannabinol called dronabinol is sold under the trade name

Table 15-3   Common Products Containing Narcotic Analgesic Drugs

Active Ingredient	Product Names
Codeine	Ambenyl with Codeine, Codimal PH 7 Syrup, Fioricet with Codeine, Fiorinal with Codeine, Guiatuss, Phenaphen with Codeine, Triacin-C, Robitussin-DAC, Tylenol with Codeine
Morphine	Avinza, Astramorph, Duramorph, Kadian, MS Contin tablets, Oramorph SR, Roxanol, Roxanol-T, Paregoric
Oxycodone	OxyContin, Oxydose, OxyIR, Roxicodone, Endocet, Percocet, Percodan, Roxicet, Roxiprin, Tylox
Hydrocodone	Anexsia, Co-Gesic, Hydrocet, Lorcet-HD, Lortab, Norco, Panacet, Vicodin, Vicoprofen, Zydone
Hydromorphone	Dilaudid
Oxymorphone	Opana

Marinol to treat nausea and vomiting in cancer patients undergoing chemotherapy, as an appetite stimulant for patients with AIDS, and also in the management of glaucoma as well as a variety of other purposes. Because Marinol is also converted into marijuana metabolite (THC-COOH), use of Marinol produces a positive test for marijuana metabolites in drugs-of-abuse testing. However, Δ^9-tetrahydrocannabivarin (THCV), which is a natural constituent of cannabis, is absent in dronabinol. THVC is metabolized by human liver into THCV-COOH, and the presence of this metabolite in addition to THC-COOH in urine indicates abuse of marijuana rather than prescription use of dronabinol.[17]

Antiretroviral therapy with the medication efavirenz in patients with acquired immune deficiency syndrome (AIDS) may cause a false-positive test for marijuana metabolite (using 50 ng/ml as cutoff level) using the CEDIA DAU Multi-level THC (Microgenics Corporation, Fremont, CA), the Triage Drug Screen (Biosite Corporation, San Diego, CA), and the Cannabinoid THCA/CTHC Direct ELISA kit (Immunalysis Corporation, Pomona, CA). In contrast, no false-positive test result was observed using the EMIT assay, the FPIA assay, or the Intercept Microplate point-of-care testing device (OraSure Technology, Bethlehem, PA). The false-positive result was due to the metabolite of efavirenz (efavirenz-8-glucuronide).[18]

BENZODIAZEPINE-CONTAINING DRUGS

Although benzodiazepines are not one of the five drugs for which testing is federally mandated, many private companies test for the presence of benzodiazepines in urine in their own workplace drug-testing programs. Benzodiazepines are one of the most frequently prescribed drugs in the United States and are used as tranquilizers, muscle relaxants, anticonvulsants, and anti-anxiety treatments. There are more than 50 different types of benzodiazepines, but not all of these are available in the United States. The most commonly prescribed benzodiazepines in the United States are diazepam, temazepam, alprazolam, lorazepam, and clonazepam. Some of the drugs in this class (for example, estazolam, temazepam, halazepam, and quazepam) are derivatives of benzodiazepine. Several drugs in the benzodiazepine class (for example, flurazepam) are short acting, while diazepam, alprazolam, and other related drugs are long acting. **Table 15-4** lists commonly available products containing benzodiazepines.

Immunoassay screening for benzodiazepines usually recognizes the presence of common drugs and metabolites after medical use or abuse. For example, one study found that the On-Line Benzodiazepine Plus assay (Roche Diagnostics, Indianapolis, IN) recognized the presence of 22 common benzodiazepines and their metabolites, including alprazolam, chlordiazepoxide, clonazepam, clorazepate, diazepam, estazolam, flunitrazepam, halazepam, lorazepam, midazolam, nitrazepam, oxazepam, temazepam, and triazolam.

Medical use of benzodiazepines produces positive drug-testing results. Based on urinary concentration of benzodiazepine, it is difficult to differentiate medical use of benzodiazepine from abuse, although benzodiazepine levels tend to be higher in the case of abuse. In one report authors screened 100 urine specimens collected from subjects attending the Leeds Addiction Unit in the United Kingdom for the presence of benzodiazepines using the EMIT assay (Dade Behring, Deerfield, IL) and later confirmed the presence of the drug in urine by high-performance liquid chromatography. The authors detected nitrazepam in 61 specimens, but none of the subjects were prescribed that drug. Similarly, chlordiazepoxide was detected in 49 urine specimens, but only five patients had a valid prescription for the drug. The authors concluded that multiple benzodiazepine abuse was evident among patients attending the Addiction Unit.[19]

Table 15-4	Product Names of Drugs Containing Benzodiazepines
Active Ingredient	**Common Product Name**
Short-Acting Benzodiazepines	
Estazolam	ProSom®, Eurodin®
Flurazepam	Dalmane®
Temazepam	Restoril®
Triazolam	Halcion®
Midazolam	Dormicum®, Versed®
Long-Acting Benzodiazepines	
Alprazolam	Xanax®
Chlordiazepoxide	Librium®, Limbitrol®
Clorazepate	Tranxene®
Clonazepam	Klonopin®, Rivotril®
Diazepam	Valium®
Halazepam	Paxipam®
Lorazepam	Ativan®
Nitrazepam	Mogadon®, Alodorm®
Prazepam	Centrax®
Oxazepam	Serax®
Quazepam	Doral®, Dormalin®

Because of the wide diversity of this class of drug, immunoassay positive specimens are usually confirmed by GC/MS for common drugs in this class, including oxazepam, diazepam, temazepam, and alprazolam. ElSohly et al analyzed benzodiazepines in 156 urine specimens from alleged victims of drug-facilitated sexual assault and observed that oxazepam was confirmed in 50% of the specimens, followed by nordiazepam (48%), temazepam (43%), and diazepam (40%), while the presence of alprazolam was confirmed in 21.8% of specimens and lorazepam in 15.4% of specimens.[20]

Tetrazepam, a muscle relaxant, is commonly prescribed in Europe (Austria, France, and Germany). Pavlic et al reported that tetrazepam is metabolized to diazepam and then to nordiazepam, as revealed by the presence of these compounds in the urine of healthy volunteers when they ingested 50 mg of tetrazepam. Both tetazepam and diazepam can be detected in urine at least 72 hours after administration of the drugs, and diazepam concentration was an average of 33% of tetrazepam concentration.[21]

EFFECT OF OXAPROZIN ON IMMUNOASSAY SCREENING FOR BENZODIAZEPINES

Oxaprozin (Daypro) is a nonsteroidal anti-inflammatory drug that cross-reacts with the various immunoassays used to screen for the presence of benzodiazepines in urine specimens. Fraser and Jowell reported that oxaprozin, if present in urine, provides false-positive screening results with three benzodiazepine immunoassays: the EMIT d.a.u. (Dade Behring, Deerfield, IL), FPIA, and CEDIA. When 12 subjects received a single standard dose of oxaprozin (1200 mg), all 36 urine specimens collected from these 12 subjects tested positive for benzodiazepines using the EMIT and CEDIA assays, while 35 out of 36 urine specimens tested positive by the FPIA assay. The authors concluded that the presumptive positive results were related to the presence of oxaprozin or its metabolites, and therefore such presumptive positive specimens must be confirmed by a different analytical technique.[22]

PRESCRIPTION DRUGS THAT CONTAIN PROPOXYPHENE

Propoxyphene, which is structurally similar to methadone, is a narcotic analgesic that is less potent than codeine. This drug is used in treating mild to moderate pain. Propoxyphene also binds to opiate receptors. This drug is sold under the trade names Darvocet, Darvon, Propacet, and Wygesic. Because propoxyphene is also abused, some workplace drug-testing programs include it in their drug-testing panel. Prescription use of this drug causes positive drug-testing results for propoxyphene because the cutoff concentration for propoxyphene in urine (300 ng/ml) can be reached after medical use of this drug.

MEDICAL EXPOSURE TO COCAINE

Cocaine is used infrequently as a local anesthetic in ear, nose, and throat surgery and also is administered topically during ophthalmitic procedures. Subjects who have undergone such procedures may test positive for cocaine (as benzoylecgonine, the major metabolite). A patient may be positive up to 72 hours after an otolaryngologic procedure in which cocaine is used as an anesthetic. Cocaine metabolite can also be detected in the urine specimen of the physician who performs the procedure.[23]

Jacobson et al studied the effect of use of cocaine-containing ophthalmic solution on urine excretion of benzoylecgonine in patients. Out of 50 subjects studied, 47 subjects (94%) tested positive for cocaine (as benzoylecgonine) 4 to 6 hours after receiving eye drops. In addition, 35 subjects (70%) showed positive results 24 hours after receiving eye drops containing cocaine. The authors concluded that ophthalmic administration of cocaine may cause positive test results up to 2 days after a procedure.[24] The combination of tetracaine, adrenaline, and cocaine is used as a topical anesthetic during the suture of simple skin lacerations. Application of such topical anesthetic also produces a positive urine test for cocaine for up to 2 days.[25]

The commercial drug Novocaine, although synthetically derived from cocaine, has a distinct structural difference from cocaine and benzoylecgonine. Therefore, use of Novocaine or other anesthetic agents, including benzocaine, tetracaine, and lidocaine, during dental procedures should not cause false-positive cocaine test results in urine testing.

 CONCLUSION

Because true-positive drug tests may result from use of a variety of prescription drugs, it is important to document medical use of such drugs during pre-employment workplace drug testing. Heath care providers need to be aware that such true-positive results can be due to use of prescription medications or due to abuse. Verification of medical use of such drugs is also important for medical review officers.

REFERENCES

1. Broussard L. Interpretation of amphetamines screening and confirmation tests. In: Dasgupta A, ed. *Handbook of Drug Monitoring Methods*. Totowa, NJ: Humana Press; 2008:379–393.

2. Papa P, Rocchi L, Mainardi C, Donzelli G. Buflomedil interference with monoclonal EMIT d.a.u. amphetamine/methamphetamine immunoassay. *Eur J Clin Biochem*. 1997;35:369–370.

3. Melason SE, Lee-Lewandrowski E, Griggs DA, Long WH, Flood JG. Reduced interference by phenothiazine in amphetamine drug of abuse immunoassay. *Arch Pathol Lab Med*. 2006;130:1834–1838.

4. Manzi S, Law T, Shannon MW. Methylphenidate produces a false-positive urine amphetamine screen. [Letter to the Editor.] *Pediatr Emerg Care*. 2002;18:401.

5. Schmolke M, Hallbach J, Guder WG. False positive results for urine amphetamine and opiate immunoassays in a patient intoxicated with perazine. [Letter to the Editor.] *Clin Chem*. 1996;42:1725–1726.

6. Kraemer T, Wenning R, Maurer HH. The antispasmodic drug mebeverine leads to positive amphetamine results by fluorescence polarization immunoassay (FPIA)-studies on toxicological analyses of urine by FPIA and GC-MS. *J Anal Toxicol*. 2001;25:333–338.

7. Shults TF. Amphetamine review and update: technical and pharmaceutical developments. *MRO Alert*. 2003;14(4).

8. Musshoff F. Illegal or legitimate use? Precursor compounds to amphetamine and methamphetamine. *Drug Metab Rev*. 2000;32:15–44.

9. Cody JT, Valtier S, Nelson SL. Amphetamine enantiomer excretion profile following administration of Adderall. *J Anal Toxicol*. 2003;27:485–492.

10. Kraemer T, Roditis SK, Peters FT, Maurer HH. Amphetamine concentrations in human urine following single-dose administration of calcium antagonist prenylamine-studies using fluorescence polarization immunoassay (FPIA) and GC/MS. *J Anal Toxicol*. 2003;27:68–73.

11. Grenhill B, Valtier S, Cody JT. Metabolic profile of amphetamine and methamphetamine following administration of the drug famprofazone. *J Anal Toxicol*. 2003;27:479–484.

12. Maurer HH, Kraemer T. Toxicological detection of selegiline and its metabolites in urine using fluorescence polarization immunoassay (FPIA) and gas chromatography-mass spectrometry (GC-MS) and differentiation by enantioselective GC-MS of the intake of selegiline from abuse of methamphetamine or amphetamine. *Arch Toxicol*. 1992;66:675–678.

13. Guay DR. Use of oral oxymorphone in the elderly. *Consult Pharm*. 2007;22:417–430.

14. Popa C, Beck O, Brodin. Morphine formation from ethylmorphine: implications for drugs-of-abuse testing in urine. *J Anal Toxicol*. 1998;22:142–147.

15. Lafolie P, Beck O, Liz Z, Albertioni F, Boréus L. Urine and plasma pharmacokinetics of codeine in healthy volunteers: implications for drugs-of-abuse testing. *J Anal Toxicol*. 1996;20:541–546.

16. Smith ML, Hughes RO, Levine B, Dickerson S, Darwin WD, Cone EJ. Forensic drug testing for opiates. VI. Urine testing for hydromorphone, hydrocodone, oxymorphone, and oxycodone with commercial opiate immunoassays and gas chromatography-mass spectrometry. *J Anal Toxicol*. 1995;19:18–26.

17. ElSohly MA, deWit H, Wachtel SR, Feng S, Murphy TP. Δ^9-tetrahydrocannabivarin as a marker for ingestion of marijuana versus Marinol: results of a clinical study. *J Anal Toxicol*. 2001;25:565–571.

18. Rossi S, Yash T, Bentley H, van der Brande G, Grant I, Ellis R. Characterization of interference with six commercial Δ^9-tetrahydrocannabinol immunoassays by efavirenz (glucuronide) in urine. [Letter to the Editor.] *Clin Chem*. 2006;52:896–897.

19. Garretty DJ, Wolff K, Hay AW, Raistrick D. Benzodiazepine misuse by drug addicts. *Ann Clin Biochem*. 1997;34:68–73.

20. ElSohly MA, Gul W, Murphy TP, Avula B. LC-(TOF) MS analysis of benzodiazepines in urine from alleged victims of drug facilitated sexual assault. *J Anal Toxicol*. 2007;31:505–514.

21. Pavlic M, Libiseller K, Grubwieser P, Schubert H, Rabl W. Medicolegal aspects of tetrazepam metabolism. *Int J Legal Med*. 2007;121:169–174.

22. Fraser AD, Jowell P. Oxaprozin cross-reactivity in three commercial immunoassays for benzodiazepines in urine. *J Anal Toxicol*. 1998;22:50–54.

23. Bruns AD, Zeiske LA, Jacobs AJ. Analysis of the cocaine metabolite in the urine of patients and physicians during clinical use. *Otolaryngol Head Neck Surg*. 1994;111: 722–726.

24. Jacobson DM, Berg R, Grinstead GF, Kruse JR. Duration of positive urine for cocaine metabolite after ophthalmic administration: implications for testing patients with suspected Horner syndrome using ophthalmic cocaine. *Am J Ophthalmol*. 2001;131: 742–747.

25. Altieri M, Bogema S, Schwartz RH. TAC topical anesthesia produces positive urine test for cocaine. *Ann Emerg Med*. 1990;19:577–579.

CHAPTER 16

Passing Pre-Employment and Workplace Drug Tests

ABSTRACT

The best way to pass a workplace drug test is not to abuse any drugs. However, there are things aside from abuse of drugs that may affect drugs-of-abuse testing. Anyone undergoing pre-employment drug testing should take certain precautions prior to the test. Awareness of these factors is essential in the pre-employment setting, where the person undergoing the testing has limited legal rights. For example, drinking excessive water prior to drug testing may produce dilute urine with creatinine concentration below acceptable limits, and the laboratory may report the urine as diluted, causing trouble for the donor. Poppy-seed cake, hemp-containing food, and certain herbal teas (like goldenseal root tea or Health Inca tea) may interfere with drug testing. It is also wise to avoid any cough or cold medicine as well as common analgesics such as ibuprofen for a few days prior to drug testing. Many prescription pain medications contain opiate, and taking such medicines will produce confirmed opiate test results. It is important for donors to list such medications on the form submitted with the specimen and have the physician prescription to document the legal use of the medication.

Workplace drug testing is widely practiced in both the government and private sectors in order to achieve a drug-free work environment. Most Fortune 500 companies, other private companies, and state and federal governments require pre-employment drug testing for new hires. Moreover, employees in security-sensitive jobs also need to undergo additional drug testing, such as unannounced random drug testing. Quest Diagnostics, a leader in the United States in drug testing, conducted 6.6 million drug tests from January to December 2007 for the general U.S. workforce.[1]

Pre-employment drug testing is a critical issue because one of the conditions of hire is successfully passing pre-employment drug testing. Moreover, potential employees have few rights to legally challenge companies who refuse to hire them based on pre-employment drug-testing results. The best way to pass a drug test is not to abuse any illicit drugs, especially drugs tested in common pre-employment panels

Table 16-1 True-Positive (Confirmed by GC/MS) Results in Drugs-of-Abuse Testing	
Cause of True Positive	**Drug Confirmed by GC/MS**
Prescription medicine containing amphetamine (e.g., Adderall, Dexedrine)	Amphetamine
Prescription medicine containing methamphetamine (Desoxyn); prescription medicines metabolized to amphetamine or methamphetamine	Methamphetamine and amphetamine
Prescription medicines containing benzodiazepines (e.g., Ativan, Librium, Halcion, Valium, Xanax)	Various benzodiazepines
Local anesthesia with cocaine (used for ear, nose, and throat procedures)	Cocaine
Prescription use of Marinol; consumption of hemp products	THC-COOH
Consumption of poppy-seed containing products	Morphine and codeine

(amphetamines, cocaine, marijuana, opiates, and phencyclidine). However, most drugs stay in urine either as the parent drug or its metabolites for a few days to a few weeks. Marijuana metabolite may stay as long as three weeks after last use. However, long-ago experiments with drugs (e.g., in high school or college) should not affect pre-employment drug testing at all. The objective of pre-employment drug testing is to identify recent abusers and regular abusers of drugs, not to identify a person who may have experimented with marijuana years ago. Nevertheless, anyone undergoing drug testing should be aware that intake of excess water, certain cold medications, and consumption of certain foods may cause problems with pre-employment drug testing as well as workplace drug testing. Moreover, drinking herbal tea made from coca leaves may cause a positive test for cocaine, and eating poppy-seed containing products results in confirmed identification of morphine and codeine in urine specimen. Taking certain

prescription medications containing opioid, benzodiazepine, or amphetamine/methamphetamine also produces positive drugs-of-abuse test results confirmed by GC/MS (**Table 16-1**).

 DILUTE URINE AND DRUG TESTING

In 2007 Japanese physicians recommended drinking more than 2 liters of water to improve cardiac health. In regards to drug testing, drinking water in excess of 2 liters should not significantly alter plasma viscosity, but it may dilute urine.[2] Drinking excess fluid may lower urinary creatinine concentration as well as specific gravity of urine, two parameters that are used to determine whether a specimen is valid for drugs-of-abuse analysis. Some drug users attempt to reduce the concentration of drugs in urine by drinking too much water a few hours before submitting a specimen or by diluting the urine after collection by adding tap water. Therefore, all laboratories perform integrity testing prior to analysis of the specimen. If a laboratory identifies a specimen as "diluted" or "substituted," a company may consider the result the same as "refusal to test" and deny employment to the person. Unfortunately, drinking excess water as a habit may cause the urine concentration to fall below the acceptable level, and a person may fail the drug test without abusing any drugs.

The effects of drinking excess water on urine creatinine concentration have been studied extensively. Many laboratories consider a creatinine value less than 20 mg/dl and a specific gravity value less than 1.003 as indicators of diluted urine. The determination of the specific gravity of a urine specimen is mandatory if the creatinine concentration is less than 20 mg/dl. SAMHSA defines a substituted specimen as having a creatinine level less than or equal to 5 mg/dl and a specific gravity less than or equal to 1.001 or greater than or equal to 1.020 (see Chapter 9). Cone et al reported that when subjects drank excess fluid (1 gallon fluid divided into 4 parts; 1 part was drunk each hour, and a total of 1 gallon of fluid consumed in a 4-hour period), creatinine concentration dropped below 20 mg/dl and specific gravity decreased below 1.003 (both indicative of dilute urine) in 1.5 to 2 hours after first intake of excess fluid. The urine test results returned to normal over a period of 8 to 10 hours.

This study also demonstrated that when subjects smoked marijuana or administered cocaine intranasally under controlled conditions and then after 22 hours started drinking excess fluid, the urinary tests results often switched from positive to negative using immunoassay screening of the drugs. This result was due to reduced concentrations of metabolite secondary to dilution of urine.[3] This study clearly shows why drug users drink excess fluid and drink herbal tea or cleansing products in order to defraud drug testing and why the criteria for accepting specimen for drugs of abuse need to be so stringent.

Individuals preparing for drug testing should also consider any diuretics they are taking, since diuretics lead to dilute urine. Diuretic therapy is used in treating hypertension, congestive heart failure, acute and chronic renal insufficiency, and other diseases. Diuretic therapy increases urine volume and ion loss (except sodium and potassium), reduces tubular absorption, and modifies diffusion, thus producing dilute urine.[4] Caffeine is also a mild diuretic. In healthy volunteers caffeine appears to produce an initial diuresis. Cone et al reported that patients taking caffeine voided a mean of 7.8 times compared with controls that voided a mean of 6.4 times on the first day of taking caffeine. The mean urine volume in a 24-hour period was 2.004 mL in the caffeine group versus 1.643 ml in the control group (placebo group), although both groups consumed similar volumes of water (2.246 ml caffeine group vs 2.102 ml in the placebo group.[5]

This diluting effect is capitalized upon by Internet companies that market flushing agents and detoxifying agents to help drug abusers pass drug tests. Many of these drinks contain caffeine, hydrochlorothiazide, or other diuretic agents to produce dilute urine. Moreover, manufacturers also recommend drinking excess water to flush out drugs from the body prior to testing. Therefore, if a urine specimen submitted for a pre-employment drug test is identified as "diluted urine" by the laboratory, employment will likely be denied.

Following the criteria of diluted urine as creatinine concentration below 20 mg/dl and specific gravity below 1.003, Fraser et al reported that 6.2% of 44,722 specimens submitted by the Correctional Services of

Canada were considered "dilute."[6] Levy et al also recently reported that 5.6% (40 specimens out of 710) collected under rigorous conditions from adolescent substance abuse programs were considered diluted.[7]

The criteria for substituted urine (creatinine concentration $\leq$ 5 mg/dl or specific gravity $\leq$ 1.001) are based on the scientific fact that it is impossible to achieve such low creatinine within normal human physiology. Barbanel et al reported that of 13,467 urine specimens, none of the urine specimens met these criteria. Although there were a few specimens that met one of the two criteria, these urine specimens were collected from patients who were neonatal, moribund, or so severely ill that none of them could possibly be part of the working population.[8]

To avoid diluted urine, it is better not to drink excessive coffee or carbonated soda containing high amounts of caffeine for 1 to 2 days prior to drug testing. Moreover, drinking excess water should also be avoided for 2 to 3 days. Drinking approximately 1 liter of fluid the day before drug testing will ensure that the creatinine concentration and specific gravity of the urine specimen will be within the acceptable limits. An individual who has polyuria due to diabetes insipidus, diabetes mellitus, or any other medical condition that produces dilute urine should discuss the condition with the physician or nurse practitioner prior to drug testing (Table 16-1).

HERBAL REMEDIES AND HERBAL TEA

Herbal tea such as goldenseal root tea may produce dark urine and thus invalidate the urine drug-testing results. In the pre-employment drug-testing scenario, it is particularly likely that a company will withdraw a job offer from the applicant. Herbal tea may also contain high amounts of caffeine, causing a diuretic effect and increased urine volume. Poppy tea is a narcotic analgesic tea that is usually brewed from dried *Papaverus somniferum* plants (poppy plants). Tea can also be prepared from seed pods or seeds. The tea is usually bitter in taste and therefore is often flavored with coffee, honey, or lemon juice. Poppy tea contains high amounts of morphine and codeine (much higher than poppy seeds), and drinking such tea would lead to positive opiate test results. Van Thuyne et al reported that the morphine content of poppy tea prepared from two specimens of a different species of poppy (*Papaveris fructus*) contained 10.4 and 31.5 μg/ml morphine, which was consumed by five subjects. The maximum urinary concentration of morphine in specimens collected from the subjects ranged from 4.3 μg/ml (4300 ng/ml) to 7.4 μg/ml (7400 ng/ml).[9] Also, tea made out of coca leaves is sold in South America. Although the sale of tea containing cocaine is illegal in the United States, consumption of Health Inca tea and Mate de Coca tea can lead to positive tests for cocaine (see Chapter 12).

Herbal dietary supplements that are sold through the Internet for recreational use contain several ingredients that can interfere with drug tests. Dennehy et al reported that of these supplements, 47% contain marijuana or 3,4-methylenedioxy-amphetamine (ecstasy), while the most common ingredients of such herbal products are ephedra alkaloids.[10] Consumption of such herbal products may lead to positive drug-testing results. Therefore, it is advisable to avoid all herbal tea and herbal products at least for one week, preferably two, prior to drug testing (**Table 16-2**). For detailed discussion of the potential effects

Table 16-2 Steps to Take to Avoid a False-Positive Drug Test
Avoid drinking excess water. It may dilute the urine specimen. Drinking 1 liter of water the day before drug testing is recommended.
Avoid drinking soda or caffeinated drinks.
If you have a medical condition that may produce dilute urine, consult your doctor or nurse prior to drug testing.
Avoid all herbal tea and herbal products for 2 weeks.
Avoid poppy-seed products for 2 to 3 weeks.
Avoid hemp-containing food or hemp oil as salad dressing for at least 3 weeks.
Avoid OTC cold medications and codeine-containing cough mixtures for 2 to 3 days, if possible, including dextromethorphan-containing cough mixtures. Make sure to list such medicines on the pre-employment testing form. Failure to disclose use of such medicine may result in a positive drug test report.
List all pain prescription medications; they may contain opioid. Be prepared to produce documentation from your physician for further verification.
Do not take any medication prescribed for another person. It is against the law.
Do not abuse drugs and try to pass drug test by using household chemicals or urine adulterants sold through the Internet. These adulterants do not work and will be easily identified by the laboratory.

of certain herbal products on drugs-of-abuse testing, see Chapter 18. Aside from causing a positive drug test, these herbal products can have acute life-threatening toxicity.

POPPY SEEDS AND HEMP PRODUCTS

Poppy seed contains morphine and codeine, and hemp oil and hemp seed contain a small amount of marijuana (THC). Eating these products may cause positive drug-testing results (see also Chapter 12). It has been well established in the scientific community that the ingestion of poppy seeds in sufficient quantities will result in the presence of morphine and codeine in urine for up to a day.

Because of the availability of information that eating poppy seeds can cause a positive drug test for opiates, some prospective employees have argued that their positive tests were due to poppy-seed muffin consumption and not opiate abuse. Courts have routinely rejected negligence claims based on arguments that an employer or drug-testing facility must inform the prospective employee/prospective employer that poppy seeds are a known cause of positive test results and could lead to a positive drug test. For example, in *Caputo v. Compuchem Labs, Inc.* (No. Civ.A. 92-6123, 1994 WL 100084, at *1 [E.D.Pa.], *aff'd* 37 F.3d 1485 [3rd Cor. 1994], *cert. denied*, 513 U.S. 1082 [1995]), the plaintiff was denied employment because her urine tested positive for morphine. The plaintiff claimed the test should not have been identified as positive because the amount of morphine was low and likely caused by ingestion of poppy-seed rolls. The court dismissed her claims and found that there was no duty on the part of the laboratory to inform the employer that the low positive could have been caused by something other than illicit drug use. Similarly, in *SmithKline Beecham Corp. v. Doe* (903 S.W. 2d 347 [Tex. 1995]), the plaintiff, in a pre-employment drug screen, tested positive for opiates in the urine. The plaintiff attributed the test result to having eaten poppy seeds prior to testing and not drug use. She contended that the testing laboratory should have notified her prospective employer that a positive test result may be from eating poppy seeds and not necessarily from illicit drug use, and that the testing lab should have asked her if she had eaten poppy seeds. The court rejected the plaintiff's arguments and held that drug-testing laboratories do not have a duty to tell prospective employees about the possible side effects of ingesting substances that might cause a positive test result. Likewise, in *Devine v. Roche Biomedical Labs.* (659 A.2d 868 [Me. 1995]), the plaintiff, in a pre-employment drug test, tested positive for opiates. The plaintiff notified the employer that the results were most likely caused by a poppy-seed muffin eaten before the test. Once again, the court found the plaintiff's arguments without merit.

Various published reports indicate that opiate concentrations in urine following consumption of poppy-seed-containing food may vary from none detected (opiate concentrations below the cutoff concentration of the opiate immunoassay screen) to urinary morphine concentration ranging from 2929 to 13,857 ng/ml (as determined by GC/MS).[11] Although in 1998 the Department of Health and Human Services increased the screening cutoff of opiate immunoassays from 300 ng/ml to 2000 ng/ml, private employers have no obligation to adopt the new cutoff value in their drugs-of-abuse testing programs.

In our experience, eating one or two commercially baked poppy-seed cakes or muffins prior to submitting a urine specimen for pre-employment drug testing may cause urinary opiate concentration above the 300 ng/ml cutoff of the immunoassays for screening of opiates in urine (see also Chapter 12). Therefore, it is advisable to avoid such foods at least for a week or two to ensure that any residual morphine or codeine has been flushed out from the system after eating poppy-seed-containing products. Some ethnic cooking uses poppy-seed paste, and such foods may contain much higher morphine and codeine compared with poppy-seed bagels or poppy-seed muffins. Such ethnic foods should be avoided at least for two weeks prior to pre-employment drug tests. Although hemp seed and hemp oil sold in the United States today contain very little (< 1%) THC, it is also advisable to avoid all hemp products for at least three weeks because marijuana metabolite stays in urine much longer than codeine or morphine. Eating poppy-seed-containing products is also problematic for unannounced, random drug testing. Individuals working in a high-security environment should be extra careful in their consumption of these food products.

COLD, COUGH, AND PRESCRIPTION MEDICATIONS

Many OTC cold medicines contain ephedrine and pseudoephedrine. Both ephedrine and pseudoephedrine have structural similarity with methamphetamine, and thus cross-react with immunoassay screening of amphetamines. In the 1990s some laboratories reported the presence of methamphetamine in several external survey specimens containing no methamphetamine but containing ephedrine and pseudoephedrine. The licenses of two NIDA-certified laboratories (NIDA-certified laboratories are now certified by SAMHSA) were suspended due to misidentification of ephedrine as methamphetamine in survey samples. The causes of misidentification are as follows:

1. Ephedrine and pseudoephedrine can be thermally dehydrated to methamphetamine at a high injector port temperature.[12] Hornbeck et al reported the GC/MS artifact peak as methamphetamine after derivatization of ephedrine/pseudoephedrine with heptafluorobutyric anhydride, 4-carbethoxyhexafluorobutyryl chloride, or N-trifluoroacetyl-1-propyl chloride. The artifact peaks were produced when the injector port temperature of GC was 300°C. The injector port temperature of GC should be maintained below 185°C to avoid thermal conversion of derivatized ephedrine/pseudoephedrine to methamphetamine.

2. The electron impact mass spectrums of trifluoroacetyl, pentafluoropropyl, heptafluorobutyl, 4-carbethoxyhexafluorobutyryl, and various carbamate derivatives of methamphetamine are similar to the corresponding derivatized ephedrine/pseudoephedrine. Because ephedrine and pseudoephedrine are eluted just after the methamphetamine peak, if the mass spectral analysis is not done carefully, ephedrine/pseudoephedrine can be misidentified as methamphetamine. Both ephedrine and pseudoephedrine are legal drugs and are found in OTC medications, so misidentification of

ephedrine/pseudoephedrine as methamphetamine has a serious medical and legal implication.

The likelihood of such misidentification is extremely low these days, however, because drugs-of-abuse tests are performed by federally certified laboratories. Nevertheless, avoiding OTC cold medicines containing ephedrine/pseudoephedrine for three to four days prior to pre-employment drug testing is advisable. If such medications can not be avoided, then these drugs (although available without prescription) should be listed in the form submitted with the pre-employment urine specimen.

In addition to ephedrine/pseudoephedrine, many OTC and prescription medications (or metabolites of these drugs) interfere with immunoassay screening for amphetamines in urine specimens. These medications include chlorpromazine, fenfluramine, mephentermine, mexiletine, N-acetyl procainamide, phenmetrazine, phentermine, phenylpropanolamine, promethazine, quinacrine, ranitidine, tolmetin, and tyramine (also see Chapters 14 and 15). Although most of these drugs have no effect on the GC/MS confirmation step for amphetamine/methamphetamine, it is important to list all medications in the pre-employment drug test form.

Dextromethorphan, a constituent of many OTC cough and cold medicines, does not interfere with immunoassay screening for opiates in urine despite some structural similarity of dextromethorphan with opioid drugs.[13] Although dextromethorphan causes false-positive immunoassays screening for phencyclidine, this drug does not interfere with the GC/MS confirmation of phencyclidine. Marchei et al reported that false-positive results for phencyclidine using the Instant-View PCP assay (Instant-View Multi-Test drugs-of-abuse panel, Alfa

Scientific Designs, Poway, CA) were due to the presence of dextromethorphan, ibuprofen, and metamizol in urine specimens. The GC/MS analysis of these specimens showed no presence of phencyclidine (PCP).[14] Another study obtained false-positive phencyclidine test results using the Syva Rapid Test d.a.u. panel (Dade Behring, Deerfield, IL) caused by the presence of venlafaxine, an antidepressant, and its metabolite O-desmethylvenlafaxine. The Syva EMIT II Plus reagent (also Dade Behring) also produced negative results.[15] These examples indicate the complexity of drugs-of-abuse testing and why all medications (OTC and prescription) taken by an individual should be listed in the pre-employment form.

Many cough medications contain codeine, morphine, hydrocodone, oxycodone, and hydromorphone, which are also found in many prescription pain medications. Use of these medications will result in positive opiate screenings and confirmation tests. A synthetic THC, dronabinol, is available as a prescription medication under the trade name Marinol. Dronabinol is metabolized to THC-COOH (marijuana metabolite), thus providing a confirmed THC test in drugs-of-abuse testing (see Chapter 15). Once again, listing all prescription medication is necessary on the pre-employment drug-testing form. Moreover, the individual may also have to present a valid prescription from his or her physician, and the physician may be contacted for more information by the human resources or medical review officer of the company where the individual is seeking employment.

It is illegal to take any prescription medication that is prescribed for a different person. This includes spouses and close family members. Failing a drugs-of-abuse test due to ingestion of any such medica-

Case Studies[16]

Case 1: A laboratory confirmed the presence of benzoylecgonine in urine and reported the test as positive for cocaine. During the interview with the medical review officer (MRO), the donor denied any cocaine abuse but informed the MRO that cocaine had been used as a topical anesthetic prior to an endoscopic procedure. The MRO verified that claim, and the medical report of the donor indicated use of cocaine hydrochloride 10 days before submission of the urine specimen for drugs-of-abuse testing. Usually, the detection window of cocaine in urine is 2 to 3 days after the last dose. Therefore, it is unlikely to test positive for cocaine 10 days after medical use, and the MRO reported the case as "positive for cocaine."

Case 2: A laboratory test confirmed the presence of methamphetamine (950 ng/ml) and amphetamine (245 ng/ml) in a urine specimen. The donor denied use of any prescription medication but informed the MRO that he had used a Vicks Vapor Inhaler. Chiral analysis revealed that approximately 90% of the amphetamine and methamphetamine in the specimen were d-isomers. Because the Vicks Vapor Inhaler contains only l-methamphetamine, the d-methamphetamine and d-amphetamine in the specimen could not have come from the use of the Vicks Inhaler but instead indicated illicit use of methamphetamine. The MRO reported the result as positive for methamphetamine.

tion can not be defended, and the person most likely will not be hired by the company. Therefore, under no circumstances should a person take a medication not prescribed to him or her. This is especially important for a prescription cough medication or prescription pain medication because many of these drugs contain codeine, morphine, or other opioids.

ADULTERANTS

Both household chemicals and adulterants sold through the Internet are used by drug abusers to cheat drug tests. In many states possession or use of such agents to defraud drug testing is against the law. Moreover, all certified laboratories follow federal guidelines to test for adulterants (see Chapters 9, 10, and 11). If an adulterant is detected in a urine specimen, the result is reported as "refusal to test" by the subject, and employment will be denied. If it appears an individual has attempted to dilute a urine specimen by using a flushing or detoxifying agent to cheat a drug test, here too the result will be reported as "refusal to test."

CONCLUSION

There are steps that non–drug users can take to avoid problems with workplace drug tests. Donors should avoid drinking excess water and caffeinated beverages in order to avoid diluted urine. Certain foods, such as those containing poppy seeds or hemp oil, should also be avoided. Furthermore, many OTC cold medications may cross-react with amphetamine immunoassays. If possible, such medicines should be avoided for a few days prior to pre-employment drug testing. Moreover, many prescription pain medications contain codeine, morphine, and other opioids. It is important for donors to list

such medications on the pre-employment form. Donors must be able to present a valid prescription on demand. Table 16-2 summarizes the recommendations in this chapter for passing drug testing.

REFERENCES

1. Quest Diagnostics. Use of methamphetamine among U.S. workers and job applicants drops 22 percent in 2007 and cocaine use slows dramatically, reports Quest Diagnostics. *Drug Testing Index.* http://www.questdiagnostics.com/employersolutions/dti/2008_03/dti_index.html. Accessed October 28, 2008.

2. Sugaya K, Nishijima, Oda M, Miyazato M, Ogawa Y. Change of blood viscosity and urinary frequency by high water intake. *Int J Urol.* 2007;14:470–472.

3. Cone EJ, Lange R, Darwin WD. In vivo adulteration: excess fluid ingestion cause false negative marijuana and cocaine urine test results. *J Anal Toxicol.* 1998;22:460–473.

4. Splendiani G, Condò S. [Diuretic therapy in heart failure.] [Article in Italian.] *G Ital Nefrol.* 2006;(Suppl 34):S74–S76.

5. Bird ET, Parker BD, Kim HS, Coffield KS. Caffeine ingestion and lower urinary tract symptoms in healthy volunteers. *Neurourol Urodyn.* 2005;24:611–615.

6. Fraser AD, Zamecnik J, Keravel J, McGarth L, Wells J. Experience with urine drug testing by Correctional Services of Canada. *Forensic Sci Int.* 2001;121:16–22.

7. Levy S, Sheritt L, Vaughan BL, Germak M, Knight JR. Results of random drug testing in an adolescent substance abuse program. *Pediatrics.* 2007;119:e843–848.

8. Barbanel CS, Winkelman JW, Fischer GA, King AJ. Confirmation of the Department of Transportation criteria for a substituted urine specimen. *J Occup Environ Med.* 2002;44:407–416.

9. Van Thuyne W, Van Eenoo P, Delbeke FT. Urinary concentrations of morphine after

the administration of herbal tea containing Papaveris fructus in relation to doping analysis. *J Chromatogr B Analyt Technol Biomed Life Sci*. 2003;785:245–51.

10. Dennehy CE, Tsourounis C, Miller AE. Evaluation of herbal dietary supplements marketed on the Internet for recreational use. *Ann Pharmacother*. 2005;39:1634–1639.

11. Hill V, Cairns T, Cheng CC, Schaffer M. Multiple aspects of hair analysis for opiates: methodology, clinical and workplace population, codeine and poppy seed ingestion. *J Anal Toxicol*. 2005;29:696–703.

12. Hornbeck CL, Carrig JE, Czarny RJ. Detection of GC/MS artifact peak as methamphetamine. *J Anal Toxicol*. 1993;17:257–263.

13. Storrow AB, Magoon MR, Norton J. The dextromethorphan defense: dextromethorphan and opioid screen. *Acad Emerg Med*. 1995;9:791–794.

14. Marchei E, Pellegrini M, Pichini S, Martín I, García-Algar O, Vall O. Are false-positive phencyclidine immunoassays Instant-View Multi-Test results caused by overdose concentrations of ibuprofen, metamizol, and dextromethorphan? [Letter to the Editor.] *Ther Drug Monit*. 2007;29:671–673.

15. Sena SF, Kazimi S, Wu A. False positive phencyclidine immunoassay results caused by venlafaxine and O-desmethylvenlafaxine. [Letter to the Editor.] *Clin Chem*. 2002;48:676–677.

16. U.S. Department of Heath and Human Services, Substance Abuse and Mental Health Services Administration. MRO Case Studies: Case #1. February 2005. http://workplace.samhsa.gov/DrugTesting/Files_Drug_Testing/MROs/MRO%20Case%20Studies%20-%20February%202005.pdf. Accessed October 22, 2008.

CHAPTER 17

Drug Testing of Hair, Oral Fluid, Sweat, and Meconium

ABSTRACT

Although the majority of workplace drug testing is performed on urine specimens, there are certain advantages of testing hair and other alternative specimens. In contrast to urine analysis, which can detect drugs a few days to a few weeks after abuse, hair analysis provides a much longer window of detection where drugs can be confirmed up to 4 months after abuse. Hair collection is also noninvasive, like urine collection, but in contrast to urine collection, hair collection is supervised, giving the person being tested no chance to substitute or manipulate the specimen. Oral fluid testing is a convenient supervised method of specimen collection. Moreover, oral fluid testing is a useful means of assessing recent drug abuse. Sweat testing is a convenient way to test for drugs several days or weeks after use and is especially useful as part of a drug rehabilitation program. Meconium testing provides useful information of maternal drug abuse and exposure of the fetus to abused drugs.

Although most pre-employment and workplace drug testing is performed on urine specimens, testing of alternative specimens such as hair, oral fluid, sweat, and meconium is also gaining widespread acceptance for drugs-of-abuse testing. Although urine tests are convenient, they do have several limitations. First, the window of detection is relatively small for urine drug testing; most drug metabolites are present for only a few days after abuse. For example, benzoylecgonine, the metabolite of cocaine, can be detected in urine only 2 to 3 days after the last exposure to cocaine. Second, the urine specimen collection process is not supervised, so the person being tested has the opportunity to add adulterates into the specimen or substitute the urine specimen with synthetic urine. In contrast, the collection of hair specimen is supervised, allowing no opportunity for manipulation of the specimen. Moreover, the window of detection for most drugs in hair is approximately 90 days or more after last exposure. Although some Internet sites and toll-free numbers sell shampoos and hair cleaners they claim will remove drugs from hair, these products have virtually no effect.

Abused drugs are also present in oral fluid after recent exposure, and in Europe oral fluid testing is gaining acceptance as a method for assessing impairment of drivers. Sweat drug testing is a good way of monitoring the progress of individuals enrolled in drug-monitoring programs. The presence of abused drugs in meconium indicates maternal drug abuse and the exposure of fetus to illegal drugs. The presence of drugs in meconium can help child protective services to remove a baby from a mother who is abusing drugs.

On April 13, 2004, the Department of Health and Human Services (DHHS) proposed a revision (*Federal Register*, Vol. 69, No. 71, p. 19673019732) to the mandatory guidelines for federal workplace drug testing. The purpose of the new guidelines is to establish scientific and technical parameters for the testing of hair, oral fluid, and sweat specimens. In addition, the DHHS is proposing guidelines for using on-site point-of-care devices for testing of urine and oral fluid for the presence of drugs. The proposed new rules affect approximately 400,000 federal employees who work in safety- and security-sensitive work environments. **Table 17-1** summarizes the applicability of different specimen types.

Hair specimens are collected from the head. The collector must clean the scissors that will be used to cut hair with alcohol wipes in the presence of the donor before cutting the hair. Approximately 1.5 inches of hair closest to the scalp must be collected from the rear of the crown toward the back. For sweat collection the federal guidelines recommend that the donor thoroughly cleans the skin, and then the collector will place two sweat patches on the upper arm or the back. The donor must wear the patches no less than 3 days and no more than 7 days before returning to the collec-

Table 17-1	Federal Guidelines by Specimen Type Collected for Drugs-of-Abuse Testing
Specimen Type	**Reason for Test**
Urine	Pre-employment drug testing
	Random drug testing
	Reasonable suspicion/cause drug testing
	Follow-up drug testing
	Return-to-duty drug testing
	Post-accident drug testing
Hair	Pre-employment drug testing
	Random drug testing
	Follow-up drug testing
	Return-to-duty drug testing
Oral fluid	Pre-employment drug testing
	Random drug testing
	Reasonable suspicion/cause drug testing
	Post-accident drug testing
Sweat (patch)	Return-to-duty drug testing
	Follow-up drug testing

Source: Federal Register, Vol. 69, No. 71, April 13, 2004, p. 19696.

tion site. For oral fluid tests, a positive test for marijuana in oral fluid must be confirmed in a urine specimen collected at the same time because oral fluid testing for marijuana is less accurate compared with testing for other drugs of abuse.

 TESTING OF HAIR SPECIMENS

Hair is composed of mostly protein (mostly keratin), lipid, water, and trace minerals (< 1%). Heavy metals such as arsenic, cadmium, and mercury have a high affinity for keratin, the most important component of

Table 17-2   Comparison of Specimen Types for Drugs-of-Abuse Testing

Specimen	Advantages	Disadvantages
Blood	Indicates recent use Has better correlation with impairment as compared with other specimen types Is difficult to adulterate	Requires difficult sample collection Requires laboratory analysis; point-of-care tests not available
Hair	Has longer detection window (weeks to years) Is relatively noninvasive Is difficult to adulterate Provides very stable specimen; stable for years Allows for repeat collection Can be used for mummified or exhumed bodies	Is unable to detect recent use Is more expensive May not be available (if subject is bald) May provoke hair color bias issues Requires laboratory analysis; can not be tested at collection site
Oral fluid	Indicates recent use Is relatively noninvasive Is difficult to adulterate Can be tested at collection site	Has shorter window of detection Is open to possibility of external/passive contamination May not be able to be produced by some individuals
Sweat	Has longer detection window (3–14 days) Is relatively noninvasive Patches are tamper resistant	Is open to passive/environmental contamination Is expensive Has questionable accuracy Requires laboratory analysis; can not be tested at collection site
Urine	Is a well-established and studied specimen type Has well-established standards among laboratories Is less expensive Has a larger menu of tests Can be analyzed at the collection site	Needs special facility for sample collection Has high adulteration potential Provides shorter detection window May be considered invasive

Source: Dasgupta A, ed. *Handbook of Drugs Monitoring Methods: Therapeutics and Drugs of Abuse.* Totowa, NJ: Humana Press, 2008. Reprinted with kind permission of Springer Science + Business Media.

hair. In 1979 Baumgartner et al published the first report demonstrating the presence of morphine in the hair of heroin addicts using radio immunoassays (RIAs).[1] This report was followed by many studies demonstrating the presence of various abused drugs in the hair of addicts. Although drugs-of-abuse analysis in hair specimens is technically more challenging than the analysis of drugs in urine specimens, there are many advantages to using hair specimens (**Table 17-2**).

However, hair testing does have one limitation: it can not detect recent drug abuse because of the lag time between recent abuse and the incorporation of the drug in hair follicles from the bloodstream and then incorporation of the drug in keratin. Nevertheless, drugs-of-abuse analysis in hair specimens is gaining widespread acceptance in forensic sciences, occupational medicine, and clinical toxicology.

Incorporation of Drugs in Hair

Hair consists of hair follicle and hair shaft. Circulating drugs or their metabolites are deposited in the hair follicle first, and eventually get trapped in the core of the hair shaft as the hair grows out of the hair follicle and then gets trapped in the keratin matrix permanently. Drugs may also get incorporated into hair from sweat, sebum, or even the external environment.

Hair grows more or less at a constant rate of 0.7 to 1.5 cm per month, at an average of approximately 1 cm per month. Usually it takes about 5 to 6 days for hair to grow from the root to appear above the scalp so that the specimen is available for detection. A hair specimen of 3 cm indicates whether a person abused drugs or not in a 3-month period. SAMHSA recommends collecting samples that are approximately 1.5 inch (3.75 cm; 1 inch = 2.5 cm) for drugs-of-abuse testing, representing a window of approximately 3 months. Moreover, analyzing hair specimen in each 1-cm segment may also provide a history of month-to-month abuse of drugs. The presence of drugs in the first, second, or third centimeter of the hair from the root of the hair is indicative of drug abuse in the first, second, or third month, respectively.[2]

Many factors affect the incorporation of drugs in hair. Therefore, higher levels of drugs detected in hair may not reflect more-frequent abuse of drugs by an individual.

Rothe et al demonstrated that there was no correlation between the doses of administered heroin and the concentrations of total opiates measured in hair specimens through a controlled study where subjects were exposed to heroin.[3] The purity of a drug, the metabolism of a drug, the frequency of abuse, as well as hair color play important roles in determining the amount of drugs and or metabolite incorporated in hair.

Another study showed that natural hair color is an important parameter in the evaluation of drug concentration in hair. Although drugs were deposited in hair specimens of subjects with both gray and pigmented hair, the incorporation of drugs and or metabolites was less in white fibers compared with pigmented fibers.[4] Hair color is due to the presence of melanin, which is synthesized in melanocytes within the hair bulb and eventually deposited into keratinocytes that mature into hair shaft. Melanin is a polymer consisting of eumelanin, which is responsible for black and brown hair color, as well as pheomelanin, which is responsible for red hair color. Drugs usually bind to eumelanin more than to pheomelanin.

Rollins et al studied the effect of hair color on the incorporation of codeine into human hair. The authors enrolled male and female Caucasians with black, brown, blond, or red hair as well as non-Caucasians with black hair. The subjects were given codeine orally. Subjects were asked not to cut their hair or use any chemical treatment but were allowed normal hygienic washing of hair. The mean hair codeine concentrations 5 weeks after dosing were 1429 pg/mg in black hair, 208 pg/mg in brown hair, 99 pg/mg in blond hair, and 69 pg/mg in red hair. In black hair, codeine concentrations were 2564 pg/mg for Asians. Using the SAMSHA guideline of 200 pg/mg as the cutoff for codeine in hair testing protocol,

100% of subjects with black hair and 50% subjects with brown hair in their study would have been reported as positive. In contrast, subjects with blond or red hair would have tested negative. Caucasians with black hair have a lower percentage of melanin compared with Asians. Authors also found a strong correlation between hair concentration of codeine and melanin concentration in hair.[5]

Yegles et al studied the effect of bleaching on the stability of benzodiazepines in hair and concluded that drug concentrations decrease significantly from bleaching of hair.[6] Low abuse of drugs may not be detected in hair treated with bleaches, perms, or dyes, but regular drug abuse will likely be detected even after chemical treatment of hair, although the concentrations of drugs may be reduced.[2] Although concentrations of other drugs incorporated in hair also decrease after chemical treatment and bleaching, Skopp et al reported that conversely, bleaching and chemical treatments also make the hair more susceptible to drug uptake from the environment.[7] Shampooing of hair has little effect on removing drugs already incorporated in hair but may be effective in removing drugs absorbed in hair due to environmental contamination.

Abuse Versus Environmental Exposure

Because drugs may be absorbed into hair from the environment, it is important to differentiate whether a positive test for drugs based on a hair specimen means that the individual abused drugs or if it was caused by environmental exposure. In one report, a couple that lived together tested positive for both tetrahydrocannabinol (THC) and cannabinol. The male subject was abusing marijuana, while the female subject denied any marijuana abuse. When hair specimens were further tested for the presence of marijuana metabolite (11-nor-Δ^9-tetrahydrocannabinol-9-carboxylic acid; THC-COOH), a significant amount was detected in the specimen from the male subject, while the specimen from the female subject did not show any presence of the metabolite. The authors concluded that the detection of marijuana metabolite in the male's hair specimen indicated marijuana abuse.[8]

Today, most shampoo products made with cannabis products contain less than 1% THC, but some of the products may contain 1% to 3% THC. Analysis of the commercially available shampoo Cannabio showed the presence of 412 ng/ml of THC as well as 4079 ng/ml of cannabidiol and 380 ng/ml of cannabinol. Three subjects washed their hair with Cannabio shampoo once daily for 2 weeks, but subsequent analysis of hair specimens for THC from these subjects indicated that regular use of such shampoo should not cause false-positive results in hair drug tests.[9] It is possible that people who are around other people smoking drugs may pick up some of the parent drugs in their hair. It is also possible that an individual not abusing drugs may passively inhale some smoke containing drugs. However, in these cases it is unlikely that the drug concentrations would be high enough to cause a false-positive result in hair analysis unless the person were exposed for many hours to illicit drugs in a contaminated environment. Moreover, hair specimens are adequately washed with buffer and or organic solvents in order to remove such environmental contaminants prior to analysis to avoid false-positive results.

The minimum criteria for the presence of drug metabolite in hair and the ratio to the parent drug can more accurately indicate drug abuse by an individual. Confirmation of marijuana use by hair analysis requires the presence of marijuana metabolite such as 11-nor-Δ^9-tetrahydrocannabinol-9-carboxylic acid (THC-COOH) or 11-nor-Δ^9-tetrahydrocannabinol (THC-OH).[2] Moreover, benzoylecgonine, the metabolite of cocaine, can be present in crack cocaine and may accumulate in hair from passive exposure, but proper washing of hair specimen prior to analysis can decontaminate hair. Therefore, the washing procedure for decontamination of hair specimen ensures that the drug present in hair specimen is due to abuse of the drug by an individual rather than environmental contamination.

Concentrations of Various Abused Drugs in Hair

Various abused drugs such as amphetamines, cannabinoids, cocaine, opiates, and phencyclidine are incorporated in hair. SAMSHA has proposed guidelines for cutoff concentrations of various drugs in hair specimens (**Table 17-3**) for the interpretation of results in hair drug analysis. For example, the concentration of marijuana metabolite at a concentration of 1 pg per milligram of hair indicates marijuana abuse. Drug concentrations in hair are measured by picograms to nanograms per milligram of hair. In one study, the maximum amounts of cocaine and benzoylecgonine detected in hair specimens were 1093.8 ng/mg and 163.7 ng/mg, respectively, while the maximum amount of cocaethylene (an active metabolite of cocaine found in persons abusing both cocaine and alcohol at the same time) was 13.9 ng per milligram in hair. In the same study, the maximum amounts of morphine, codeine, heroin, and 6-acetylmorphine (metabolite of heroin) detected in subjects were 291.3 ng/mg, 68.4 ng/mg, 146.4 ng/mg, and 220.8 ng/mg, respectively. Similarly, the minimum

amounts of cocaine and benzoylecgonine detected in hair specimens were 200 pg/mg and 100 pg/mg, respectively. The minimum amount of cocaethylene detected was also 100 pg/mg. For THC, the minimum level detected was 3 pg/mg, while the minimum THC-COOH detected was 1 pg/mg.[2]

Hair Drug Testing for Mothers and Babies

Drug testing in hair of neonates and mothers is a good way to evaluate maternal drug abuse as well as exposure of the fetus to abused drugs. Because of the immediate and long-term problems associated with newborns born to mothers who abused drugs during pregnancy, such abuse should be identified soon after birth to take appropriate legal steps to protect such newborn babies. Urine analysis can identify only recent abuse. The analysis of meconium also has limitations, so negative results do not exclude any drug abuse during pregnancy. In contrast, analysis of hair from newborns may provide evidence of the mother's drug abuse weeks to months prior to delivery. Maternal drug abuse is a serious health hazard to the fetus. In 1987 Parton et al first demonstrated fetal exposure to cocaine by analysis of hair specimens collected from 15 babies.[10] More recently, authors compared cocaine and benzoylecgonine concentrations in hair specimens from mother/child pairs and observed a positive correlation between cocaine concentrations in the infants' hair and maternal cocaine and benzoylecgonine concentrations. However, median cocaine concentration was 10-fold higher in mothers compared with neonates (3.56 ng/mg vs 0.31 ng/mg of hair). However, there are cases where the mother's hair showed the presence of cocaine and benzoylecgonine,

Table 17-3   SAMHSA-Proposed Initial Screen and Confirmation Cutoff Concentrations of Drugs-of-Abuse in Hair Specimens

Analyte	Screen Test Cutoff Level (pg/mg)	Analyte	Confirmation Test Cutoff Level (pg/mg)
Marijuana metabolite	1	Marijuana metabolite (THC-COOH)	0.05
Cocaine metabolite	500	Cocaine	500
Opiate metabolite	200	Cocaine metabolite[b]	50
Phencyclidine	300	Morphine	200
Amphetamine[a]	500	Codeine	200
MDMA	500	6-acetylmorphine[c]	200
		Phencyclidine	300
		Amphetamine	300
		Methamphetamine[d]	300
		MDMA	300
		MDA	300
		MDEA	300

Source: Federal Register, Vol. 69, No. 71, April 13, 2004, p. 19697.

*Abbreviations:*MDMA, methylenedioxymethamphetamine; MDA, methylenedioxyamphetamine; MDEA, methylenedioxyethylamphetamine.

a. Methamphetamine is the target analyte for amphetamine screen.

b. Cocaine metabolites include benzoylecgonine, norcocaine, and cocaethylene.

c. Specimens must also contain morphine at a level 200 pg/mg or higher.

d. Amphetamine must be present at a concentration greater than or equal to 50 pg/mg.

while the infant's hair tested negative. The median concentration of cocaine in mothers whose infants also tested positive was 7.24 ng/mg, compared with a median cocaine concentration of 1.25 ng/mg in mothers whose infants tested negative. The authors concluded that fetal hair grows in the third trimester, and hence a positive neonatal hair testing result indicates maternal drug abuse during pregnancy.[11]

Adulteration of Hair Specimens

The collection of hair specimens is supervised, and therefore it is unlikely that an individual can substitute a hair specimen or attempt to adulterate a hair specimen during collection. However, several shampoos available for sale through the Internet are claimed to help a person pass a drug test. Clear Choice Hair Follicle Shampoo ($35) claims to remove all residues and toxins within 10 minutes of use. One application is sufficient for shoulder-length hair, and the effect can last for 8 hours. Root Clean hair cleansing system shampoo is also commercially available. Rohrich et al studied the effect of Zydot Ultra Clean shampoo on drug concentrations in human hair and observed that all drugs that were originally present in hair specimens were also present after a single application of shampoo, although a slight decrease was observed in cocaine, monoacetylmorphine, and THC concentrations. The authors conclude that Zydot Ultra Clean shampoo can not remove drugs in sufficient amounts to cause a positive hair specimen to test negative.[12]

Analysis of Drugs in Hair Specimens

Unlike urine specimens, which can be analyzed directly using immunoassays, drugs need to be extracted from hair prior to analysis. First, hair specimens must be washed with organic solvent and buffer to remove environmental contamination of drugs in order to avoid false-positive drug-testing results. Various solvents such as methanol, isopropyl alcohol, hexane, and buffers such as phosphate buffer are used to wash the hair specimen. Then, washed specimens are digested with acid, alkali, or neutral buffer to extract drugs. However, digestion in an alkaline medium (e.g., 1 molar sodium hydroxide or an acidic medium using 0.1 normal hydrochloric acid) results in hydrolysis of acetylmorphine or acetylcodeine. Using a neutral medium such as a buffer at pH 7.4 or methanol, the hydrolysis of acetylated opiates can be minimized.[13] After digestion, drugs are extracted in organic solvent and reconstituted with the appropriate buffer, followed by screening for the presence of drugs using the appropriate immunoassays.

The first requirement of the immunoassay screening is that the digest should not be the denatured antibody used in the immunoassay. Therefore, a strong acid or alkali digest must be neutralized during the immunoassay. Enzymatic digestion is superior to chemical digestion for further analysis of specimens using immunoassays. Moreover, immunoassays must be calibrated using the spiked-hair digest standard to correct for any matrix effect. Because the concentration of drugs is lower in hair compared with urine, these immunoassays are often used near their limit of detection.[14]

Although enzymatic digestion can be performed under mild conditions at neutral pH, but in contrast to acid or alkali digestion, which can be completed in few hours, a much longer incubation time (up to 24 hours) may be needed for completion of enzymatic digestion. Schaffer et al used proteinase-K, dithiothreitol, and detergent for enzymatic digestion of hair specimens. Specimens were digested overnight at 40°C. After digestion all specimens were extracted using solid-phase extraction columns and derivatized for liquid chromatography–tandem mass spectrometric analysis.[15] However, GC/MS can also be used for confirmation of drugs of abuse in hair specimens that tested positive by the immunoassay screening procedure. Drugs that have been confirmed with GC/MS can withstand legal challenges in a court of law.

TESTING OF ORAL FLUIDS

Testing of saliva or oral fluid is a recent development in drugs-of-abuse testing. Oral fluid originates from major salivary glands, minor salivary glands, oral mucosa, as well as gingival cervices. The mixture of fluid is called "oral fluid," "whole saliva," or "mixed saliva." Drugs are transported from blood to oral fluid by passive diffusion. Drugs and metabolites in plasma are rapidly distributed to salivary glands and then diffuse into saliva within minutes of parenteral administration. Drug molecules (molecular weight < 500) that are not ionized and not bound to serum proteins can diffuse passively to oral fluid. Usually, the parent drug molecule, which is more lipophilic than the metabolite, diffuses more rapidly to oral fluid from circulation.

The diffusion of drugs to oral fluid is also pH dependent. Concentrations of drugs in oral fluid correlate to concentrations of drugs in blood. Therefore, drug concentrations in oral fluid correlate to the degree of impairment, while the drug concentrations in urine correlate poorly with impairment. For example, Menkes et al demonstrated that there is a correlation between THC concentrations in saliva and intoxication in individual subjects.[16] Cone demonstrated correlation between salivary concentrations of morphine and pupil measurements as well as behavior in individuals abusing morphine.[17]

Oral fluid collection is easy and noninvasive. Moreover, oral fluid collection does not require the presence of any medically trained personnel, and oral fluid can be tested at the site of collection by point-of-care devices. Drug testing of oral fluid is a quick, useful way to assess people involved in driving, operating machinery, or any other task requiring a high level of psychomotor functioning.[18] One of the major uses of oral fluid testing is to identify people who are driving under the influence of drugs.

A few countries have passed legislation to allow saliva as a valid matrix for screening and confirmation of drugs of abuse in suspected individuals. The United Kingdom's Railways and Transportation Safety Act of 2003 gives a constable the power to administer a preliminary test to individuals suspected of being under the influence of drugs who are driving or attempt to drive or are in charge of a motor vehicle on a road or other public place. The allowed preliminary tests include breath tests, impairment tests, and tests of saliva or sweat. In December 2003 the State of Victoria in Australia passed legislation to allow police to perform roadside oral fluid tests for cannabis and methamphetamine.

Despite the progress in drug testing in oral fluids, more work is needed to improve both the sensitivity and the specificity of onsite screening devices, particularly for testing for marijuana and benzodiazepines. The possibility of passive contamination of oral fluid also needs to be explored in more detail.[19] Table 17-2 summarizes some advantages and disadvantages of oral fluid tests.

Concentrations of Drugs in Oral Fluid Specimens

The expected concentrations of abused drugs in oral fluid are in low nanogram levels, making testing of drugs in oral fluids a major analytical challenge. **Table 17-4** lists the proposed SAMHSA cutoff values for drugs-of-abuse testing of oral fluids. For example, the proposed cutoff for THC in the screening assay is 20 ng/ml, while the proposed cutoff in the confirmation assay is 8 ng/ml. For cocaine metabolite, the proposed cutoff concentration is 20 ng/ml, while the confirmation test cutoff is 8 ng/ml. These cutoff values are significantly lower than the cutoff values used for urine testing. For example, in urine the cutoff value for screening of cocaine metabolite is usually 300 ng/ml.

Cone et al studied disposition of drugs of abuse in oral fluids using a large number of specimens (approximately 635,000 specimens). A total of 8679 specimens constituted the data base, where at least one drug was confirmed positive (1.4% of specimens positive). Oral fluids were collected using the Intercept Oral Fluid Collection device (OraSure Technologies, Bethlehem, PA) and initially screened for amphetamines, benzodiazepines, cannabis, methadone, and opiates using the Intercept Micro-Plate Enzyme Immunoassays (OraSure Technologies). Presumptive positive specimens

Table 17-4   SAMHSA-Proposed Initial Screen and Confirmation Cutoff Concentrations of Drugs-of-Abuse in Oral Fluid Specimens

Analyte	Screen Test Cutoff Level (ng/ml)	Analyte	Confirmation Test Cutoff Level (ng/ml)
Marijuana or metabolite	4	THC (parent drug) (THC-COOH)	2
Cocaine metabolite	20	Cocaine or benzoylecgonine	8
Opiate metabolite	40	Morphine	40
		Codeine	40
		6-acetylmorphine	4
Phencyclidine	10	Phencyclidine	10
Amphetamine[a]	50	Amphetamine	50
		Methamphetamine[b]	50
MDMA	50	MDMA	50
		MDA	50
		MDEA	50

Source: Federal Register, Vol. 69, No. 71, April 13, 2004, p. 19697.

Abbreviations: MDMA, 3,4-methylenedioxymethamphetamine; MDA, 3,4-methylenedioxyamphetamine; MDEA, 3,4-methylenedioxyethylamphetamine.

a. Methamphetamine is the target analyte for amphetamine screen.

b. Amphetamine must be present at a concentration greater than or equal to the limit of detection of the confirmation test.

were confirmed by GC/MS or GC combined with tandem mass spectrometry. The authors observed that opiate-positive tests dominated in legal/treatment settings, while cannabis positive specimens were most common in workplace drug testing. The lowest observed concentrations of cocaine, benzoylecgonine, and cocaethylene in oral fluids were 2.0 ng/ml, 2.1 ng/ml, and 2.4 ng/ml, respectively, where the corresponding highest observed concentrations were 16,770 ng/ml, 2999 ng/ml, and 9864 ng/ml, respectively. The minimum observed THC concentration in oral fluid was 0.3 ng/ml, and the maximum observed concentration was 382 ng/ml. For methamphetamine, the lowest observed concentration was 20.2 ng/ml, and the highest observed level was 203 ng/ml. Although the lowest observed amphetamine concentration in oral fluid was 12.2 ng/ml, the highest observed concentration was 23,476 ng/ml.[20]

The detection windows for abused drugs in oral fluid specimens are shorter than the detection windows of drugs in urine specimens. Nevertheless, drugs are present for a significant time after use in oral fluid. Amphetamine can be detected in oral fluid for 20 to 50 hours after abuse. (For comparison, amphetamine can be detected in urine for 1 to 3 days after exposure.) Cocaine can be detected in oral fluid for 5 to 12 hours after a single dose. 6-acetylmorphine, the metabolite of heroin, is present in oral fluid for 0.5 to 8 hours, while morphine can be detected in oral fluid for 12 to 24 hours.[21] Niedbala et al measured the salivary concentrations of THC after smoking of marijuana. The last positive specimen for THC was 31 hours using the immunoassay and 34 hours using the GC/MS method. However, the metabolite of THC (THC-COOH) can be detected in urine for up to 58 hours.[22]

Analysis of Oral Fluids

Spitting is the simplest way of collecting oral fluid, but the specimen may contain food particles, cell debris, or mucous. Stimulation of saliva formation using sour candy or citric acid crystals can result in a sufficient amount of oral fluid for both screening assays and confirmatory tests by GC/MS. Various devices—such as Intercept, Salivette, OralScreen, DrugWipe, Cozart, OraLine, and Toxiquick—are commercially available for collection of oral fluid specimens. Oral fluid specimens collected using such devices are usually cleaner than specimens collected through spitting.

Some of the collection devices available commercially use some form of propriety diluent to mix with the collected oral fluid. Typically, the absorption pad used to collect the oral fluid is added to diluent in the collection tube following mixing. After that the solution can be used directly for drug testing (both screening and GC/MS confirmation). For example, the Intercept collection device consists of an absorbent foam pad with diluent, the DrugWipe collection device is a swipe only, and the Salivette consists of a cotton wool swab that is filtered and centrifuged.[23]

After collection the presence of drugs in oral fluids can be tested at the collection sites for quick results (within 30 minutes) using point-of-care devices for testing oral fluids. Currently there are 12 such devices commercially available. Examples of such devices are the Cozart RapiScan saliva sample kit, the Oratect II oral fluid drug screening device, OralScreen, and SalivaScreen. Some of these devices (Cozart RapiScan, DrugRead) provide an electronic readout, while other devices (DrugWipe, OralScreen) use handheld photometers or handheld cartridges requiring visual inspection.[23] Moreover, oral fluids can be transported to a laboratory for further testing by immunoassays. The results obtained by these point-of-care devices are presumed positive. In legal cases, further confirmation of the presence of such drugs should be verified using a more sophisticated analytical technique such as GC/MS.

Adulteration of Oral Fluid Specimens

The main advantage of oral fluid testing is that the donor has little chance to adulterate the specimen. Already in use in the transportation and insurance industries, saliva testing is becoming more common in workplace and roadside testing for driving under the influence of drugs and criminal justice. Insurance companies often rely on saliva-based drug testing. Home test kits for testing of oral fluid are also available. The Saliva Multi-Drug Screen Test 5 (which tests for THC, cocaine, opiate, methamphetamine, and benzodiazepine) is commercially available.

Following the increasing popularity of oral fluid testing, products are now being marketed to help drug users pass such tests. Some commercially available products claim to be able to help a person pass saliva-based drug testing. However, the effectiveness of such products in escaping detection by drug tests has not been clearly established by scientific research. Wong et al studied the effects of commercially available adulterants and food stuffs on oral fluid drug testing. An on-site oral fluid drug screen (Oratect) showed no effect of American or ethnic food (Asian, Hispanic) on drug tests when food was consumed 30 minutes before analysis. Similarly, common beverages such as orange and apple juice did not cause any false positives in drugs-of-abuse tests. Cosmetics, toothpaste, mouthwash, and cigarettes also did not show any effect. The authors also evaluated the commercially available oral fluid adulterants Clear Choice, Fizzy Flush (Health Tech, Macon, GA), and Spit n Kleen Mouthwash (A-Z Enterprise, Sparks, NV) for their abilities to cause a false negative in drug testing. They reported that these products are not capable of destroying drugs of abuse in saliva specimens.[24]

████   SWEAT TESTING

Sweat and sebaceous glands are distributed throughout the body. The highest concentrations of sweat glands are found in the hands, while sebaceous glands are concentrated more on the forehead. Both glands can deliver drugs to sweat and sebum. Drugs probably enter into sweat by passive diffusion from blood to sweat glands. Usually a parent drug is present in higher concentrations in sweat than its metabolites are. Sweat may be collected as liquid perspiration on sweat wipes or with a sweat patch. Sweat patches that are waterproof and tamper resistant are available commercially and can be worn comfortably for weeks to a month. For example, the sweat-collection device PharmaCheck uses a transparent film that allows oxygen, carbon dioxide, and water vapor to escape but can retain drugs excreted in sweat. The skin should be cleaned thoroughly before application of the sweat patch. The normal pH of sweat is 5.8, but its pH may increase to 6.4 during exercise. The change of pH may affect diffusion of drugs to sweat. Despite variations in sweat production by individuals, drug testing for sweat can be successfully performed for cocaine, opiates, benzodiazepines, cannabis, buprenorphine, and methylenedioxyethyl-amphetamine.[25] The main advantage of sweat monitoring is that it provides a long window of continuous monitoring of an individual (weeks to months).

Concentrations of Drugs in Sweat

Concentrations of drugs vary widely among individuals as well as among different collection devices. In general, concentrations of drugs are significantly lower in sweat compared with urine. Therefore, sensitivity screening techniques are required for analysis of drugs in sweat. SAMHSA proposes a cutoff of 4 ng/patch for THC, while the confirmation cutoff is 1 ng/patch (**Table 17-5**).

In one study involving 198 injured drivers, 22 subjects tested positive for THC based on urine drug analysis, while 16 tested positive using forehead wipe (THC concentration: 1-152 ng/pad). No metabolite of THC was detected in sweat.[26] Huestis et al reported that cocaine and codeine concentrations were higher when sweat specimens were collected using the Hand-Held Fast Patch compared with the Torso Fast Patch. The values were also higher than the values reported with PharmChek sweat patch. The Hand-Held Fast Patch device is applied to the palm of the hand, while the Torso Fast Patch is worn on the abdomen. Both devices utilize heat-induced sweat

Table 17-5   SAMHSA-Proposed Initial Screen and Confirmation Cutoff Concentrations of Drugs-of-Abuse in Sweat Patch

Analyte	Screen Test Cutoff Level (ng/patch)	Analyte	Confirmation Test Cutoff Level (ng/patch)
Marijuana metabolite	4	Marijuana (parent drug) (THC-COOH)	1
Cocaine metabolite	25	Cocaine or benzoylecgonine	25
Opiate metabolite	25	Morphine	25
		Codeine	25
		6-acetylmorphine	25
Phencyclidine	20	Phencyclidine	20
Amphetamine[a]	25	Amphetamine	25
		Methamphetamine[b]	25
MDMA	25	MDMA	25
		MDA	25
		MDEA	25

Source: Federal Register, Vol. 69, No. 71, April 13, 2004, p. 19697.

Abbreviations: MDMA, 3,4-methylenedioxymethamphetamine; MDA, 3,4-methylenedioxyamphetamine; MDEA, 3,4-methylenedioxyethylamphetamine.

a. Methamphetamine is the target analyte for amphetamine screen.

b. Amphetamine must be present at a concentration greater than or equal to the limit of detection of the confirmation test.

stimulation and a larger cellulose pad for increased sweat collection. Sweat specimens can be collected within 30 minutes using these devices, whereas the Pharm-Chek sweat patch is usually worn for 5 to 10 days. The authors reported that cocaine and codeine were the primary analytes detected in sweat. Peak cocaine and codeine concentrations ranged from 33 ng/patch to 3579 ng/patch and 11 ng/patch to 1123 ng/patch, respectively, using Hand-Held Fast Patch devices, compared with 22 ng/patch to 1463 ng/patch for cocaine and 22 ng/patch to 1463 ng/patch for codeine using Torso fast patch devices. The peak concentrations of drugs were observed 4.5 to 24 hours after dosing, while drugs were detected up to 48 hours after exposure. Metabolites of cocaine and codeine were also detected in sweat patches but in considerably lesser concentrations than the respective parent drugs.[27]

In another study, authors investigated excretion of amphetamine and methamphetamine in human sweat after controlled oral methamphetamine administration. The authors reported that methamphetamine was measurable in sweat within 2 hours of administration. The median amphetamine concentration in the sweat patch was 63.0 ng/patch (range: 16.8–175 ng/patch) after a low dose of amphetamine and 307 ng/patch (range: 199–607 ng/patch) after a high dose of amphetamine. The corresponding amphetamine values were 15.5 ng/patch (range: 6.5–40.5 ng/patch) for the low dose and 53.8 ng/patch (range: 34.0–83.4 ng/patch) for the high dose administration of methamphetamine. All patches worn for 1 week after dosing tested negative for amphetamine and methamphetamine.[28]

Analysis of Sweat Testing

One advantage of sweat testing is that once the patch is in place it is difficult to contaminate the patch in order to invalidate drug testing because the outer polyurethane layer is impermeable to molecules larger than water. Adulterants applied to outer layers do not reach the collection pad.[29] Drugs can be extracted from the sweat collection patch followed by analysis using enzyme immunoassays with appropriate matrix correction for screening of drugs present in sweat specimens. However, presumptive positive specimens must be confirmed by an alternative method such as GC/MS.

Sweat drug testing has limitations, and it is premature to replace urine drug testing with sweat drug testing in both clinical and research settings. Chawarski et al reported that sweat patches have low acceptability among patients enrolled in their study, where 54.3% of patches were removed by the research personnel, and only 35.1% patches were obtained exactly 7 days after their application. Moreover, sweat drug testing has low sensitivity; only one-third of illicit opiate abuse was detected by sweat testing compared with urine drug testing.[25] Moreover, using the SAMHSA-recommended cutoff values for testing of cocaine, sweat testing misses a significant number of cocaine abusers.[30] Therefore, improvements are needed to increase the current level of sensitivity and specificity of sweat testing.

 ## TESTING OF DRUGS IN MECONIUM

Drug abuse during pregnancy is a serious problem that has significant impact on neonatal health and development. Prenatal use of illicit drugs has been associated with decreased birth weight, preterm delivery, withdrawal symptoms, birth defects, and a variety of other problems. Cocaine abuse during pregnancy may cause cardiac defects, endocardial cushion defect, genitourinary defects, atrial septal defect, ventricular septal defect, and other abnormalities in newborns. Maternal abuse of methamphetamine or amphetamine may cause cardiac malfunction and musculoskeletal defects. Mirochnick et al demonstrated an inverse correlation between the concentration of benzoylecgonine (cocaine metabolite) in meconium and birth weight, length, and head circumference in newborns.[31] Parental drug abuse can be detected by maternal report, urine drug testing of pregnant mothers, hair analysis, as well as analysis of meconium. Meconium provides a higher sensitivity and longer window of detection than other traditional drug-testing protocols such as urine drug testing.

Meconium is an infant's first bowel movement. It is dark green to black in color and odorless because the bacteria that produces the foul odor of feces are usually absent in meconium. The formation of meconium probably starts at 12 weeks of gestation. Most abused drugs are capable of crossing the placenta through passive diffusion because of the small molecular weights of abused drugs. Fetal swallowing is considered to be the mechanism by which drugs are concentrated in meconium. Collection of meconium is noninvasive and relatively simple, and the analysis of meconium for drugs is useful to assess fetal exposure to drugs of abuse during pregnancy. Meconium is collected by scraping the content of a soiled diaper, and 0.5 g of meconium is the minimum requirement for drugs-of-abuse testing.[32]

Cocaine crosses the placenta through passive diffusion. The concentration of cocaine and its metabolites decreases rapidly 48 hours after birth, but another metabolite, benzoylecgonine, remains detectable for an additional few days. The parent cocaine along with several metabolites, including benzoylecgonine, ecgonine methyl ester, norcocaine, benzoylnorecgonine, m-hydroxybenzoylecgonine, and cocaethylene have been indentured in meconium. A highly polar metabolite of cocaine, m-hydroxybenzoylecgonine, is the only compound found in one-fourth of screened positive meconium samples for cocaine. Different cocaine metabolites can be associated with specific patterns of drug abuse in pregnant women. Cocaethylene, nor-cocaethylene, and ecgonine ethyl esters are associated with concurrent abuse of cocaine and alcohol, while anhydroecgonine and anhydroecgonine methyl esters are pyrolytic products of cocaine, indicative of "crack cocaine" abuse.[33] Other drugs and metabolites such as amphetamine, methamphetamine, methadone, and THC-COOH have been detected in meconium.[32]

Concentrations of Drugs in Meconium

Meconium testing for cocaine and its metabolites is more sensitive than urine drug testing for establishing fetal exposure to cocaine. Lewis et al analyzed both urine and meconium specimens from newborns within 3 days of birth. The authors analyzed 54 paired urine and meconium specimens. Out of 54 paired specimens, 39 specimens tested negative for cocaine in both urine and meconium, 10 specimens were negative for cocaine in urine but positive for cocaine in meconium, 4 specimens were positive for cocaine in both urine and meconium, and 1 specimen tested positive in urine and negative in meconium. Therefore, 25.9% of meconium specimens tested positive; in contrast, only 9.3% of urine specimens tested positive. The authors concluded that meconium testing for cocaine is more sensitive than urine drug testing.[34]

The amount of drugs found in meconium may also vary significantly among neonates depending on duration and magnitude of exposure. In one study, meconium from babies born to cocaine-dependent mothers showed cocaine concentrations in the range of 0.1 to 0.78 μg per gram of meconium.[35] In another study, authors found that 80% of newborns born to cocaine-dependent mothers showed the presence of cocaine in their meconium. The cocaine concentrations ranged from 0.14 to 19.91 μg/g of meconium. In the same study, 55% of babies born to mothers with a history of morphine abuse showed morphine concentrations of 0.41 to 14.97 μg/g of meconium, and 60% of babies born to mothers with a history of cannabinoid (marijuana) abuse showed cannabinoid concentrations of 0.05 to 0.67 μg/g of meconium. The concentrations of metabolites were highest for the first two days after birth, while some meconium showed the presence of drugs even on the third day. Eight urine specimens from these newborns showed no presence of drugs, while the corresponding meconium specimens tested positive for drugs.[36] This study also demonstrates the superiority of meconium testing over urine testing for drugs of abuse in babies born to mothers with history of drug abuse.

Analysis of Meconium

After extraction of drugs from meconium using organic solvents, the extract can be dried and reconstituted with the appropriate buffer for analysis with the appropriate immunoassays. Moriya et al extracted meconium with chloroform/isopropanol (3:1 by vol) and used enzyme multiplied immunoassay technique (EMIT; Dade Behring, Deerfield, IL) immunoassays for screening of drugs of abuse. The lower limit of detection of benzoylecgonine, methamphetamine, morphine, and phencyclidine (PCP) were 250, 730, 110, and 100 ng of drug/g of meconium. When the authors analyzed meconium from 50 infants born to mothers who abused drugs during pregnancy, 12 specimens tested positive for benzoylecgonine, 7 for opiates, and 1 for PCP. The authors also used GC/MS for confirmation of benzoylecgonine and PCP in meconium.[37]

Although the presence of drugs in meconium can be confirmed by GC/MS, a more sophisticated technique than GC/MS, such as liquid chromatography combined with tandem mass spectrometry, can also be used for confirmation of drugs in meconium. Coles et al described a sophisticated method for analysis of codeine, morphine, hydrocodone, hydromorphone, oxycodone, and 6-acetylmorphine in meconium, urine, plasma, and whole blood using liquid chromatography and tandem mass spectrometry.[38] The authors claim that this is the first time the presence of 6-acetylmorphine, a metabolite of heroin, has been confirmed in meconium, providing definite proof of illegal heroin abuse by pregnant mothers.

CONCLUSION

Although the majority of drugs-of-abuse testing is performed on urine specimens, use of alternative specimens for drug tests has certain advantages. In contrast to urine, where drug or metabolites are present for only a few days to a week, hair testing can establish drug abuse in an individual over a period of several months. Drugs usually appear in oral fluid immediately after abuse, so oral fluid testing is useful to identify recent drug abuse. Twelve different point-of-care devices are commercially available for testing of oral fluid at the site of collection, although oral fluids can also be sent to laboratories for analysis. A few countries have passed legislature to approve oral fluid testing in drivers suspected of driving under the influence of drugs and in other similar situations. Sweat testing is also useful for showing drug abuse over a week or longer, but it has limitations. Analysis of meconium is useful for evaluating levels of drugs of abuse in newborns born to mothers suspected of abusing drugs. Moreover, meconium testing is more sensitive and superior to urine drug testing for identifying newborns whose mothers abused drugs during pregnancy.

REFERENCES

1. Baumgartner AM, Jones PF, Baumgartner WA, Black CT. Radioimmunoassay of hair for determining opiate-abuse histories. *J Nucl Med.* 1979;20:748–752.

2. Tsanaclis L, Wicks JF. Patterns in drug use in the United Kingdom as revealed through analysis of hair in a large population sample. *Forensic Sci Int.* 2007;170:121–128.

3. Kintz P, Bundeli P, Brenneisen R, Ludes B. Dose-concentration relationship in hair from subjects in a controlled heroin-maintenance program. *J Anal Toxicol.* 1998;22: 231–236.

4. Rothe M, Pragst F, Thor S, Hunger J. Effect of pigmentation on the drug deposition in hair of grey-haired subjects. *Forensic Sci Int.* 1997;84:53–60.

5. Rollins DE, Wilkins DG, Krueger GG, et al. The effect of hair color on the incorporation of codeine into human hair. *J Anal Toxicol.* 2003;27:545–551.

6. Yegles M. Marson Y, Wennig R. Ingluence of bleaching on stability of benzodiazepines in hair. *Forensic Sci Int.* 2000;107:87–92.

7. Skopp G, Potsch L, Moeller MR. On cosmetically treated hair: aspects and pitfalls of interpretation. *Forensic Sci Int.* 1997;84:43–52.

8. Uhl M, Sachs S. Cannabis in hair: strategy to prove marijuana/hashish consumption. *Forensic Sci Int.* 2004;145:143–147.

9. Cirimele V, Kintz P, Jamey C, Ludes B. Are cannabinoids detected in hair after washing with Cannabino shampoo? *J Anal Toxicol.* 1999;23:349–351.

10. Parton L, Warburton D, Hill V et al. Quantitation of fetal cocaine exposure by radio immunoassay. *Pediatr Res.* 1987;21:372.

11. Garcia-Bournissen F, Rokach B, Karaskov T, Koren G. Cocaine detection in maternal and neonatal hair: implications to fetal toxicology. *Ther Drug Monit.* 2007;29:71–76.

12. Rohrich J, Zorntlein S, Potsch L, Skopp G, Becker J. Effect of shampoo Ultra Clean on drug concentrations in human hair. *Int J Legal Med.* 2000;2:102-106.

13. Balikova MA, Habrdova V. hair analysis for opiates: evaluation of washing and incubation procedures. *J Chromatogr B Analyt Technol Biomed Life Sci.* 2003;789:93–100.

14. Cassani M, Spiehler V. Analytical requirements perspective and limits of immunological methods for drugs in hair. *Forensic Sci Int.* 1993;63:175–184.

15. Schaffer MI, Wang WL, Irving J. An evaluation of two wash procedures for the differentiation of external contamination versus ingestion in analysis of human hair samples for cocaine. *J Anal Toxicol.* 2002;26:485–488.

16. Menkes DB, Howard RC, Spears GFS, Cairns ER. Salivary THC following cannabis smoking correlates with subjective intoxication and heart rate. *Psychopharmacology.* 1991;103:277–279.

17. Cone EJ. Testing human hair for drugs of abuse: 1. Individual dose and time profiles of morphine and codeine in plasma, saliva, urine and beard compared to drug induced effects on pupils and behavior. *J Anal Toxicol.* 1990;14:1–7.

18. Dryer KR, Wilkinson C. The detection of illicit drugs in oral fluid: another potential strategy to reduce illicit drug related harm. *Drug Alcohol Rev.* 2008;27:99–107.

19. Verstraete AG. Oral fluid testing for drivers under the influence of drugs: history, recent progress, and remaining challenges. *Forensic Sci Int.* 2005;150:143–150.

20. Cone EJ, Clarke J, Tsanaclis L. Prevalence and disposition of drugs of abuse and opioid treatment drugs in oral fluid. *J Anal Toxicol.* 2007;31:424–433.

21. Verstraete A. Detection times of drugs of abuse in blood, urine, and oral fluid. *Ther Drug Monit.* 2004;26:200–205.

22. Niedbala RS, Kardos KW, Fritch DF, et al. Detection of marijuana use by oral fluid and urine analysis following single-dose administration of smoked and oral marijuana. *J Anal Toxicol.* 2001;25:289–303.

23. Drummer OHG. Drug testing in oral fluid. *Clin Biochem Rev.* 2006;27:147–159.

24. Wong RC, Tran M, Tung JK. Oral fluid testing: effects of adulterants and foodstuffs. *Forensic Sci Int.* 2005;150:175–180.

25. Chawarski MC, Fiellin DA, O'Corner PG, Bernard M, Schottenfeld RS. Utility of sweat patch testing for drug use monitoring in outpatient treatment for opiate dependence. *J Substance Abuse Treat.* 2007;33:411–415.

26. Kintz P, Cirimele V, Ludes B. Detection of cannabis in oral fluid (saliva) and forehead swipe (sweat) from impaired drivers. *J Anal Toxicol.* 2000;24:557–561.

27. Huestis MA, Oyler JM, Cone EJ, Wstadik AT et al. Sweat testing for cocaine, codeine, and metabolites by gas chromatography-mass spectrometry. *J Chromatogr B Biomed Sci Appl.* 1999;733:247–264.

28. Barnes AJ, Smith ML, Kacinko SL, et al. Excretion of methamphetamine and amphetamine in human sweat following oral methamphetamine administration. *Clin Chem.* 2008;54:172–180.

29. Forgerson R, Schoendorfer D, Fay J, Spiehler V. Quantitative detection of opiates in sweat by EIA and GC-MS. *J Anal Toxicol.* 1997;21:451–458.

30. Kacinko SL, Barnes AJ, Schwilke EW, Cone EJ, Moolchan ET, Huestis MA. Disposition of cocaine and its metabolites in sweat after controlled cocaine administration. *Clin Chem.* 2005;51:2085–2094.

31. Mirochnick M, Frank DA, Cabral H, Turner A. Relation between meconium concentration of the cocaine metabolite benzoylecgonine and fetal growth. *J Pediatr.* 1995;126:636–638.

32. Gareri J, Klein J, Koren G. Drugs-of-abuse testing in meconium. *Clin Chim Acta.* 2006;366:101–111.

33. Xia Y, Wang P, Bartlett MG, Solomon HM, Busch KL. An LC-MS method for comprehensive analysis of cocaine and cocaine metabolites in meconium. *Anal Chem.* 2000;72:764–771.

34. Lewis DE, Moore CM, Leikin JB, Koller A. Meconium analysis for cocaine: a validation study and comparison with paired urine analysis. *J Anal Toxicol.* 1995;19:148–150.

35. Browne SP, Tebbett IR, Moore CM, Dusick A, Covert R, Yee GT. Analysis of meconium for cocaine in neonates. *J Chromatogr.* 1992;575:158–161.

36. Ostrea EM, Brandy MJ, Parks PM, Asensio DC, Naluz A. Drug screening of meconium in infants of drug-dependent mothers: an alternative to urine testing. *J Pediatr.* 1989;115:474–477.

37. Moriya F, Chan KM, Noguchi TT, Wu PY. Testing for drugs of abuse in meconium of newborn infants. *J Anal Toxicol.* 1994;18:41–45.

38. Coles R, Kushnir MN, Nelson GJ, McMillain GA, Urry FM. Simultaneous determination of codeine, morphine, hydrocodone, hydromorphone, oxycodone and 6-acetylmorphine in urine, plasma, whole blood and meconium by LC-MS-MS. *J Anal Toxicol.* 2007;31:1–14.

CHAPTER 18

Herbal Remedies and Drugs-of-Abuse Testing

ABSTRACT

Although considered safe by the general population, herbal remedies can actually be very toxic. The popular remedy kava may cause liver damage. St. John's wort, a popular herbal antidepressant, induces metabolism of many drugs, thus causing treatment failure. Different recreational herbal products sold through the Internet contain hallucinogens, ephedra alkaloids, and even illicit drugs. Consuming such drugs not only may cause positive test results in drugs-of-abuse testing but also may cause severe toxicity requiring immediate medical attention. These recreational herbal supplements may contain drugs such as marijuana, cocaine, opiates, and benzodiazepines. Ingestion of these herbal products prior to drug testing would cause positive test results. Other herbal drugs of abuse may contain lysergic acid hydroxyethylamide (LSA), mescaline, ephedra-containing alkaloids, atropine, and a variety of other active ingredients that act as hallucinogens or stimulants. Ingestion of these compounds in high amounts may produce severe adverse reactions requiring hospitalization. It is important to avoid such herbal supplements not only for health reasons but also to avoid a positive drug-testing report in workplace drug testing.

Herbal medicines are readily available worldwide from stores without prescriptions. In the United States, sales of herbal medicine increased from $200 million in 1988 to over $3.3 billion in 1997.[1] Currently, it is estimated that the world market for herbal remedies is U.S. $60 billion, with an annual growth rate between 5% and 15%.[2] The typical user of herbal medicines in the United States has a college degree and falls in the age group of 25 to 49 years. In one study, 65% of subjects stated that they thought that herbal medicines are safe.[1] Gulla et al performed a survey of 369 patient-escort pairs coming to emergency departments. Of these, 174 patients used herbal products. The most common herbal product used was ginseng (20%), followed by echinacea (19%), ginkgo biloba (15%), and St. John's wort (14%).[3]

In the United States, most herbal products are classified as dietary supplements or foods and are marketed pursuant to the Dietary Supplement Health and Education Act of 1994. In Germany, herbal monographs called the German Commission E monographs are prepared by an interdisciplinary committee using historic information; chemical, pharmacological, clinical, and toxicological studies; case reports, epidemiological data; and unpublished manufacturer's data. If an herb has an approved monograph, it can be marketed. In 1997 Australia created a Complementary Medicine Evaluation Committee to address regulatory issues regarding herbal remedies.

Although most people in the general population consider herbal supplements safe and effective, medical literature indicates that severe organic toxicity and even death may occur from prolonged use of herbal supplements. Certain herbal supplements such as Asian ginseng, ginkgo biloba, saw palmetto, feverfew, valerian, and echinacea are considered relatively safe because there are few reports of adverse reactions due to use of such supplements. In contrast, prolonged use of herbal supplements such as kava, germander, and chaparral can produce severe hepatotoxicity. Escher et al described a case in which severe liver damage was associated with kava use. A 50-year-old man took 3 to 4 kava capsules daily for 2 months (maximum recommended dose: 3 capsules). Liver function tests showed 60- to 70-fold increases in concentrations of the liver enzymes AST (aspartate aminotransferase) and ALT (alanine aminotransferase). Tests for viral hepatitis were all negative. In addition, the patient tested negative for cytomegaly virus (CMV) and human immunodeficiency virus (HIV). The patient eventually received a liver transplant.[4] In January 2003 kava extracts were banned in the entire European Union and Canada, and in the United States, the Federal Drug Administration (FDA) strongly cautioned against using kava. There have been at least 11 cases of serious hepatic failure and 4 deaths directly linked to kava extract consumption, and there are also 23 reports indirectly linking kava with hepatotoxicity.[5] **Table 18-1** lists common toxic herbal supplements.

HERBAL REMEDIES AND ADVERSE EFFECTS

Besides kava, other herbal supplements have been associated with death. Haller and Benowitz evaluated 140 reports of ephedra-related toxicity that were submitted to the FDA between June 1997 and March 31, 1999. The authors concluded that 31% of the cases were definitely related to ephedra toxicity and another 31% were

Table 18-1	Toxicity of Some Commonly Used Herbs
Herbal Supplement	**Toxicity**
Kava	Hepatotoxicity
Comfrey	Hepatotoxicity
Germander	Hepatotoxicity
Chaparral	Hepatotoxicity Nephrotoxicity Carcinogenic
Borage	Hepatotoxicity Carcinogenic
Ephedra	Cardiovascular
Chan su	Cardiovascular
Calamus	Carcinogenic
Licorice	Pseudoaldosteronism Hypertension Heart failure

possibly related. Of the reports of ephedra toxicity, 47% involved cardiovascular problems and 18% involved problems with the central nervous system. Hypertension was the single most frequent adverse reaction, followed by palpitation, tachycardia, stroke, and seizure. Ten events resulted in death, and 13 events caused permanent disability.[6] In 2003 the FDA issued warnings against use of ma huang and related herbal weight-loss products that contain ephedra. Consuming ephedra-containing herbal supplements also results in positive amphetamine tests in the screening for amphetamines in urine specimens. Death from consuming chan su, a Chinese medicine, has been reported.[7] Oleander-containing herbal supplements is also associated with severe cardiotoxicity. Osterloh reported a case of death due to consumption of oleander tea.[8]

 ### INTERACTION OF ST. JOHN'S WORT WITH WESTERN DRUGS

Although not directly related to this topic, interaction of St. John's wort, a popular herbal antidepressant, with many Western drugs has clinical significance. Self-medication with St. John's wort may cause treatment failures due to significant reductions in plasma drug concentrations because St. John's wort increases the metabolism of drugs that are metabolized though the liver by inducing liver enzymes. Moreover, St. John's wort also induces metabolism of drugs that are not primarily processed by the liver by modulating P-glycoprotein. Published reports indicate that St. John's wort significantly reduces steady-state plasma concentrations of cyclosporine, tacrolimus, amitriptyline, digoxin, fexofenadine, indinavir, methadone, midazolam, nevirapine, phenprocoumon, saquinavir,

simvastatin, theophylline, and warfarin.[9,10] Increased clearance of oral contraceptives has also been reported. Moreover, herbal remedies are not prepared using rigorous standards, and concentrations of active ingredients may vary widely. St. John's wort containing low concentrations of hyperforin (< 1%) may not cause interactions with Western drugs.[11] **Table 18-2** lists the common drugs that interact with St. John's wort.

 ### CONTAMINATION OF HERBAL SUPPLEMENTS

Heavy metal contamination, adulteration with Western pharmaceuticals, and prohibited animal and plant ingredients are regularly reported in herbal remedies. Lead, mercury, and arsenic intoxication have been reported with the use of Ayurvedic medicines. Saper et al reported that of 70 Ayurvedic medicines tested, 13 preparations contained lead (range: 5.0–37,000 µg/g) and

Table 18-2 Common Drugs That Interact with St. John's Wort	
Alprazolam	Methadone
Amitriptyline	Midazolam
Atazanavir	Omeprazole
Cyclosporine	Oral contraceptives
Digoxin	Ritonavir
Imatinib	Simvastatin
Indinavir	Tacrolimus
Irinotecan	Theophylline
Lopinavir	Verapamil

Source: Reprinted with permission from Dasgupta A. Drug-herb and drug food interactions and effects on therapeutic drug monitoring. In: Hammett-Stabler CA, Dasgupta A, eds. *Therapeutic Drug Monitoring: A Concise Guide* (3rd ed.). Washington, DC: AACC Press; 2007.

6 contained mercury (range: 28.0–104,000 µg/g) and/or arsenic (range: 37–8130 µg/g).[12] Lead poisoning due to use of Ayurvedic medicine has been documented in the literature.[13] Ko reported that 24 out of 254 Asian patent medicines collected from herbal stores in California contained lead, 36 products contained arsenic, and 35 products contained mercury.[14]

Labeling of herbal products may not accurately reflect their content. Adverse events or interactions attributed to a specific herb may be due to misidentification of plants, contamination of plants with pharmaceuticals or heavy metals, or manufacturing or quality-control problems, including substitution of one herb for another.[15] The adulteration of Chinese herbal products with pharmaceuticals is a serious problem because these drugs are not listed in the package insert. Of 2069 samples of traditional Chinese medicines collected from 8 hospitals in Taiwan, 23.7% contained pharmaceuticals, most commonly caffeine, acetaminophen, indomethacin, hydrochlorothiazide, and prednisolone.[15,16]

Lau et al reported a case of phenytoin poisoning in a patient who used Chinese medicines. This patient was treated with valproic acid, carbamazepine, and phenobarbital for epilepsy but was never prescribed phenytoin. She consumed three bottles of a Chinese proprietary medicine in addition to her prescribed medicines. She showed a toxic phenytoin level of 48.5 µg/ml in her blood. Analysis of her Chinese medicines showed adulteration with phenytoin, although the product leaflet stated that the preparation contained only Chinese herbs.[17] A fatal case of hepatic failure due to contamination of a herbal supplement with nitroso fenfluramine has been reported. Analysis of the herbal supplement also revealed the presence of fen-

fluramine.[18] Cole and Fetrow reported presence of colchicine in ginkgo biloba and echinacea preparations. They also reported a case of a 23-year-old woman who showed a serum digoxin level of 3.66 ng/ml after taking an herbal cleansing product. One product called "plantain" was found to be contaminated with *Digitalis lantana* as an unlabeled constituent.[19]

 ## HERBAL SUPPLEMENTS THAT DO NOT INTERFERE WITH DRUGS-OF-ABUSE TESTING

Table 18-3 lists common herbal supplements that do not produce false-positive results in urine drug screens by enzyme immunoassays. Markowitz et al studied the effect of eight common herbal supplements on urine drug tests using enzyme immunoassays (Synchron LX system; Beckman Coulter, Fullerton, CA). Ninety subjects participated in eight different herbal supplement studies. Baseline urine specimens as well as post–herbal treatment urine specimens were analyzed for the presence of drugs of abuse. One specimen from a subject taking only ginkgo biloba tested positive for amphetamine in the screening assay. The presence of amphetamine was subsequently confirmed by GC/MS. Because other subjects taking ginkgo biloba did not show a positive screen for amphetamines, the authors concluded that amphetamine in the urine specimen of one subject was due to amphetamine abuse and not to ingestion of ginkgo biloba. No other urine specimen showed any positive test results. The authors concluded that ingestion of these eight herbs should not result in false-positive results in drugs-of-abuse testing.[20] The active ingre-

dients of these herbal supplements have no structural similarity with any known abused drugs. Winek et al studied the effect of 50 herbal supplements on drugs-of-abuse testing by the fluorescence polarization immunoassay (FPIA; Abbott Laboratories, Abbott Park, IL) and thin-layer chromatography. The authors demonstrated that none of these herbal supplements interfere with drugs-of-abuse testing.[21]

HERBAL SUPPLEMENTS CONTAINING HALLUCINOGENS

Several recreational herbal supplements marketed through the Internet contain hallucinogens. Use of these supplements may cause severe toxicity. Although lysergic acid diethylamide (LSD) is a synthetic and very potent hallucinogen not found in nature, the closely related compound LSA (lysergic acid hydroxyethylamide), which has one-tenth the potency of LSD, is found in nature. LSA is found in seeds of morning glory (*Ipomoea violacea*) and Hawaiian baby woodrose (*Argyreia nervosa*). Seeds of morning glory are abused as a substitute for LSD. When seeds are chewed on an empty stomach, the hallucinogenic effect may start within 1 hour and may last 6 to 10 hours. LSA is listed as a Schedule III drug by the U.S. Drug Enforcement Agency. The seeds of Hawaiian baby woodrose are sold through the Internet and contain LSA. After being soaked in water, seeds can be crushed and eaten for hallucinogenic effect. Routine urine drugs-of-abuse tests do not reveal any presence of LSD or even LSA.[22] Other hallucinogenic plants like peyote cactus and magic mushrooms are discussed in Chapter 13.

Table 18-3	Common Herbal Supplements That Do Not Interfere with Urine Drug Screen by Enzyme Immunoassay	
Arnica	Peppermint tea
Barley grass	Rose hips herb tea
Camellia sinensis	Rosemary
Chimaphila	Sage
Comfrey leaf tea	Saw palmetto
Cranberry extract	Senega
Garlic	Siberian ginseng
Ginkgo biloba	St. John's wort
Ginseng tea	Strawberry
Green tea capsules	Sunflower seeds
Korean ginseng tea	Thymus
Licorice tea	Turkish bay leaves
Papaya herb tea	Valerian extract

ABUSE OF KHAT

Khat (*Catha edulis*) is a flowering evergreen shrub native to East Africa and also found in Arabian countries. Dried plant material is chewed like tobacco and is abused. Although sold in some European and African countries in the open market, khat is illegal in the United States. The major active constituent of khat is cathinone [S(-)-a-aminopropiophenone), which is a sympathomimetic amine that has structural similarity with amphetamine. Khat also contains weaker psychoactive compounds, including phenylpropanolamine, norephedrine, and norpseudoephedrine. Khat is also known as "herbal ecstasy" because it has central nervous system stimulant effects similar to those of amphetamine. Cardiovascular complications from khat use are similar to the complications observed with amphetamine abuse.[23] Moreover, increased blood pressure and heart rate are also observed in individuals abusing khat.[24]

Methcathinone is an illicit drug also known on the street as "cat" or "ephedrine." It is a methyl derivative of cathinone, which is found naturally in the khat plant. This illicit drug can be easily manufactured by oxidation of pseudoephedrine in underground laboratories. Methcathinone can produce neuropsychiatric symptoms, including agitation, insomnia, and tremors. Belhadj-Tahar and Sadeg reported a case of a 29-year-old woman who was admitted to the hospital with coma due to drug toxicity. The family claimed that she was taking an amphetamine-like drug. Her blood alcohol level was 167 mg/dl, and analysis of urine showed the presence of benzodiazepines and high levels of amphetamines (methcathinone: 17.24 mg/L, ephedrine: 11.60 mg/L, and methylephedrine: 11.10 mg/L). The analysis of serum also showed the presence of methcathinone (0.50 mg/L), methylephedrine (0.19 mg/L), and bromazepam (8.89 mg/L). The authors concluded that ingestion of alcohol and bromazepam altered the typical symptoms of methcathinone-induced intoxication—namely, hypertension and convulsion. The authors further stated that the identification of methylephedrine, which is an impurity in the synthesis of methcathinone, can serve as a tag indicating fraudulent synthetic origin of methcathinone.[25]

Cathinone and methcathinone cross react with the amphetamine immunoassays because of the structural similarities of these compounds with amphetamines (**Figure 18-1**). The presence of cathinone and methcathinone in urine should be confirmed by using GC/MS. Paul and Cole reported the presence of cathinone in 2 urine specimens (range: 118 and 3266 ng/ml) that screened positive for amphetamines and methcathinone in 6 urine specimens (range: 13–91 ng/ml) that also screened positive for amphetamines using immunoassay screening.[26] However, cathinone and methcathinone, if present in urine, do not produce a positive screen with all amphetamine assays. One study showed negative response in all urine specimens except one using the FPIA screening test for amphetamines where the presence of cathinone in urine was suspected. In contrast to the FPIA assay, the Mahsan-AMP(300) on-site immunoassay (Mahsan Diagnostika, Reinbeck, Germany) provided positive tests for amphetamine in 7 out of 8 cases. The concentration of cathinone varied from 0.1 mg/L to 28.8 mg/L in urine specimens. The authors commented that the on-site test for amphetamine is more sensitive than FPIA for detecting the presence of cathinone in urine specimens.[27]

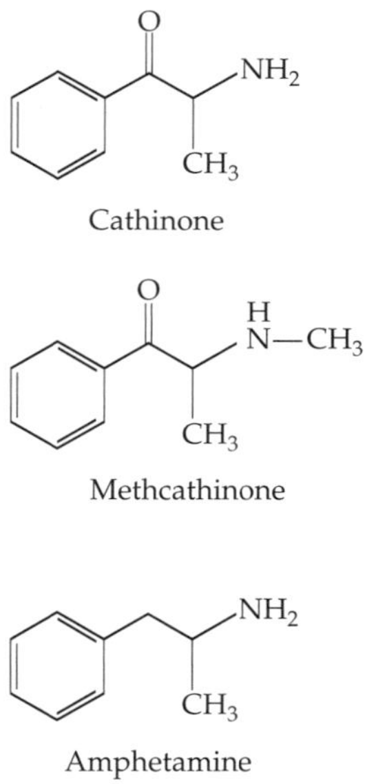

Cathinone

Methcathinone

Amphetamine

Figure 18-1. *Chemical Structures of Cathinone, Methcathinone, and Amphetamine*

ABUSE OF JIMSON WEED

Jimson weed (*Datura stramonium*), also known as "angel's trumpet," is a common plant that grows in the United States, Canada, Europe, and other parts of the world. The main ingredients of jimson weed are belladonna alkaloids (atropine and scopolamine). This plant is poisonous, but people, especially teenagers, abuse this plant for the hallucinogenic and euphoric effects of the belladonna alkaloids. Flowers and other parts of the plants can be chewed or boiled in hot water to make tea for abuse, or this plant can be smoked to induce euphoric effects.

The most common symptoms of poisoning from jimson weed are anticholinergic effects, including dry mouth, rapid heart beat, visual hallucinations, and also cardiac arrest. Hayman reported toxicity from ingestion of jimson weed in a group of 7 people. All subjects suffered severe hallucination, and one person drowned in shallow water because of hallucination.[28] One approach to investigate abuse of jimson weed is hair testing. Kintz et al described a very sophisticated liquid chromatography combined with tandem mass spectrometry to analyze hair specimens for the presence of atropine and scopolamine. The authors detected scopolamine in three segments of hair from an abuser, and the concentrations of scopolamine varied from 14 to 48 pg/g of hair. No atropine was detected.[29]

HERBAL SUPPLEMENTS CONTAINING ILLICIT DRUGS

Many products are marketed through the Internet as alternatives to illicit drugs. Herbal ecstasy often contains ephedra alkaloid combined with guarana or kola nuts that contain caffeine. Severe cardiovascular toxicity may be encountered due to ingestion of herbal ecstasy.[30] Nguyen et al reported contamination of an Internet-marketed nutraceutical with the illicit drug amphetamine. A 25-year-old woman presented with abdominal pain after ingesting an imported herbal weight-loss product. The urine specimen showed the presence of amphetamine. The herbal product was found to be contaminated with an amphetamine derivative banned by the FDA.[31]

Dennehy et al surveyed 119 recreational dietary supplements available through the Internet (54% of the Web sites were in the United States) and observed that 47% of the products were contaminated with illicit drugs, typically marijuana (48%), 3,4-methylenedioxyamphetamine (ecstasy; 23%), LSD (14%), cocaine or cocaine mixed with amphetamine (13%), and mescaline (magic mushroom; 5%). A small percentage of these supplements (5%) were also contaminated with benzodiazepines, opium, and flunitrazepam. The authors reported that the major ingredients of recreational herbal supplements are ephedra alkaloids (27%), *Salvia divinorum* (Salvia, a hallucinogenic plant native to Mexico; 17%), kava (10%), guarana (source of caffeine; 10%), *Acorus calamus* (contains asarone, which is converted in the body to trimethoxyamphetamine and has psychedelic effect; 10%), and damiana (damiana and lettuce opium are smokable herbs with relaxing effects; 10%).[32]

POSITIVE DRUG TESTS DUE TO HERBAL SUPPLEMENTS

Ingestion of recreational herbs contaminated with illicit drugs such as marijuana, cocaine, LSD, or amphetamine should result in a positive drug test from a workplace drug-testing program. Consumption of herbal diet pills containing ma huang may result in a positive amphetamine screen. Contamination of many preparatory Chinese herbs, especially products imported from China and other Asian countries, may be contaminated with Western drugs, including benzodiazepines. Consumption of such products may cause positive results in the test for benzodiazepines. A recent report indicates that drugs such as promethazine, clomethiazole, chlorpheniramine, diclofenac, chlordiazepoxide, hydrochlorothiazide, triamterene, diphenhydramine, and sildenafil citrate were found in Chinese herbal products and patent medicines collected from New York City's Chinatown.[33] Another report revealed the presence of diazepam, indomethacin, and acetaminophen in herbal powder imported from Pakistan.[34]

CONCLUSION

Use of common herbal remedies manufactured in the United States should not cause false-positive test results in pre-employment or workplace drug testing. However, abuse of herbal recreational supplements sold through the Internet may cause positive results in drugs-of-abuse testing because these products may be contaminated with illicit drugs such as marijuana, cocaine, amphetamine, LSD, or benzodiazepines. The adulteration of Chinese herbal medicines manufactured in China or other Asian countries may be contaminated with Western drugs, including benzodiazepines. Moreover, herbal diet pills may contain ephedra and amphetamine derivatives that may cause positive amphetamine test results. Ephedra-containing alkaloids are toxic, and deaths have been reported from ephedra-containing products like ma huang.

REFERENCES

1. Mahady GB. Global harmonization of herbal health claims. *J Nutr*. 2001;131:1120S–1123S.

2. Kartal M. Intellectual property in the natural product drug discovery, traditional herbal medicine and herbal medicinal products. *Phytother Res*. 2007;21:113–119.

3. Gulla J, Singer AJ, Gaspari R. Herbal use in ED patients. [Abstract.] *Acad Emerg Med*. 2001;8:450.

4. Escher M, Desmeules J. Hepatitis associated with kava, an herbal remedy. *Br Med J*. 2001;322:139.

5. Clouatre DL. Kava Kava: examining new reports of toxicity. *Toxicol Lett*. 2004;150: 85–96.

6. Haller CA, Benowitz NL. Adverse and central nervous system events associated with dietary supplements containing ephedra alkaloids. *N Eng J Med*. 2000;343:1833–1838.

7. Ko R, Greenwald M, Loscutoff S, et al. Lethal ingestion of Chinese tea containing ch'an su. *West J Med*. 1996:164;71–75.

8. Osterloh J. Cross-reactivity of oleander glycosides. [Letter.] *J Anal Toxicol*. 1988;12:53.

9. Venkataraman R, Komoroski B, Strom S. In vitro and in vivo assessment of herb-drug interactions. *Life Sci*. 2006;78:2105–2115.

10. Hu Z, Yang X, Ho PC, Chan SY, et al. Herb-drug interactions: a literature review. *Drugs*. 2005;65:1239–1282.

11. Williamson EM. Interactions between herbal and conventional medicines. *Expert Opin Drug Saf*. 2005;4;355–378.

12. Saper RB, Kales SN, Paquin J, et al. Heavy metal content of ayurvedic herbal medicine products. *JAMA*. 2004;292:2868–2873.

13. Dunbabin DW, Tallis GA, Popplewell PY, Lee RA. Lead poisoning from Indian herbal medicine (Ayurvedic). *Med J Aust*. 1992; 157:835–836.

14. Ko RJ. Adulterants in Asian patent medicines. *N Eng J Med*. 1998;339:847.

15. Huang WF, Wen KC, Hsiao ML. Adulteration by synthetic therapeutic substances of traditional Chinese medicine in Taiwan. *J Clin Pharmacol*. 1997;37:344–350.

16. Vander Stricht BI, Parvasis OE, Vanhaelen-Fastre RJ. Remedies may contain cocktail of active drugs. *BMJ*. 1994;308:1162.

17. Lau KK, Lai CK, Chan AYW. Phenytoin poisoning after using Chinese proprietary medicines. *Hum Exp Toxicol*. 2000;19:385–386.

18. Lau G, Lo DS, Yao YJ, Leong HT, Chan CL, Chu SS. A fatal case of hepatic failure possibly induced by nitrosofenfluramine: a case report. *Med Sci Law*. 2004;44:252–263.

19. Cole MR, Fetrow CW. Adulteration of dietary supplements. *Am J Health-Syst Pharm*. 2003;60:1576–1580.

20. Markowitz JS, Donovan JL, DeVane CL, Chavin KD. Common herbal supplements did not produce false positive results on urine drug screen analyzed by enzyme immunoassay. [Letter to the Editor.] *J Anal Toxicol*. 2004;28:272.

21. Winek CL, Elzein EO, Wahba WW, Feldman JA. Interference of herbal drinks with urinalysis fort drugs of abuse. *J Anal Toxicol*. 1993;17:246–247.

22. Richardson WH, Slone CM, Michels JE. Herbal drugs of abuse: an emerging problem. *Emerg Med Clin N Am*. 2007;25:435–457.

23. Kuczkowski KM. Herbal ecstasy: cardiovascular complications of khat chewing in pregnancy. *Acta Anaesthesiol Belg*. 2005;56:19–21.

24. Al-Motarreb A, Baker K, Broadley KJ. Khat: pharmacological and medical aspects and its social use in Yemen. *Phytother Res*. 2002;16:403–413.

25. Belhadj-Tahar H, Sadeg N. Methcathinone; a new postindustrial drug. *Forensic Sci Int*. 2005;153:99–101.

26. Paul BD, Cole KA. Cathinone (Khat) and methcathinone (CAT) in urine specimens: a gas chromatography-mass spectrometric procedure. *J Anal Toxicol*. 2001;25:525–530.

27. Toennes SW, Kauert GF. Driving under the influence of khat-alkaloid concentrations and observations in forensic cases. *Forensic Sci Int*. 2004;140:85–90.

28. Hayman J. Datura poisoning: the angels' trumpet. *Pathology*. 1985;17:465–466.

29. Kintz P, Villain M, Barguil Y, et al. Testing for atropine and scopolamine in hair by LC-MS-MS after Datura intoxia abuse. *J Anal Toxicol*. 2006;30:454–457.

30. Zahn KA, Li RL, Purssell RA. Cardiovascular toxicity after ingestion of "herbal ecstasy." *J Emerg Med*. 1999;17:289–291.

31. Nguyen MH, Ormiston T, Kurani S, Woo DK. Amphetamine lacing of an Internet-marketed nutraceutical. *Mayo Clin Proc*. 2006;81:1627–1629.

32. Dennehy CE, Tsourounis C, Miller AE. Evaluation of herbal dietary supplements marketed on the Internet for recreational use. *Annals Pharmacother*. 2005;39:1634–1639.

33. Miller GM, Stripp R. A study of Western pharmaceuticals contained within samples of Chinese herbal/patent medicines collected from New York City's Chinatown. Leg Med (Tokyo). 2007;9(5):258–264.

34. Dowman JA, Khattak FH, Elliott S, et al. Herbal medicine containing hidden prescription drugs. *Rheumatology (Oxford)*. 2006;45:1309–1312.

APPENDIX

The Substance Abuse and Mental Health Services Administration (SAMHSA) published a final notice to the revision to the Mandatory Guidelines for Federal Workplace Drug Testing Programs in the November 25, 2008 issue of the *Federal Register*. The revision addresses the collection of urine specimens, the revised cut-off concentrations for certain abused drugs, and the testing for adulterants, as well as various other issues. These new guidelines will be effective in 2010. One highlight of these revisions is the inclusion of designer drugs MDA (3,4-methylenedixoyamphetamine), MDMA (3,4-methylenedixoymeth-amphetamine), and MDEA (3,4-methylenedixoyethylamphetamine) in the list of drugs that should be tested in urine specimens. The revised cut-off concentrations of various drugs are given in Table 1 while the confirmation cut-off concentrations are given in Table 2. In order to implement these changes, manufacturers of the screening assays should modify their assays to achieve precision and accuracy at the lower modified cut-off concentrations using proper calibrators and controls. Modification of gas chromatography/mass spectrometric (GC/MS) confirmation assay also may be needed depending on the practice guidelines of individual laboratories.

Table 1 Revised Cut-off Concentration of SAMHSA–Mandated Drugs

Drug or Drug Class	Immunoassay (ng/ml)
Amphetamines	
Amphetamine/ Methamphetamine[a]	500
MDMA	500
Marijuana Metabolite	50
Cocaine metabolite	150
Opiates	
Codeine/Morphine[b]	2000
6-Acetylmorphine	10
Phencyclidine	25

a. Methamphetamine is the target analyte for screening test.
b. Morphine is the target analyte for screening test.
Source: SAMSHA. *Federal Register.* 2008; 73(228): 71857–71907. http://edocket.access.gpo.gov/ 2008/E8-26726.htm. Accessed January 5, 2009.

Table 2 Revised Confirmation Cut-off Concentration of SAMHSA–Mandated Drugs

Drug or Drug Class Confirmation	GC/MS (ng/ml)
Amphetamine	250
Methamphetamine[a]	250
MDMA	250
MDEA	250
MDA	250
Marijuana Metabolite (THC-COOH[b])	15
Cocaine metabolites (Benzoylecgonine)	100
Morphine	2000
Codeine	2000
6-Acetylmorphine	10
Phencyclidine	25

a. If methamphetamine is confirmed by GC/MS, then amphetamine must be present at a concentration of > 100 ng/ml in order to call the methamphetamine test positive.
b. THC-COOH is 11-nor-Δ^9-tetrahydrocannabinol-9-carboxylic acid, the major metabolite of marijuana.
Source: SAMSHA. *Federal Register.* 2008; 73(228): 71857–71907. http://edocket.access.gpo.gov/2008/ E8-26726.htm. Accessed January 5, 2009.

INDEX